Prime Movers

Prime Movers

Define Your Business or Have Someone Define it Against You

Rafael Ramírez

and

Johan Wallin

JOHN WILEY & SONS, LTD
Chichester · New York · Weinheim · Brisbane · Singapore · Toronto

Other Wiley Editorial Offices

John Wiley & Sons, Inc., 605 Third Avenue,
New York, NY 10158-0012, USA

WILEY-VCH Verlag GmbH, Pappelallee 3,
D-69469 Weinheim, Germany

Jacaranda Wiley Ltd, 33 Park Road, Milton,
Queensland 4064, Australia

John Wiley & Sons (Asia) Pte Ltd, 2 Clementi Loop #02-01,
Jin Xing Distripark, Singapore 129809

John Wiley & Sons (Canada) Ltd, 22 Worcester Road,
Rexdale, Ontario M9W 1L1, Canada

British Library Cataloguing in Publication Data

A catalogue record for this book is available from the British Library

ISBN 0-471-89944-5

Typeset in 12/15 Garamond by MHL Typesetting Ltd, Coventry
Printed and bound in Great Britain by Biddles Ltd, Guildford and King's Lynn
This book is printed on acid-free paper responsibly manufactured from sustainable forestry, in which at least two trees are planted for each one used for paper production.

Contents

Foreword

Doing business is to solve dilemmas creatively. Anybody can do business from a position privileged by geography, access to raw materials, or political protection (though getting into that position in the first place may take precious skills). But in principle, being successful in business means doing difficult things better than others, or before others.

A century or so ago a new manufacturing paradigm hit the world. Called Industrialism, it not only meant a different way to manufacture, but it also spawned new modes of organization, and new types of institutions. Briefly, it was a new mode of thinking. Productivity increased dramatically, with wealth and welfare following. With Fayol, Taylor, and others, management theory was born. Naturally, it was concerned with helping economic actors to play the game of Industrialism more efficiently, i.e. of increasing productivity. As the state – particularly the European welfare state as we know it – was built, its service systems to citizens was modeled on Industrialism: efficient production of services (intangible products) to cover 'manifest needs' among citizens.

Perhaps the apotheosis of this paradigm was in the 1960s. But the seeds of change were already there. Post-modern values began to manifest themselves, and with the oil shock of 1974 doubts started to arise as to whether we were on the right track. The future did not seem so certain anymore. With more demanding customers, lower growth, and with the Japanese having taken over as world champions of manufacturing, the business scene changed. Management theory was invaded by new words and concepts: quality, service management, customer satisfaction, customer loyalty, strategic human resources management, time-based management, to name but a few. These were symptoms that the real world issues had changed.

My own interpretation (see *Service Management*) was that customers had now become the scarce resource, and that manufacturing (or more broadly production) capacity now had to fight for customers, rather than customers having to fight to get access to production capacity. Many companies began to change their worldview: they now began to see business as coming from customers, not from factories or products. The factory or the product had been a means to establish a customer base; now the largest investments had been made in relationships with that customer base. It was discovered that the costs of marketing and distribution were often larger than costs of manufacturing. And since customers increasingly began to want the efficient use of products as opposed to just the products, business companies discovered that they had to build service systems.

For example, according to *The Economist* (18 September 1999 issue, p. 29), in 1980 85 percent of the profits of General Electric came from selling products. Today 75 percent of the profits come from selling services (including selling the use of products).

The service sector seemed to rise inexorably. Partly, this was a bookkeeping trick because of increased outsourcing, and partly it was a result of the increased 'unbundlability' of the economy which necessitated 'rebundling-facilitating services' for increased individualization of offerings to customers. But fundamentally it reflected the shift from producing products to supporting the use of assets in the whole economy and for literally every business.

And here we have what is probably the most important dilemma pervading all business: on the one hand, the logic of efficiency in production, and on the other hand the logic of customer orientation and individualization to be competitive. This is a true dilemma. Making all cars similar and black may imply tremendously efficient production; making all offerings maximally customer-oriented ascertains customer satisfaction and loyal customers.

Business comes from the factory and the product. Business comes from the customer. Both are true. Both are wrong. A particular era may favor one or the other view. But in the longer term creatively doing business means creatively solving the dilemma.

In the early 1980s I had the opportunity, together with colleagues, to begin to address this dilemma. In the beginning we did it from the customer's point of view. True to the post-1974 paradigm we looked at customers not as an abstract collectivity (a 'market') but as a set of individual actors (a 'customer base') of flesh and blood. We found that it was as relevant to calculate individual customer profitability as it was to calculate factory profitability or product profitability. We found that by combining a quantitative analysis of customers with qualitative and quantitative studies of what customers were trying to achieve for themselves – not just in relationship to the 'supplier' – we could establish a much better basis than before to develop unique and individualized offerings to them. And by working backwards from the customer base and its diversity, into the production systems, we could often invent, together with our clients, very cost-efficient ways to individualize customer offerings or streamline offerings for different customer clusters or segments.

Business comes from the factory. Business comes from customers. We began to see means of resolving the eternal dilemma.

The resolution of this dilemma is the overall topic of this book, which reports on progress in this area. It does so by recognizing the dilemma and specifically depicting business as the matching of resources and customers. More specifically, it achieves its goal by addressing the dilemma at three different levels.

The first level is related to technology. One of the most striking developments of recent years is the effect that information technology and an increasingly free market economy has had on asset unbundlability and therefore asset liquidity – and, as a consequence, on asset rebundlability. If the name of the game is matching assets and customer bases, then new information technology (and some other technologies) can achieve this much better than ever before, and it can do so increasingly in real time and interactively. This book describes, concretely, the power of interactive resource planning management (IRP) *when framed by this overall notion of business.*

Second, the book does so by succinctly identifying the various *business* capabilities required to perform in today's business world, given the emerging business logics as depicted above. It also identifies the *management* capabilities required to make business capabilities develop into competences that match customers. Thus, it separates and reunites what I once came to call the 'WOB' and the 'WOM': the World Of Business with its inherent logic and the World Of Management. It does so recognizing that business capabilities is the stuff that business is made from but that we need a social context – the task of management – in which the stuff that business is made of can come together into a functioning whole. The world of business and the world of management, though closely related, are all too often confused.

At all three levels, the authors offer an in-depth, creative but practical analysis and framework. The overall idea, the theoretical foundation, of their work is strong – but they apply a thorough engineering approach to it, providing the nuts and bolts of how to translate the framework into practice.

Still, the book rests on the foundation of a powerful framework. And it is also at this conceptual, abstract level that the basic dilemma of 'business from production' versus 'business from customers' is addressed. In the process a number of holy cows and taken-for-granted notions are slaughtered and replaced by more powerful schemes. Indeed, a number of the established metaphors of business are shown to be highly constraining and preventing us from taking a different vantage point from which we can see more opportunities.

For example, business is traditionally described as going 'from seeds to needs'. Instead of this chainlike metaphor the notion of co-production is used. And the stuff that economic actors transact – 'products' or 'services' or 'offerings' – are seen not as *objects transacted* but as *organizers of co-productions*, linking assets and capabilities and competences of business companies with customers and their value-creating processes.

Likewise, the notion that we do not make money from customers but from our customers' successful value creation is advocated. For the company this means that we must go beyond understanding 'needs' to understanding 'value-creating processes' and to match them with our own capabilities, as manifested in offerings.

This view is absolutely fundamental to me. I believe that language is often constraining, and that we need new metaphors to see new opportunities. Two of the words that I consistently try to eradicate from my own language are 'needs' and 'consumers'. Why? Because 'needs' is something that is much easier to apply at the bottom of the Maslow ladder than toward the top of it, and because we can learn much more about how to help customers by understanding their value-creating processes than by thinking in terms of needs. And as to 'consumers' the whole notion of consumption implies 'destruction', whereas I find it derogatory to characterize people as 'destroyers of value', as well as extremely unhelpful when we think about business. I prefer to think about people as 'value creators' rather than as 'value destroyers'. The English language has another word which is much more useful and creatively descriptive and therefore much better as a metaphor: 'consummate'. To consummate is to complete, fulfill, create.

To me people should be seen as consummators, not consumers. And this, in essence, is the metaphor suggested by this book.

So what we see is that the old dilemma is not only challenged and addressed but actually expanded and rephrased. It is no longer a matter of matching production and the market or customers. It is a matter of mobilizing assets and capabilities – not just internal capabilities but a much broader set of 'addressable' capabilities – with the value-creating processes of customers. In this way, both the notions of what a company is, what a customer is, and what an offering is, have all been rephrased and expanded into much more powerful metaphors than the constraining ones traditionally used in business.

Also, instead of using traditional models of business or product life cycles the book proposes a scheme which includes but transcends such models. It introduces a typology of business models in which the emphasis is on renewal on the capability side or on the customer value-creating process side. What results is a strong typology of contingent strategic logics. Managers and shareholders would be wise to distinguish between them rather than mixing them up.

This book, then, is very powerful both in its overall ideas and in showing how they can be implemented. Indeed, the authors argue that idea and implementation are not two phases but two sides of the same coin. I agree with this. As we move into a faster, real life interactive world – aided by new technology and also by emancipation from conceptual prisons into stronger metaphors, the distinction between idea and implementation indeed becomes blurred.

But we must not mistake this dimension for another one. It is sometimes argued that strategy and operations have now merged into one. Still, my experience tells me that in this new, boundaryless world, boundaries have never been more important. In the old times a business company was identified by its products, its buildings, its people. Mostly there was no special need for theorizing about what the company was. No longer. In the new situation, and as amply demonstrated in this book, there is a greater need than ever to think, and to think with a high conceptual quality, about what really is the identity and destiny of a company. The New York marathon may be full of people who run very fast and efficiently. But the world increasingly belongs to those who define new games, and then have the capacity to implement them. These are the Prime Movers.

Richard Normann
La Celle St Cloud

Acknowledgements

The title of this book, *Prime Movers*, we owe to our colleague Richard Normann, who invented this notion to describe the breed of firms that not only adapt to the changes in the environment, but actually drive environmental changes.

This book is a continuation of the work which Richard Normann and Rafael Ramírez started, with a multi-client project called 'Business Logics for Innovators', in the late 1980s, and which produced the book *Designing Interactive Strategy*, also published by Wiley in 1994.

We have been lucky to be able to continue this work by working clinically, that is combining knowledge application and testing, knowledge generation, and knowledge sharing. Thus, the work of which this book is a result builds on four main, parallel, initiatives.

One initiative is a research project on value co-production directed by Rafael Ramírez since 1994, generously financed by the Fondation HEC. Special thanks are due to the three doctoral students who helped in this context: Fabienne Autier, Denis Bourgeois, and Flavio Vasconcelos. Several joint and individual publications resulted from this effort, which are cited in the book.

A second initiative is the research for a doctoral dissertation at the Helsinki University of Technology carried out by Johan Wallin since 1989, resulting in a thesis to be published in 2000. This research has been directed by Professor Tomi Laamnen, whose contributions also have influenced part of the conceptual framework presented in this book.

Interactions between these two initiatives have given rise to a number of joint papers, presented at the Strategic Management Society conferences in Phoenix, Barcelona, and Berlin, which are also cited in the book.

The third initiative concerns work done by each of the authors in the 'competence-based management' series of conferences organized by professors Aimé Heene and Ron Sanchez. In particular, some of the ideas in Chapters 3 and 4 are based on papers that Johan Wallin presented at the Ghent (1995) and Oslo (1998) conferences.

The fourth initiative concerns strategy-consulting engagements undertaken by the authors with their clients. These allowed us to 'ground' and test our ideas in actual practice, and to refine them accordingly. In addition to thanking our clients for making these enriching co-learning opportunities possible, we also want to express special thanks to the SMG consultants who helped us in these initiatives: Rolf Jansson, Mikael Huhtamäki, Peter Nou, and Eskil Ullberg.

Many internal discussions with SMG colleagues, and in particular with Richard Normann, helped us along the way. The interest of the thinking in this book was confirmed in the 'Business Concept Innovation' workshop which SMG organized in Zurich together with Studio Ambrosetti, Global Business Network, and Crédit Suisse in November 1998. Special thanks to Richard Normann and Ulf Mannervik, who organized the workshop, for the exchanges we enjoyed with them in preparing for, during, and upon debriefing the event. Thanks too to the participants and key individuals in the other sponsoring organizations for the enriching discussions of which the workshop consisted.

In addition to the four initiatives, different lectures and presentations made by the authors on both sides of the Atlantic in diverse settings (executive education sessions, conferences, colloquia, learning journeys, workshops, classrooms) allowed us to both test and further our ideas. In particular, we acknowledge the quality of exchanges we enjoyed in the 'Customer of the Future' workshop organized by Global Business Network in NYC in October 1999.

We thank the senior executives in the organizations we analyze in this book who agreed to be interviewed, and/or who took the time to read drafts of our research, which allowed us to correct errors and find missing pieces in their companies' stories.

Finally, we gratefully acknowledge the editorial support which Diane Taylor and her colleagues at John Wiley and Sons offered. Special thanks also to Chris Murray for his help in making our English more understandable and accessible. We are also extremely thankful to Teija Virtanen who untiringly drew and redrew new versions of the numerous figures of this book, and who co-ordinated draft versions between Helsinki and Paris during the whole joint writing period. Jagdeep Kapoor and Katharina Balasz helped in updating and checking information and its presentation.

Rafael Ramírez
Johan Wallin
Paris and Helsinki

The New Logic of Value Creation   1

> If Yves Saint Laurent presents a new collection in Paris that features see-through fabrics, he will set new standards (or create a trend) for other fashion houses to follow. Other fashion designers are not obliged to follow Yves Saint Laurent's example. There is no legal or official contract that requires them to do so. Yet several designers will feature see-through fabrics in their next collection.

The role that Yves Saint Laurent plays here is that of a 'referent' organization:[1] an organization that, through its pre-eminence, *de facto* shapes how others in its field of activity will behave.

In this book, we have adopted and extended the concept of referent organization. We apply it to prime movers: organizations that are taken to be pre-eminent in their business, becoming different in relation to others playing similar roles (such as other fashion designers for Yves Saint Laurent); by rethinking relations with other key counterparts involved in, or linked to, their business. These key counterparts include:

- Customers
- Employees and/or their representatives
- Suppliers
- Investors
- Regulators
- Interest Groups
- Other relevant stakeholders

Prime movers 'move' businesses by getting others to follow the way they design (or co-design) the business. For example:

- **Microsoft** has been the prime mover in disk operating systems.
- **Dell** became the prime mover in Internet-based computer selling.
- **Boeing** has been the prime mover in civilian jet sales, though it is now contested in this role by **Airbus**.
- **Benetton** has been a prime mover in franchise-based clothes retailing, though it is now contested in this role by **The Gap**.
- **EF Education** is the uncontested prime mover in second language education in Europe.
- **Disney** has twice been a prime mover in children's entertainment.
- **IKEA** is a prime mover in low-cost home furnishing.
- **Nokia** has become a prime mover in cellular phones.

These prime movers do not succeed alone. In many cases, well over half (sometimes as much as 90 per cent, as is, for example, the case with IKEA) of what they sell is actually produced by others. These prime movers influence what these others do, and together with them reshape old businesses into new configurations – or shape entirely new businesses.

Prime movers have a big say in how their customers use what they sell to them. Some prime movers who have created new businesses from scratch (such as Sony did with the 'Walkman' or 3M with the 'Post-It') did not interact with customers, for the business they created had no customers to start with. But in many cases the prime movership occurs in a more evolutionary way, with a first design being co-developed with customers. Here, a more intensive interaction with customers is evident. The emergence of Xeroxing, and then of the 'Document Company Xerox', which we review in Chapter 2, is an example of such an interaction.

Prime movers also play a key role in influencing how employees, unions, regulators, investors, consumer groups, and other counterparts create value.

For example, Nouvelles Frontières, the French travel services group, has pioneered relations with both employees and unions which have 'set it apart' and created a 'referent' against which other travel companies compare themselves. Amazon.com created web-based relations with customers, who for example review books for others, which are emulated by competitors. E-Bay exploited the interactivity of the Internet to organize auctions, making commercial relations that would have not existed at all possible for different types of actors.

RECONFIGURATION

Incumbent prime movers are challenged more than ever before.

You may be happy doing business, even putting out one commercially successful innovation after another, when out of the blue, a company you have never heard of is suddenly taking customers (and customer revenues!) away from you. This company may be based in another country. It may be from an industry in which you never considered yourself to be involved. On your 'competitive radar screen' it may be 'catalogued' as one of your customers.

Ryder Systems, operating out of Miami Florida, successfully took customer revenues away from its truck-manufacturing suppliers, by providing leased trucks (*and* leased trailers, *and* logistical packages, *and* insurance, *and* administrative support, *and* human resources, *and* inter-operator efficacy improvement services, *and* maintenance *and* repair services, *and* spare parts).[2] The truck makers had considered Ryder to be a customer. Suddenly, Ryder became a competitor.

In the same way, shipyards considered ship management companies, who manage ships for shipping concerns, to be 'downstream' from them in a value chain. Yet, some of the advanced ship management companies have transformed themselves into 'prime movers', offering, like Ryder, services such as repair and maintenance, chartering, manning, administration, insurance, registration, and so on to shipowners. It is such companies that now 'call the shots', specifying what the shipyard should do to render the vessel as effective as possible for the shipowner – a task once the responsibility of the shipyard itself.

New players have more options to exploit than ever before. They use these options to challenge incumbents. The weapon with which new players challenge incumbent prime movers is what we call 'reconfiguration'. In retail industries, a firm that successfully reconfigures its business is called a 'category killer'. Examples are firms such as 'Toys R Us', Dell Computers, e-Bay, or IKEA, which create totally new ways of doing business, thereby setting the 'standard' – which often includes unprecedented cost effectiveness against which others will be judged.

Reconfiguration is about finding out new ways of doing business by **reallocating roles among players** that enhance value creation effectiveness – evaluated in ways we explore in Chapter 3, and which often (but not always) involve lower costs. This is what prime movers have done to established incumbents, allowing them to become incumbents themselves. And in turn, this is how challengers can, and do, challenge these incumbent prime movers.

To reallocate roles, assets must be mobilized in time and space. Assets are becoming more 'liquid' because they can flow more easily across time and space. This enhanced liquidity renders them more easily moved, bundled, and separated.

ASSET LIQUIDITY

Wired Magazine editor Kevin Kelly tells us that the physical weight per dollar value of US exports has been cut in half in the past six years.[3] Logistic capabilities render physical assets more easy to move. So-called 'intangible assets' can be moved by wire and cellular technology, stocked optically, and moved again – be they aircraft designs, brand rights, legal agreements, musical compositions, or personal reputations. Finally, people move more frequently and more cheaply from place to place, and time zone to time zone.

As people, intangible-intensive 'software' and information, and physical assets become more liquid, they become replaceable (literally) in place and time, and in relation to each other. This opens up opportunities for new sets of configurations to be designed and actually put in place with unprecedented ease.

THE ARGUMENT THIS FAR

- Asset liquidity drives reconfigurability.
- Reconfigurability renders business incumbents easier to challenge.
- Prime movers are those who reconfigure, and then dynamically defend their reconfiguration best, thereby shaping the configurations their counterparts play by.

BUSINESS

To carry out business, two elements, plus a way of connecting them, are required. First, one needs customers. Second, one needs to secure access to capabilities.[4] Finally, one needs to connect those capabilities to customers through 'offerings'. Viable businesses are those in which customers pay an organization for effectively accessing, configuring, and providing capabilities in the forms of 'offerings'.[5]

We shall see in this book that this perspective of business is fundamentally different from one which considers 'products' (instead of capabilities) and 'markets' (instead of customers). More specifically, we consider that businesses link (a) not so much customers as such, but *customers' own value creation* to (b) *capabilities and resources* – within the supplying firm *and* outside it, which the firm owns *or* accesses, and then packages in (c) sets it makes available to enhance (a) customers' value creating.

'Prime mover' firms that successfully re-interpret existing links between (a) and (b), change the roles of other economic actors involved.

> For instance, the adoption of 'smart' card technology by Cartes Bancaires, the French inter-bank pay-card consortium, involved the banks themselves, account holders, retailers, the national phone company, suppliers of terminal equipment, regulators, VISA and Master-Card, and other parties. As we see in Chapter 10, this configuration proved to be extremely successful.

The configuration of roles and/or of actors that prime movers create is what we call a 'value constellation'. A value constellation provides, from the customer's point of view, new offerings. If the new offering is competitive, the business that offers it will also be competitive.

OFFERINGS

Offerings are the key unit of analysis for business design and redesign. They are different from 'markets'. Offerings compete in markets, and as we see in the following chapter, are valued in different ways by different parties in those markets. Innovative offerings can generate entirely new markets. Offerings join economic actors with each other. They are outputs *and* inputs. Offerings thus also distinguish one economic actor from its counterpart. They entail work-sharing between 'supplier' and 'customer', and as such suppose activities by each.[6]

Offerings involve:

- Work by people on the supplier's part.
- Work by people on the customer's part.
- Risk taken up by the customers (or insured by them).
- Risk taken up (or insured) by the supplier.
- Physical assets.
- Utilization of software, infrastructure, and/or supporting processes.
- Information.
- (Possibly) work by third parties which customers accessed themselves.
- (Possibly) work by third parties that the supplier has accessed for the customer.

We will examine offerings in greater detail in Chapters 3 and 4.

THE BOOK EXPLAINED

The book builds on the above concepts and framework, illustrating the analyses we make with practical examples from firms such as VISA, Caterpillar, Nokia, ABB, Xerox, Tetra Pak, and Cultor.

It attempts to guide managerial choices, and outline steps that can be followed to prevent other companies from outconfiguring one's business – or to enable one to reconfigure a business. It does so as follows:

- Explains the rise of, and interest of, value constellations – what others might call networks or webs.
- Overviews the usefulness of analyzing business in this manner, particularly as Internet and other information technologies intervene.
- Argues that the impact of such technologies in effect requires thinking of value creation in terms of value constellations.
- Introduces elements of the conceptual framework of value creation that we further develop in Chapters 3 and 4 of the book.
- This conceptual framework is based on the idea that firms which successfully reinterpret their businesses, changing the roles of their economic counterparts, define the value constellations in which they do business. We call such firms 'prime movers', as they are the ones which reconfigure the roles and positions of others in the new value constellation.

It is this framework which the book explores, further develops, and renders operational.

In Chapter 2, we review how Xerox became a prime mover – twice. This story grounds the analyses in the following chapters. It also vividly illustrates the very important point that becoming a prime mover may mean having to become it again – and again!

In Chapter 3, we look at how value is seen from both the customer's, and the supplier's perspective, offering formulae which allow these two to be compared and related to each other. The notion of 'offerings' is introduced here as the central unit of analysis. We illustrate this with an analysis of how the market for internet browsers developed.

In Chapter 4, based on the above, we offer a new architecture with which to think of value creation. Our starting point is here that the firm is a part of a larger context. Firms have to define their business models to exploit the potential for value creation this context holds for them. We illustrate the concepts we introduce with an example from ABB.

In Chapter 5, we explore customer orientation, one of four possible priorities of the business model. Companies wanting to give their highest strategic attention to their existing customer relations have continuously to develop new capabilities and offerings to keep these customers' business. We use Caterpillar's remarkable relations with its dealers and their customers as an illustration.

In Chapter 6, we apply the architecture of value creation to companies that want to give their highest strategic attention to capabilities, better exploiting the cost effectiveness and scale benefits which this obtains. The development of the French market for overnight delivery services offers an example.

In Chapter 7, we examine how prime movers 'colonize' their own immediate business environment, by applying the new architecture of value creation developed in Chapters 4 to 6. Such actors 'make markets' to serve them – the central actor. We use Nokia as an illustration of this strategy.

In Chapter 8, we examine how prime movers 'colonize' the context of actors, for which they become an element in their immediate business environment. They do this by getting these actors to co-operate with each other. These prime movers also apply the new architecture of value creation developed in Chapters 4 to 6, but in a different way. We use VISA, and in particular their French partner – Groupement Cartes Bancaires – as an illustration of this strategy.

In Chapter 9, we examine how prime movers can go beyond the 'colonizing' of business environments, actually reshaping these fundamentally in their market making. Such prime movers take the architecture of value creation developed in Chapters 4 to 6 to its logical limits. We use the Tetra Pak company as an illustration of this strategy.

In Chapter 10, we critically examine what is meant by 'value creation'. We present two different views on this issue. We look at the implications of thinking of value as 'co-produced', rather than 'produced'. We examine how information technology makes co-production mandatory, and close by looking at how values and value relate to each other.

Configuration and Reconfiguration

2

The case of Xerox Corporation shows how a company can become a prime mover – twice.

- How, after years of struggle, Xerox developed the technological and marketing *capabilities* that matched customers' *value creation logics*.
- How the first *configuration* of Xerox's relationship with its customers was threatened by new competitors.
- How Xerox *reconfigured* its relationship by shifting the focus from copies to what was being copied: the document.

XEROX'S ORIGINS, AND ITS HISTORY UNTIL 1995[1]

Xerox's history up to 1995 can be described as the creation, success, and crisis of a first business configuration ('photocopying'). The crisis of the first configuration led to the creation, and success of a second configuration ('documenting'). In developing each configuration, Xerox played a key role – which we call the 'prime mover' role – in establishing relations between itself and

- Customers,
- Suppliers/partners, and
- Competitors.

The initial, 'photocopying' configuration was constructed in the 1950s. It was very successful until the mid-1970s, when the strategic competences its capabilities had created became strategic rigidities.[2] These rigidities made it difficult for Xerox to see the dangers, and seriously delayed reaction, leading the company into a serious crisis.[3] The crisis contained elements which were interpreted in ways that allowed Xerox to address its problems, and then to create a new configuration.

We review the stages of this story below.

THE CONSTRUCTION OF THE FIRST CONFIGURATION

Xerox took an invention 'nobody wanted' and turned it into a multi-billion dollar industry. It took over 20 years from the first elaboration of the technology (1938) to the first commercial success (1959).

At the very origin of 'xerography' technology[4] is a man: Chester Carlson. This graduate from the California Institute of Technology was struck by the wasted energy required to copy or duplicate documents. So in the early 1930s, he began to explore technical alternatives that would allow people to 'make copies at a push of a button'. From the beginning he decided not to try to improve existing technologies, but instead went looking for a new one.

At that time, several copying technologies were available. First, there was the mimeograph (first commercially released in 1887). It relied on chemical technology and produced awful smells. Then there was carbon paper, associated with the typewriter (available since 1890 – the notion of 'carbon copy' is still used in 'e-mails' as 'cc'). Various unsophisticated photographic machines were also available, starting in the 1910s. They used technologies derived from photography (the best known product was Photostat). Finally, the offset printing press had been available since 1930. It produced far superior quality copies, but was reserved to sizeable offices, due to its price and its overall dimensions.

None of these existing technologies satisfied Chester. The mimeograph, carbon paper, and offset presses were, technically, duplicators, not copiers. To use them, it was necessary to create a special master page which would then be duplicated. The long inflexible processes involved, with the possible exception of carbon paper, were only worthwhile if you planned to make a lot of copies of the same documents. The photographic machines represented a first step of freedom from the master page, but the technology had many limitations: it was cumbersome, expensive and unreliable. Thus, it was confined to limited uses, such as copying legal documents.

Carlson turned to the little known field of photoconductivity – where he learned that when light strikes a photoconductive material, the electrical conductivity of that material is increased – and started experimenting. It took him eight years of spare-time work (with another physicist he hired) to come to prove the viability of his technology, which produced its first copy in 1938.

This is how his first copies were made:

- First, a special photoconductive surface is given an electrostatic charge. The key principle is that the charge will only hold in the dark and will disappear once it is exposed to light.
- Next, a printed page is placed in close proximity to the surface, and light is shone on it so that an image of the printing is projected onto the surface. Because of the light, the surface keeps its charge only in the places occupied by the dark ink.
- The surface is then dusted with ink powder. Ink only sticks to the charged portion, creating a mirror image of the printed page.
- This image is then transferred to a blank sheet of paper.
- Finally, to render the image permanent, heat is applied which melts the ink and fuses it to the page.

Carlson applied for, and received, many patents for his invention. But he spent the next six years trying to sell it to every important office-equipment company in the US ... without success. Remington Rand, RCA, General Electric, and IBM all declined the offer.

In 1944 Carlson finally found an unexpected sponsor in the Battelle Memorial Institute, a non-profit industrial research organization.[5] In 1947 Haloid, a photographic paper maker proposed itself as a manufacturer for the new technology in exchange for royalties to Battelle and Carlson, and participation in the development costs.

One of the first things Haloid did was to suggest renaming the Carlson process. Electrophotography, the original name, was not very appealing.

Following the recommendation of a professor in classical languages, they created a name derived from the Greek language: Xerography (*Xerox* for dry and *Graphein* for writing). After further development, Haloid finally introduced the first commercial Xerographic copier, the Model A, in 1949.

Model A was a very big and complicated machine. It was derived from different technological fields – namely, mechanics, chemistry, and optics. It was, as described in a recent history of Xerox 'part a chemical plant, part an optical device, and part a mechanical device (paper mover)'.[6] It was not automatic, and it was very difficult to use. The 39-step process to make one copy was very difficult to get right, and it was also very long. Only a specialist having studied the manual for a while could be able to make a single copy!

Model A was far from a commercial hit. It only convinced a few customers who found it a simpler, cheaper way to make paper masters for offset printing presses. Ford was one of these. This niche market was not sufficient. The Xerographic copier was far from the easy-to-use concept Carlson had been attempting.

Meanwhile, competitors were managing to release new, substitute products which could offer functions comparable to those targeted by Haloid: devices helping to make copies of office papers without using a master page. For this, they explored various technologies:

- 3M introduced the 'Thermo-Fax' in 1950. It used heat from an infrared lamp to create images on special paper.
- American Photocopy's 'Dial-A-Matic Autostat' came out in 1952. It used a process similar to that of ordinary photography.
- Kodak's 'Verifax', which appeared in 1953, used chemical developers.

The common features of these pioneer devices were relatively low costs: just a few cents per copy. Yet, they had several flaws. They worked only with specially treated papers, sold only by the manufacturers, and the copies themselves were rather poor. Copies made from Verifax and Autostat had to be dried off to be of any use, and those from Thermo-Fax were so sensitive to heat that they would get darker and darker as they lay on the office desks.

Haloid kept on allocating resources for further developments, which had at that point mounted to astonishing levels: between 1947 and 1960, Haloid spent about 75 million dollars on Xerography, far more than it had earned during those years. Many flaws and problems had slowed down the development process:

- The sticking of the paper to the photoreceptor.
- The residues of toner.
- The jamming of the copy paper (known as 'mis-puff').
- Fires.

Thus, every initiative that could either save money or bring more in was welcome. Newly issued shares were sold whenever it was possible. One of the confident acquirers (most were difficult to convince) had been the University of Rochester. Managers were paid in stock rather than cash, and some of them even lent personal savings to the company.

The actual outcome of this development was still very uncertain at the time. Yet Joe Wilson, grandson of the founder, and then CEO of Haloid, thought it would be wise to develop an overseas presence and insure a patent protection there. Thus, in 1956, he managed to persuade an English motion picture firm, the J. Arthur Rank Organization, to launch a joint venture with Haloid that was called Rank Xerox. The venture was granted the exclusive rights to exploit the xerographic patents throughout the world, except in America and Canada. In the same period, Haloid adopted the trademark 'Xerox': an abbreviated form of xerography defined with reference to 'Kodak' (a short word starting and ending with the same letter).

In 1959, Haloid finally managed to overcome the technical problems, or at least to limit their negative implications. It released a new product: the 914. History will recall the 914 as the first hit product of Xerox. However, this was far from obvious at the time.

The 914 was very different from the existing products on the market. It looked roughly like an L-shaped table, and measured nearly 1.2 meters (4 feet high) . . . It was nearly the size of a small U-Haul trailer, and weighed about 650 pounds.[7] Other copiers existing in the market at that time were small enough to squeeze on the top of a good-sized desk. In addition the 914 was extraordinarily expensive to manufacture (it cost 4,000 dollars to produce), while existing copiers in the market were sold for between 300 and 400 dollars. As we shall see, the high production cost was later interpreted in a way that gave Xerox an extraordinary competitive advantage.

Compared to these apparent handicaps, the distinctive advantages of the Xerox 914 were that:

- it could use ordinary plain paper;
- it was very easy to use: all one had to do was place a sheet of paper face down on the glass window on top of the machine, select the number of copies desired (up to a maximum of fifteen), then push the button;
- it was reasonably fast, producing the first copy in 2 seconds, and the next ones in 7-second intervals; and
- the quality of the copy was good.

These were the reasons for the 914 becoming a major breakthrough.

But because of the high production cost, there was what appeared to be a major remaining flaw: the price. Just imagine Haloid's top management at the time. Beyond the important technical problems to overcome, they, the promoters of Xerography, also faced the commercial problem of figuring out how to convince potential customers of the usefulness of this new copier. Xerox copiers exceeded both the size and the price of existing devices.[8]

The breakthrough

Marketing innovations were at least as important as technical breakthroughs in making Xerox copiers successful.

These consisted in:

- leasing the machine (vs. selling it),
- offering a two-day cancellation warranty,
- charging customers on the number of copies made.

These three choices allowed Xerox to set the conditions to begin *creating value for and with its customers* which, to this day, have proven to be extremely successful.

First, the leasing option made Xerography an affordable solution. Later, when model changes happened at a faster rate, this allowed Xerox to master the customer relationship, for leases come to an end at predetermined dates. This is an important advantage in terms of keeping the customer relation. The reason is that the expiration of the lease contract is predetermined, allowing Xerox to launch its customer-retention marketing efforts at times which are known in advance. If the machine were sold, it would be impossible to know when the customer will think of replacing it, making the timing of marketing relationship renewal efforts much more of a guessing game.

Second, the two-day cancellation warranty allowed Xerox products to go into the company, and be tried by potential users, at virtually zero risk to the company or order-issuing department within it. The charge-per-copy principle made the technology 'cheap' from an up-front investment point of view. So people tried out the offering, at a low cost. That the offering could be seen as becoming 'expensive' from a long-term cash flow point of view became irrelevant – by the time the finance department figured out the yearly or monthly cost, the high value which the offering had demonstrated for users made the price look 'reasonable'.

Finally, all these marketing innovations helped Xerox sales reps to bypass the in-house copying expert: the head of the customers' Reproduction Departments (nicknamed 'Charlie Print-pants'). Due to his position, Charlie would have been the first one to evaluate the technology in terms of its quality/reliability aspects. Ease of use had no value as a feature for him – in fact, the value of this particular feature, from Charlie's point of view, was negative. The integration costs of Xerox's offering were lower than established alternatives which had been offered into Charlie's shop. Yet Charlie's very existence inside companies resided in part on his unique role in addressing the difficulties, and thus cost, of integrating copying offerings into staff units and line operations. Going around Charlie Print-pants for Xerox reps was important, as he was objectively threatened by the new Xerography device.[9] In the value equations we examine in the next chapter, we see that the low integration costs of Xerox's offering for users allowed them to avoid requesting Charlie's advice. Xerox reps and users thus jointly colluded to out-configure Charlie from having a say in the new configuration they jointly brought about.

Thus, once the Xerox machines had entered a company department, users started creating value with the machines. They paid for what they used only, so neither the buying department, the finance department, nor Charlie Print-pants could block the entry. The relatively wide distribution of users also distributed the cost into different budgetary lines, and so it was not easy for accountants to discover the true cost of the machine – until it was 'too late' (by then, perceived value had far exceeded the cumulative cost).

Demand for copies increased faster than anyone had expected, as uses which had not been anticipated by Xerox appeared. People were not only using copiers to make copies of original documents (the use which had been anticipated) but also to copy copies, time and again, to pass on information more quickly. In fact, thanks to the new possibilities offered by the technology, people expanded the use of Xerography beyond two-dimensional documents, to three-dimensional objects, a totally unexpected use of the technology. For example, police officers discovered the 'Xeroxed receipt', which was a copy of the contents of an arrested person's wallet, which was much more accurate and easy to do than a detailed written description listing each and every item. In the same way, Food and Drug Administration employees photocopied labels pasted on medicine bottles and food packages, instead of using typewritten copies of these.[10]

The history of xerography's development does away with the simplistic notions of 'technology push' or 'market pull'. Here supplier and customers co-constructed a business. The co-construction between suppliers and customers manifested innovative relationships between

- technologic and commercial capabilities, and
- value creation by customers.

This manifestation took the form of

- offerings.

In doing so, Xerox and its customers evolved their relationships into a market. They did so through mutual learning, through co-developing understandings and co-constructing roles, that allowed each party to generate value. Xerox configured many value-creating activities with users, which had previously been either highly cumbersome, or nonexistent.

The unexpected commercial success of Xerox's first model illustrates what can be called a co-construction of a market. Once the conditions of appropriation by the customers were met, then they began using the machines in unexpected and in unplanned ways, thereby creating value for themselves – and for their customers. These innovative behaviors were recognized by Xerox, which further facilitated them, supporting such developments through new offerings.

THE CONSOLIDATION AND EXPLOITATION OF THE FIRST CONFIGURATION: 1959–70

For the two years following the 1959 introduction of the 914, Xerox worked at making the most of this first successful meeting with users and customers. While improving the products and developing its offering range, Xerox exploited the basic configuration it established with its customers. This configuration relied on:

- leasing copiers instead of selling them;
- offering continuous technical support with the lease;
- regularly upgrading the machines.

The exclusive and official goal of this period was growth. It consisted of two elements:

1 Expanding the customer base, applying the same configuration of relationships to *more customers*. The two-day cancellation warranty was a powerful means to gain more customers.

2 Maintaining the loyalty of established, convinced customers, while inciting them to make *more copies*.

This was Xerox's 'instant growth' concept: it consisted in renewing the machine rented to the customers regularly, exchanging them with better and more powerful ones. Success relied on the assumption, which turned out to be correct, that the more powerful the machine, the higher the capacity, and the more copies people make.

This configuration was extraordinarily successful throughout the 1960s. Xerox expanded from 900 employees in 1960 to 24,000 in 1966. In 1959 Haloid-Xerox sales were $32 million; in 1961, the first full year of the 914 model sales, they rose to $61 million; and by 1968, they were $1,125 billion. The profit was $2.5 million in 1961, and reached $138 million in 1968. More generally, the number of copies made within the US rose from 20 million in the mid-1950s, to 9.5 billion in 1964, to 14 billion in 1966. The pre-eminence of Xerox as a configurer of this activity can be seen in the use of the word 'Xeroxing' instead of 'photocopying' to denote this activity.

This exploitation of a winning relationship with customers was all the more easy as Xerox had no competitors in the plain paper copy market. Xerox enjoyed a 95 percent market share in the 1960s, as a result of its numerous patents on the Xerography technology. A schematic representation of the configuration Xerox managed to build is shown in Figure 2.1.

'Customers' in Figure 2.1 mostly depicts middle-to-large-sized companies. More precisely, the 'customers' were the department heads, or purchasing managers, of customer companies. Xerox used a direct (manufacturer-controlled) sales-and-service force. This still distinguishes it from its Japanese competitors, who have relied on an indirect sales-and-service force (independent, sometimes exclusive, dealers and distributors). Xerox developed a strong key account management program with which it tried to establish continuing relationships with the customer.

In Figure 2.1, 'competitors' refers to copying companies that did not have the same technology (remember: competitors' technology required special paper and was based on either photographic or chemical

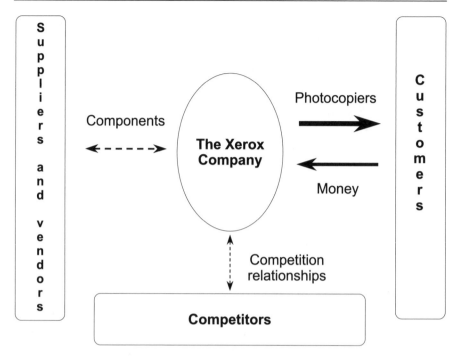

Figure 2.1 Xerox's first configuration.

technology). Xerox nearly had a monopoly of plain paper copiers until 1970. IBM first introduced its 'Copier' series in 1970, and Kodak its popular and high-performance 'Ektaprint' series in 1972. It was only in 1975, when the Federal Trade Commission decided that Xerox would have to license its patents without royalties, that competition really started to hit Xerox. As a result, up to this 1975 decision, Xerox simply dominated (potential) competitors.

The capabilities in the configuration which Figure 2.1 illustrates were

- Xerox's patent-protected monopoly on Xerography for plain paper copying until 1975, combined with the fact that Xerography was superior to alternative technologies,
- Xerox's successful management and operation of a direct sales and service force for distribution to medium and large businesses, and
- Xerox's leasing/financing/upgrading capabilities, enabling it to retain customers effectively.

Key account management, along with the leasing relationship, were decisive elements of the configuration depicted in Figure 2.1, which helped Xerox to retain customers, even well after some of its products started to become technically outdated, falling behind those of some competitors. Strong customer relations protected Xerox from losing too many customers, even if it had difficulty in meeting competitors' ever shorter development cycles, focused on faster machine renewal, and important performance and feature enhancements.

THE GROWING 'QUESTIONING' OF THE SUCCESSFUL CONFIGURATION: 1970–80

The first determining element, which began the crisis of the first successful ('photocopying', or 'Xeroxing') configuration we surveyed above, was the entrance of newcomers seeking to reconfigure Xerox's offering. Note that success had made Xerox 'the' incumbent *prime mover*.

As mentioned above, IBM entered the copier market in 1970, using licensed Xerox technology. Kodak and Ricoh appeared on the market shortly thereafter, with their own technology. The offerings these new competitors developed destabilized Xerox's established configuration, for they changed the relationship between suppliers and customers.

The newcomers enhanced the hardware dimension of the offering by lowering its cost, improving its quality, and adding new features such as liquid toner.

They transformed the software dimension of the offering by adding document handling, and by changing the pricing logic. As they had succeeded in slashing production costs, machines could now be sold and rented (not just leased). This not only altered the established work sharing between supplier and customer, but also opened up possibilities for new risk-sharing formulae – for example allowing servicing to be unbundled and out-sourced. New pricing possibilities emerged. Thus, in its rental option, IBM offered 'Top Stop Pricing' in which customers were allowed to stop paying for their copies beyond a certain monthly amount of copying.

In parallel to this 'invasion',[11] Xerox experienced defaults in its own established offering: it encountered quality and reliability problems in its machines, and service-related complaints were more and more evident. Customers began canceling contracts and defecting to the invaders in increasing proportions. All these changes involved the first major questioning *ever* of Xerox's established (incumbent) pricing and leasing policy. Leasing, once a competitive advantage, was becoming more and more a competitive weakness.

Yet, in spite of all these signals, Xerox made no radical changes in the configuration (illustrated in Figure 2.1) at that time. The only significant change was replacing leases with sales whenever possible. The dominant reaction consisted in trying to find more customers (in order to replace the lost ones) through more aggressive commercial actions, and hiring more service representatives in order to fix the growing quality problems.

This 'solution' did not work well. In 1975, Xerox installed just 1 percent more copiers than it removed. Competitors meanwhile started flooding the market with new products. From 1971 to 1978, no less than 77 new plain paper copiers were introduced in the US market; and another 80 from 1978 to 1980. Yet, during the 1970s, Xerox introduced only three completely new copiers!

THE CRISIS: 1980–85

Not surprisingly, Xerox's success had made the company con-servative,[12] and it did not see the limitations of its existing configuration early enough. Its competitive capabilities had become competitive rigidities.[13]

The turning point of this situation was reached by the early 1980s, when Xerox painfully recognized that competitors had begun to set the standards for the copying business. As CEO David Kearns put it at the time, 'The Japanese are selling copiers at the costs it takes for us to manufacture them'. Xerox, which had for such a long time defined the market and its standards, found itself below the market standards – not only in terms of cost, but also in terms of quality. The conclusions of a benchmark survey launched by Xerox were clear: as a Xerox senior manager put it 'it was not a case of being out in left field. We weren't even playing the same game.'

Japanese companies had six to eight times less inventory than Xerox. For every employee, there were 1.3 overhead support employees at Xerox, while only 0.6 support employees per employee in Japanese companies. The unit manufacturing costs of the Japanese were 66 percent those of Xerox.

The deterioration of Xerox's position was rapid: Xerox's market share of installed copiers dropped from 80 percent in 1976 to 13 percent in 1982.

Within the span of a few years, 10 Japanese companies had entered the business. The major ones were Canon, Ricoh, Sharp, Minolta, and Toshiba. They offered reliable and cheap products, and moved from their beachhead at the low end of the copier market to higher positions. Canon struck first, in 1981, introducing a line of middle-volume copiers. Whereas 1981 was one of the best years for Xerox, with operating profits of $1.25 billion, these dropped to less than half the year after.

As a first reaction to this by now critical situation, 1981 saw a broad restructuring of the company. Xerox reorganized along Strategic Business Units, and laid off 12,000 people between 1981 and 1982. Then, a large-scale Quality Program was launched, which led to a major cultural change for Xerox. In fact, from the inward-looking company it had become, virtually insensitive to changing customer logics, the culture and concrete functioning of Xerox became once again more outward looking, and alert to creating value with and for customers. Quality at Xerox was defined as 'meeting customer requirements'. The program instituted formal customer satisfaction measurement systems, and linked these to compensation and promotion. It supplied people at all levels with appropriate problem-solving tools.

This program proved to be a significant success. Dramatic improvements in manufacturing costs and customer satisfaction were evident beginning in 1983. At the same time, at the end of 1982, the third generation of Xerox copiers was released: the 10 Series. This product, accompanied by the Quality Program, was a big success in the marketplace, and was largely responsible for Xerox's first recovery signs (in 1983) that enabled Xerox to claw back and reclaim market share.

Another release of new Xerox copiers took place in 1988 (the 50 series). This fourth generation consisted of sophisticated copiers which included more digital, microelectronic components, and greatly contributed to strengthen Xerox's recovery. With this new release, Xerox managed to turn the situation around, as Paul Allaire (then Xerox President) put it for the release: 'We are setting the benchmark against which our competitors must be judged.' This recovery gained further credibility with Xerox's winning of the Baldrige National Quality Award, also in 1988.

By the end of the 1980s, Xerox regained 19 percent overall market share in the copier market. From 1984 to 1988, the number of defective parts dropped from 10,000/million to 325/million, and customer satisfaction increased by 38 percent. In September 1990, Xerox was confident enough to offer a Customer Satisfaction Guarantee for all its customers (replacement of the machine at the expense of Xerox).

And yet, the established (Figure 2.1) configuration of Xerox's relationship with its customers remained mostly unchanged. Xerox had managed to enhance the characteristics of its existing offering, but had not basically changed it. Xerox's offering was centered on 'boxes' sold to clients with 'after-sales' service. Even the 'forced' change from leasing to selling – for some of the machines – was not a significant re-configuration of the established business model.

THE SEARCH FOR A NEW CONFIGURATION: 1985–95

Winning the 'Quality' battle helped Xerox deal with immediate threats from new entrants, re-establishing the company's competitiveness, and safeguarding the established configuration. Yet, Xerox could not rest. Profound questions about the company's future remained – questions such as:

- What is Xerox's positioning?
- How does Xerox differentiate itself from the competition?
- What is Xerox's 'distinctive competence'?[14]
- Is the move from analog (electo-mechanical and chemical) technologies to digital ones (electonic/programmable) inevitable?
- If so, what are the implications for the company?

These questions brought to the forefront key unresolved issues for the company. With the help of hindsight, we can see that these issues included:

- *Lack of clear business idea.* Xerox declared that 'we are not only a copier company' and expanded into the financial business area (as a result of investments decided by CEO D. Kearns, in 1984). But how Xerox defined its business was not sufficiently clear and explicit.

- *Lack of agreement on the evolution of technology.* Xerox's copier-engineering community in the late 1980s did not accept the move from analog to digital technologies as 'inevitable'. Many studies and arguments indicated that analog technology would always be advantageous for copiers. While analog advocates were right within their own logic, they found it hard to admit that digital copiers could ever be something other than a one-for-one replacement of analog (light-lens) copiers.

- *Hesitations about 'system activities'.* The existing Systems Group delivered numerous products during the 1980s (laser printers, personal computers, workstations, etc.). Most of these products did poorly in the marketplace. Even exceptions, such as the laser printer, and in particular the 9700 printer that served as an output device for IBM mainframes, were considered as evidence that Xerox could not exploit the overall potential of such 'systems' products well. For example, Xerox failed to address the low end of the market for laser printers, leaving it to Hewlett-Packard, which quickly dominated it. Yet, as the digital world progressed, 'system' activity was taken to be more and more 'strategic'. What directions to take? How to relate it to the copier activity? How to resolve the tensions between the two activities?

- *No specific definition of Xerox's sustainable competitive advantage against competitors.* The widespread impression was that, even if the Quality battle was won, it would be hard to maintain Xerox's position in the long run. There was a sense that the cost and quality battle was a never-ending one.

And so, in 1985 – 10 years after the Federal Trade Commission's decision on xerography patents – the Corporate Strategy Office initiated a process to define Xerox's strategy for the 10 coming years (1985–95). This process was called 'Xerox '95'. It was the first structured process ever developed at Xerox to think about the future strategic directions for the company.[15]

To define this strategy, Xerox's top management team proceeded through a collective, interactive exploration process. It was focused on the major identified threat for Xerox at that time – that 'paper will go away' – and aimed at discussing two key questions:

- 'What is our business?'
- 'What is our strategy?'

The beginning of the process confirmed Xerox's lack of clarity and focus. There was no unanimity of any kind within the senior team concerning questions such as 'What business are we in?' or 'What are Xerox's distinctive strengths and weaknesses?' (the key questions submitted to the senior team by the Corporate Strategy Office). The company in effect had emerged from the recovery of its first crisis with no common view about what its future should be.

The 'Xerox '95' process team began examining alternative positioning and strategy options. As a result of their analyses, and the identification of major external issues, the team finally put forward four possible strategies for Xerox's future:

1   The '*System Strategy*'
    - Basic assumption: The world of paper is going away.
    - Resulting positioning: 'We should move aggressively in the 'systems' activity. We should be second after IBM.'
    - Code name = the 'Chrysler' strategy (in second position behind GM at the time).
2   The '*Copier Strategy*'
    - Basic assumption: We are a copier company, and have exceptional capabilities in the copying field ... If we remain the best in

copying, we will retain the need for paper, which will not go away.

- Resulting positioning: 'Leadership position in the copying industry.'
- Code name = the 'Boeing' strategy.

3   The '*Direct Sales Force Strategy*'

- Basic assumption: We have a world-class sales force. We can sell office equipment, supplies, and even furniture. Just give us other products to sell, and we will sell them, too.
- Resulting positioning: 'Let's become a selling company.'
- Code name = the 'Sears' strategy.

4   The '*Financial Strategy*'

- Basic assumption: If we just exit from businesses in which we lose money, we will recover.
- Resulting positioning: 'Let's position the company on short-term, profitable, activities.'
- Code name = the 'BMW' strategy.

After having collectively weighed the pros and cons of each of these four strategies, CEO David Kearns took the recommendations of the group and came up with the following choice: 'I want a modified Boeing strategy.'

At the time, this was widely interpreted as meaning that he wanted Xerox to remain a key (ideally, dominant) player in its 'core business' (copiers), while expanding its capability range and its markets. In other words, it meant that Xerox would enter the electronic world, and address the whole document problem.

The most important aspect of Kearns' decision was the focus on the document. He and his team reasoned that paper was not going to go away, but that its use, its value logics, would change. Paper would be used less for creating, storing and transmitting documents, and more as a transient display medium for reading them and commenting on them.

An important risk was that with more convenient printers, documents would be printed out, thrown away, and then printed out again. However, the real point [of the strategy] was that our customers are not interested in paper per se, but in the content on it: the document. If we focused on that [i.e the document] and how to help them deal with it in paper or electronic form, our business would prosper no matter how technology evolved.' (R. Levien, Head of Corporate Strategy).[16]

The new strategic direction was communicated internally in January 1986. It is known as the 'Document Processing Strategy'.

IMPLEMENTING A NEW CONFIGURATION: THE DOCUMENT PROCESSING STRATEGY

The major assumption of the Document Processing Strategy was that the development of electronics would not mean the disappearance of paper. Paper would remain the preferred media for communication: 'Paper will continue to be the primary tool of the office.' Yet, the *relationship* between paper and electronics would become crucial: this is where Xerox would position itself if it wanted to remain a leader in the document business in the coming years.

Thus, the Document Processing Strategy established *for the first time a focus on the document as a business.* The 'document' was defined as 'recorded information structured for human comprehension' (R. Levien, Head of Corporate Strategy). Documents were considered to be 'the life blood of the office, its raw material and final product'.

This strategy resulted in a shift in the position of Xerox's offerings in relation to the paper and digital formats of documents.

Xerox's initial copying technology (Xerography) had enabled documents to go only from a paper to a paper format. As we saw above, 'system' activities had extended Xerox into the electronic format, with offerings allowing documents to go from the electronic to the paper format in the form of printing, and from paper to paper through an intermediary electronic format in the form of faxing. Becoming a leader in document processing meant that Xerox had to position itself as linking electronic and paper in any direction. The new strategy in effect meant that Xerox would have to invest in scanning technologies, and to provide the means to integrate and manage information flowing both from digital to paper and paper to digital formats.

As a result, the document processing strategy formalized the necessity to have state-of-the-art capabilities in all the technologies which enable users to build bridges for documents, between electronic and paper formats, so as to enhance information and communication effectiveness. This new positioning implied three important changes in Xerox's offerings.

First, it implied that the offering provided by Xerox to its customers would have to shift from 'stand alone boxes' (i.e. the actual copiers), to 'systems reprographics' (i.e. inter-linked series of boxes in modular systems). These modular systems would perform copying, as well as document capture, storage, processing, communication, and printing. Xerox's new goal was to link its capabilities on printing, copying, faxing, and scanning together; and also connect them with other vendors of computer (and 'network') systems. Thus, the new positioning implied three new imperatives:

- more diverse products that are
- consistent and interconnected and
- compatible with other offerings

Second, the shift from 'copying' to 'document processing' meant that Xerox had to change the role its offerings played in the value creation of its customers. Internally, this came to be seen as offering customers not only 'relieving' products – products that make a task easier – but also 'enabling' services – services that enable customers to do more. As Paul Allaire, CEO, explained:

> Our strategy is designed to enable our customers to effectively utilize their entire information base; by providing [*them with*] products and software that will enhance the ease with which people can create, reproduce, distribute, and file documents; by enabling users to move seamlessly back and forth between electronic and paper document.[17]

Third, Xerox would have a more strategic role in its customer's business:

> Connecting the company's document base to its electronic environment
> is a key to realizing the full potential of its investments in information
> systems. We believe that a company's ability to gain a competitive edge
> in the future will depend on its ability to effectively utilize its entire
> information base. Our strategy is designed to enable our customers to
> do that.[18]

Internally, the practical consequences of this new strategy were understood as a need 'to move toward systems'; that is, to reach a new position between the paper and electronic formats of documenting. The new position was closer to the electronic format than the paper-oriented copying configuration one had been.

> The new strategy was a resolution of an internal conflict between those
> who were pushing for a copier focus and those pushing for a system
> focus. [The document processing concept] provided an answer to this
> since it acknowledges that the two were merging and that the key
> concept was the document.[19]

THE SEARCH FOR NEW WORDING

The wording used at the time to depict these ideas, Document Processing, did not satisfy Xerox's top management.

As Dr Roger Levien, Vice-President of Corporate Strategy, put it 'we had a good strategy, but internally, people did not get enthusiastic about the notion.' The top management team had defined the 'Document Processing' concept as a *data* processing concept. Internally, however, people did not get it. They associated 'Document Processing' with *paper* processing. A problem was that the notion was often defined in terms that were too legal or technological, which failed to explain the strategic interest of the concept. As a result, some people saw Document Processing as being 'low-tech', and many believed it was a major departure from the company's core strengths, and even identity.

This was of great concern for top management. If the Document Processing idea was not well received within the company, one could assume it would be even worse for people outside the company. The key question was: '*How to market this idea for the outside?*'

So in the late 1980s, David Kearns (then CEO) and Paul Allaire (appointed President in 1987) decided to hire a marketing person from the outside, Len Vickers, coming from GE, to work on this challenge.

Vickers was aware of the new document focus which the company had chosen to pursue. It was consistent with his own view of the business. According to a member of the strategic department:

> Len Vickers came with a strong personal point of view: 'I don't understand technology, and I am not interested in it. Rather, I am interested in the document as a business process. That is why I think we should understand the customer's business process.'

Len Vickers spent a few months figuring out how to market this idea. One day he called Roger Levien and said, 'Let's do it flat-footed: how about "the Document Company"?' Levien answered: 'Not bad!' Paul Allaire immediately accepted this new concept.

In fact, according to Len Vickers himself, this new wording was not only both a marketing and strategic necessity, it also was a symbolic imperative for the recently appointed CEO to 'leave his mark'. 'Paul Allaire had the vision, I gave voice to it.'[20]

Once this new wording was found, it was communicated internally and externally very quickly. Top management accepted the 'Document Company' wording in the spring of 1990, and communicated it to the general public that summer. This speed is explained by the important, and potentially lethal, resistance to the new wording:

> When I said, 'The document is the right idea' . . . it created a huge push back, a lot of resistance in the company. The biggest resistance was not coming from the technical people but from the marketing side because 'The Document Company' was about seeing things differently . . . I spent a lot of time addressing this resistance.[21]

The first people that needed to be convinced were the senior management team members. The aim was to persuade them that 'the Document' was not only the right *issue* but also the right *word*. Len Vickers and Nancy Wiese (Director of Worldwide Strategic Advertising for Xerox) delivered a presentation and shot a commercial for this purpose. They remember having chosen to address every negative feeling 'Document' provoked among people, both emotionally and rationally. The speech they gave that day and the commercial they presented[22] were very well received by the senior team. Nancy Wiese reports that the audience applauded, which was unusual in senior team meetings.

The next assignment was to convince the rest of the Xerox workforce, from managers to rank-and-file employees. Many people in Xerox were skeptical. In part, this skepticism was justified: many ideas had been launched in the recent past – 'Architecture of Information', 'New Directions' – but nothing had come out of these. Thus, people were wary of any new 'big' idea or 'concept'. To counter this, Len Vickers decided to run an advertisement for the general public. 'It was the only way to persuade inside people,' Vickers explains. 'It gave credibility and legitimacy to our claim.' If Xerox was going to be seen in the 'document' way by outsiders, it would make insiders accept it.

In effect, therefore, the new 'Document Company' wording was communicated both to insiders and outsiders (including customers and financial actors) at the same time. The 'Document Company' was communicated before top management had a clear idea of what it implied on a practical level. Intention preceded action. Vickers: 'When we announced the new strategy, we were not ready. First, we made the claim, then we implemented it.'

THE DOCUMENT COMPANY XEROX AS OF 1995

The new wording began a new strategic era, which as a process took on the name of 'Xerox 2000'. 'Xerox 2000' continued the reconfiguration of Xerox's business that began with 'Xerox '95'. As with its predecessor, it would concern the 10 coming years (1990 to 2000). The process began in January 1990 and ended in January 1991. Whereas 'Xerox '95' led to a concept labeled 'document processing', 'Xerox 2000' was shaped and oriented by the new wording: 'The Document Company.'

As Len Vickers put it, 'Xerox 2000' consisted in 'thinking of the future with the Document glasses – wearing the Document glasses to identify all the new opportunities, in terms of technology, threats, competition ...'

Thus, 'Xerox 2000' was the process which put flesh on the 'Document Company' bones. In many respects, it set Allaire's agenda for the remainder of his tenure (aged 60 in 1998, he would have to retire by 2000 at the latest[23]).

The key 'Document Company' strategy which the 'Xerox 2000' process produced was:

> Xerox, The Document Company, will be the leader in the global document market providing Document Services (products, systems, solutions, and support) that enhance business productivity (i.e. enable individuals and organizations to be more effective and productive). Our leadership will be based on superior document technologies, linked to a superior understanding of the document and its role in our customers' business processes. We will understand and anticipate customers' document needs and provide services that exceed their expectations.

A graphic representation of this strategy, *centered on customer value creation* called 'the (customers') Document cycle', is shown in Figure 2.2. Note that the 'copy' function is now one out of 16 items in customers' documenting.

This strategy built on the Document Processing themes of 'Xerox '95'. It meant Xerox would provide products *and* services focused on the whole document cycle of its customers. Xerox would now be present at every stage of its customers' document cycles including, as its web-page indicated in 1998, 'input, receipt and capture; management: archiving, retrieval, creation, replication, summarization, abstraction; and output: digital distribution, printing and duplication, viewing and use'.

Yet, some new themes also emerged in 'Xerox 2000':

- Xerox's distinctive capabilities are its technology *and* its understanding of documenting cycles. There is an emphasis on the 'understanding' capabilities of Xerox in addition to the more classical mastery over 'technologies'.
- Xerox is producing 'solutions' said strategy head Levien: 'The Document Company strategy changed what Xerox claimed it brought to the customer: we are no longer selling only products but also services, solutions. We are solution providers.'

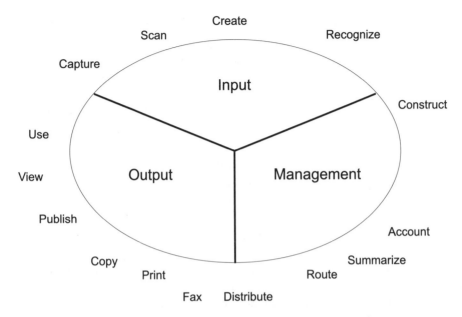

Figure 2.2 Xerox's strategy, in terms of customers' documenting cycles.

- Xerox's goal is to increase the customers' productivity.

The 'Document Company' strategy allowed Paul Allaire, the newly appointed CEO, to reconfigure the business in three, mutually reinforcing ways.

1   *It refocused the company by redefining the business.* The new strategy offered an opportunity to get rid of non-performing investments in financial activities, concentrating on Xerox 'core' activities. As Len Vickers puts it:

> Paul Allaire disliked the new businesses we had got into: financial businesses, insurance. . . . He thought there were plenty of opportunities in our core business, but that we had to redefine what it was. . . . He needed to have an idea which would allow him to get rid of the financial businesses, and a way to show that our core business was still profitable.

Paul Allaire confirmed afterwards:

We [*now*] have a focus on what we know and what we do well. We failed in the past when we went outside our [*area of expertise*]. We know the office, we know the documents, we have superior technology and we know our competitors.'[24]

The Document Company concept shifted attention from the *production* of the offering to its *role* in customers' value creation.

Xerox had forgotten a fundamental thing: that it was in the copies, in the document, business as opposed to the copiers business. (Len Vickers)

The Document Company strategy allowed

a change in our driving force, our focus. From technology driven (we have a technology and we sought to apply it on everything), we became market driven. The Document notion pulled us into many marketplaces we were not in. Now we have to follow the Document everywhere. (Pierre Danon, head of the Publishing Division until 1999, then, CEO of Xerox Europe)

2   *It supported Xerox's transition from analog to digital technologies, and organized their integration, while allowing it to remain active and strong in analog technology.* Micro-electronics technology brought an inescapable shift from analog toward digital technologies in many applications and markets. Xerox's top management perceived this both as a major threat and as an opportunity. The new strategy repositioned Xerox *vis-à-vis* this evolution. The Document Company Strategy 'provided a meaningful way to unite the company, which had been technically and geographically divided. It pushed us to be more "system" oriented: to integrate our two offerings (i.e. copiers and systems), previously disjointed'. (Len Vickers)

3   *It reconfigured the strategy so that price-centered competition would not be central.* This is a major advantage of the new strategic position:

Selling boxes, whatever their value is, is sooner or later being condemned to being a peripheral seller. Xerox, as it is today, has no future as a box seller, no matter what these boxes are: copiers, printers, etc. . . . We chose not to compete on price, this is the game for the small, reactive companies, not ours. If we were playing this game we would not need the Systems Research Centers – PARC and Rank Xerox Research Center: they would not contribute to that strategy. (Hervé Gallaire, R&D Director, Europe until 1999, then head of R&D for the whole of Xerox)

We positioned ourselves as solution providers because we did not want to become a commodity hardware producer: i.e. people producing pieces of hardware ... this would have obliged us to compete on a low-cost basis. If we want to be a leading company, we have to deliver solutions. (Roger Levien)

The focus on the value-creating potential within the customer base meant that Xerox positioned its offerings as 'strategic' for the customer, and thus had to change the counterparts with whom Xerox interacted in client companies. This is graphically illustrated in the new 'documenting' configuration, in Figure 2.3 below.

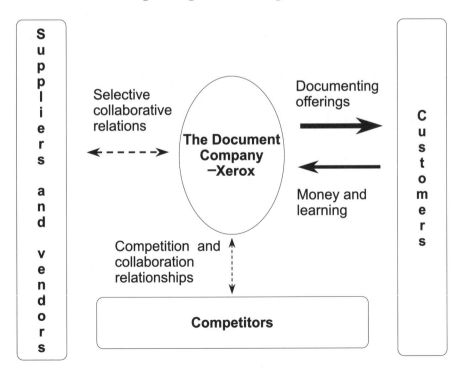

Figure 2.3 The 'documenting' configuration.

HOW THE 'DOCUMENT COMPANY' RECONFIGURATION CREATED NEW MARKETS

Xerox came to offer a credible set of 'Document' offerings supporting the whole document cycle very rapidly. Starting with high-end markets, Xerox released the 'Docutech' in 1990. It was the first offering to concretize the bridge between the paper and electronic domains, and revolutionized the printing of documents.[25] As such, it demonstrated the viability and interest of the 'Documenting' strategy.

The 'Docutech' offering was then extended to other market segments. First, it was developed for the offices market. For example, the 'Document Center System 35' introduced in 1995 was a multi-capability system including printing, scanning, faxing, and copying functions. It could be accessed either from a PC or on a walk-up basis. The offering, as it was meant to, allowed office workers to navigate easily between digital and paper documents.

In 1997, Xerox evaluated Document Center Systems to be a billion-dollar business within five years. A next step was to extend these offerings to individual and small office customers. In 1995, a line of multi-function products costing less than $600, the Xerox Document Center 250, was made available. It too integrated fax, print, copy, and scan functions, linked to the user's PC.

Xerox offerings in color printing and copying also experienced very active development. First considered as an enhanced offering, color allows customers to communicate better, to optimize document use. As is mentioned in the Xerox web page, studies show that 'highlighting' color improves decision-maker performance, as it

- improves the time to locate a target word within a document by up to 74 percent;
- the time to comprehend by up to 29 percent; and
- the accuracy of comprehension by up to 77 percent.

France Telecom, one of Xerox's main French customers, used color in an effective way to highlight the move from 8 to 10 digit phone numbers, with messages appearing in an unusual, attention-grabbing green color background within the usual blue/red monthly bill.

Xerox, through its reconfiguration, also managed to reach new customers and to create new markets.

The best example is the creation of a 'print-on-demand market', created with the introduction of the Docutech in 1990. Its new technology (digital print-on-demand) allowed Xerox to approach new customers. With their publishing products they entered the reprographic department in the large organizations, and then went to the printer people. They had never approached this kind of customer before ... Today, the printer people represent 80 percent of Xerox's publishing market.

These 'printer people' were progressively convinced by the new technology. It offered them totally new ways to do their business. Before, printing companies were obliged to print large quantities to leverage their huge printing costs. Xerox's innovation made it economically possible to print small quantities of documents, with the same quality as before. It eliminated costly stocks, and even the need for physical storage. Wiley, the publisher, uses this to reduce print run size, and to reprint as demand requires.

The expansion of Xerox's offerings in 1994 and 1995 (for example, the 6135 Production Publisher) allowed customers to share and manage documents to be printed across countries and continents.

By 1996, Docutech technology had created a $1.4 billion business with more than 10,000 systems installed worldwide.

In a similar way, Xerox has been instrumental in developing the market for Personal Copying and Printing (an activity it launched in 1988). The business grew from $200 million in 1993, to $300 million in 1994, and $400 million in 1995. A new configuration of relationships has also been developed with these customers, for example, selling through retailing channels and including maintenance agreements with resellers.

Examples of customers' value creation, significantly affected through the use of 'Document Company Xerox' offerings, are:

- _Whirlpool_'s Swedish manufacturing operations for microwave ovens for the worldwide market switched to print-on-demand on a

Docutech 135 for oven user guides. Lead time for the booklets was cut from three weeks to eight hours.

- *Handelsblatt*, Germany's business and financial daily, produces an A4-size evening newspaper for Lufthansa. Business Class passengers receive the latest news on eight pages including the closing quotes of the Frankfurt Stock Exchange. With the help of Xerox Business Services' Documents Direct, the newspaper is printed in 12 locations and distributed on all domestic flights from 4:30 p.m. onwards, only 20 minutes after the copy deadline.

CONCLUSION: SIGNIFICANCE OF THIS STORY

Xerox struggled for years, for decades, until it found how to relate a set of capabilities with the logics of customer value creation. The relationship became an offering, 'photocopying', that became very successful. The fact that even today we often use the word 'Xerox' to mean 'photocopy' attests to this success better than anything else.

With time, both the (a) relevance of the set of capabilities, and (b) the customer value-creation logics evolved. And so the fit between (a) and (b) became less tight, and the offering that manifested it lost its competitiveness.

Because the capability sets of new entrants matched customer value-creating logics better, these new entrants developed offerings that out-competed those of the incumbent companies.

At first Xerox sought to copy its invaders' relative strengths. It decreased costs and enhanced quality. Yet it took Xerox about 10 years to begin rethinking how to find a radically different relationship, between a new set of (a) capabilities and (b) its understanding of customers' value creation. And finally they succeeded. They came up with the notion of 'documenting', which is argued here to be a new radical innovation, in the same way as photocopying was.

Yet documenting itself is under attack, just as photocopying came to be attacked. Only this time, the attacks on Xerox's second configuration have come much faster. And so, as we write this book, we see Xerox struggling with moving from 'documenting' to 'knowledge management'. The time it has taken to define and grow a new configuration, lead it, then seeing it attacked has taken only a few years – not a few decades, as was the case with photocopying.

As development cycles shorten, thinking about who will out-configure present configurations becomes very important indeed. Obviously, it is important for the incumbents who have configured (or reconfigured) a business, and who are its 'prime movers'. It is also what any attacker seeking to take on the prime mover role in its place is also thinking about.

Reconfigure or be reconfigured. That is the question. That is the strategic question for senior managers everywhere: do we play by our own rules or by others. If we do it by our own, who will challenge us doing so, and how? If we do it by others, how can we create rules that we, and hopefully others, will also play by? How can we prevent others from becoming prime movers at our expense? How can we become the prime mover?

It is these questions which this book explores.

The Perception of Value 3

DEVELOPMENT OF THE UNDERSTANDING OF HOW VALUE IS CREATED

This chapter:

- Shows how from *the customer's point of view,* an offering's value is created in the interaction between the customer and his or her customers or counterparts. In other words, a company's offerings have value to the degree that customers can use them as inputs to leverage their own value creation.
- Presents a *value-creation framework* which structures the interactivity between a company, the company's customers, and the customers' customers and the offerings that manifest this interactivity.
- Explains how a value-creating offering is *three-dimensional,* encompassing hardware (the physical product), software (technical or customer service support, for example) and peopleware (in the form of a long-term partnership, for example).
- Shows how a value-creating offering shifts the focus of a company's strategy from a product/market strategy to the design of *value constellations.* Value constellations concern the group of actors who are involved in co-producing value-creating offerings.

We end this chapter with an in-depth example of a value constellation in action.

HOW CUSTOMERS PERCEIVE VALUE

Why customers are important

As mentioned in Chapter 2, understanding how customers perceive value has become very important for management. Recent studies have shown the direct link between customer retention and profitability. One such study in the US insurance brokerage industry showed that the firm with the highest pretax profit margin also had the highest degree of customer retention.[1]

Just as companies are recognizing the value of loyal customers, however, customers themselves are becoming less loyal. Companies are therefore taking aggressive steps to keep their customers. Merrill Lynch has their sales people rewarded not just on commissions generated but also on enhancing the value of 'assets under management'. Merrill has found that the value of 'assets under management' is increased most effectively when it helps loyal customers make money. In the same way, MBNA, a fast growing major US credit card company, has incentives tied to customer loyalty.

The bottom line is that growth in profits, and shareholder value, are greatly affected by ongoing relationships with loyal customers.

Different customers see products differently

The notion of 'customer base management' describes how firms systematically act in order to cultivate their customer relationships. They aim to achieve the best possible fit between their own activities and their customers' perceptions of value.

To manage a customer base, it is essential to see the world from the point of view of the customer. Different customers see things differently. Let's take the example of a white shirt, and five possible customers.

For the first customer the shirt would represent just a piece of clothing. It is important that it fulfills a certain physical function. In this case value for the customer is based on the price of the shirt in relation to its physical specifications (for example, the quality of the fabric).

A working woman with limited time for shopping may consider the purchasing of a shirt in a similar way as the first one, except for one thing.

She wants to be able to get the shirt with a minimum of time spent on the actual shopping event. She may therefore have a similar evaluation in respect of price and quality, but she will additionally pay attention to the logistics of getting the shirt. For example, she may order through catalogs, a home-shopping network or the Internet. For her the question of how to get the product becomes decisive.

Another buyer of a white shirt is looking for something which will become an integral part of her wardrobe. The shirt is not just an individual piece of clothing, but it has to fit in with the material, design, and so forth of her other clothes. It will enhance – or not! – her own personality, in her mind. Thus, image is a key consideration in the purchasing decision of this buyer.

Many environmentally conscious consumers have started to judge products based on their environmental impact. This might encourage clothes sellers to specify the origin of the material used, the environmental impact of the production process, and whether the material can be recycled or not.

The buyer of the shirt could also be a fashion student who buys the shirt to learn about design. This student might later reverse engineer the shirt and compare it with several other designs.

All of the above customers may end up buying the same shirt, but for completely different reasons!

By appreciating these differences, we can establish strategically intelligent links not only with each customer individually, but also with the ensemble of customers with whom we carry out our business. The above examples help us to take a more in-depth look at the notion of 'value added'.

How is value produced from the point of view of the customer?

Suppliers usually argue that what they sell has 'value added' when they can present some new feature of their product or service. But this so-called 'added' value is in fact only 'added' for the supplier!

From the customers' point of view, what a supplier brings is not 'value added', but – at least most immediately – an extra cost ('cost added').

An offering may indeed become more valuable for customers as a result of new or additional features with which the supplier has decided to extend it. However, in many situations customers do not actually experience this added value at the time of the acquisition. They experience the 'extra' value (if they experience it at all) much later, upon actually using the offering to create value (when the buyer wears the shirt, for example).

Why later? The reason is that the actualization of value takes place – that is, value is *actually* manifested – in *the actual relationships between a customer and his or her customers or counterparts.* In other words, for customers, value is not 'added' in the interaction between customer and supplier (when the customer buys the shirt) but in the interaction between the customer and the customer's customer or counterpart (when the buyer wears the shirt and her family and others see it on her). In co-productive terms, value is manifested thanks to the 'enabling' which the supplier brings to the customer's own value creating activity. By 'enabling' we mean 'supporting', or 'making possible'. Thus, for example, using portable computers enables authors of books to write faster and in more flexible ways, than if they were to do it by hand or by typewriter. Modems and phone companies and software enable this writing to be shared by co-authors, faster and more effectively than it would be to share it by mail or fax – which would mean rewriting the whole text each time a correction or improvement is suggested by the co-writer.

It is thus not at the interface with the supplier that value is manifested for a customer, but at the interface between the customer and the customer's customers or counterparts. Take the example of the white shirt.

- The first two examples may represent customers who consider their families as their primary counterparts. In our terminology we could call the family members 'customers' of the mother. For her it is important the family budget is spent in a sensible way, considering the multitude of interests that have to be met within the family. In the second case the issue of budget additionally includes the question of how the mother disposes her time. The ultimate definition of the value of the offering, therefore, will be determined by the customer in relation to her customers, even if the product bought, in this case the shirt, primarily was for herself.

- The third case involved a customer who is very conscious about (who much values) how she is judged by other people around her, as in her mind this ultimately defines her image. Again here the value has to be related to the context represented by the customer's counterparts.

- The same can be said about the fourth, environmentally conscious customer. Here value is not only manifested in other people, but in a general concern about how our behavior affects the future of our planet. But again it is a question about value in relation to someone else – future generations, for whom the buyer acts as a surrogate guarantor.

- The final example puts the value of the shirt in relation to a time perspective. The learning derived from the purchasing and subsequent reverse engineering is pursued in order to become something new. This 'becoming something (new)' is of value in the customer's perception because of how the new role will enable the actor to be valued (in her mind) by other people whose valuing she values.

These examples demonstrate that value is established in terms of the current or planned interaction which customers have with their interest group, valued counterparts or, a term we use for all of the above situations, 'customers'. These 'customers' may not buy anything from the customer in question. They only need to be valued by the customer, and what the customer has bought will help enhance the value of the interactions the customer has with them. 'Customers' in this broad sense can thus include family, friends, future generations, or designer colleagues. Value is 'co-produced', interactively, in the sense that it requires the customer and her customers to appreciate the shirt's specific supporting role – enhancing their mutual valuing of their interaction. The customer may have some predisposition, expectations, plans, and/ or opinions regarding the eventual value of the shirt. But the value of the shirt will not be truly and finally determined until the customer can determine the value of the interactions she actually entered into with the help of the shirt.[2]

In sum, value is not 'objective'. That is, it does not reside 'in' the object itself. If it did, a white shirt would have the same value no matter which customer bought it.

At the same, however, value is not totally 'subjective' either. Beauty, for example, is said to be subjective, as reflected in the proverb, 'Beauty is in the eye of the beholder'. The beholder is supposed to independently determine the beauty of an object (or person). Yet taste, which is co-produced socially, will intervene and guide the beholder's preferences. The five different customers cited above do play a role in determining the value of the shirt. But they too do not value the shirt in total independence. As shown above, a customer cannot determine the value of an offering independent of the interactions (involving other actors) that he or she has had or is expecting to have.

Rather than being objective or subjective, interactive value is, in fact, 'actual'. It is 'actual' in the sense that it requires *action* on the part of both the customer, and his or her customers, and the supplier for the value to become (actually) possible. Once the actions take place, they become *facts*. Actual value is thus dependent on 'action' and inter*action*, which upon taking place 'actually', becomes 'factual'.

With this understanding of customer valuation, the notion of 'end customer' – a customer at the end of a value chain that passively receives the value produced by the supplier – has lost its significance. Somebody buys an offering, seeking to co-create value with others, for themself, for the other, and/or for third parties. We buy in order to create value, with others or in relationship to them. And we seek value-creating opportunities, which guide much of our buying.

Understanding these value-creating opportunities for one's customers becomes the true challenge for any seller. The interface between one's customers and their own different customers, establishes the value that one's customers are seeking to produce. It is the supplier's role of actually helping customers to create value (with their counterparts) that convinces a customer to buy from that supplier.

Estimating value before the interactions

Some offerings, such as cars, can be 'test driven' before acquisition. Other offerings, such as visits to the dentist, cannot.

The second type of offering in particular poses a problem for prospective buyers, who have to estimate the value of what they plan to acquire before having the possibility of actually valuing it.

Before a customer can wear a shirt, he or she has to pay for it. In other words, they have to establish how valuable the offering is going to be for them. They may do so based on their expectations of how the offering will enable them to interactively create value. For the reasons surveyed above, to evaluate the value of the offering before acquiring it, the customer has to consider which counterparts they want to interact with, how these interactions can create value for the other counterparts and for themself, and under which circumstances these interactions will take place.

The connotations that a given interaction holds for us, how we value it, are subjected to the particulars of the situation in which the interaction takes place. Aspects of the situation which affect valuation include the mood of the counterparts; the extent to which other possible interactions intervene; how the actual interaction relates to other interactions; and the setting of the interaction (the physical setting, the weather, etc.). Offerings are thus valued 'contingently', that is, depending on which place they hold in relation to other actions and interactions with which they are connected. Thus for example, the buyer's valuation of a shirt may be totally distracted if their mobile phone rings to inform them that a member of their family has just been rushed to hospital because of a car accident.

The offering consequently is not something that exists, independently, *in itself*. It both resulted from and contributes to a *bundle of activities* that enable the buyer to perform his or her activities in a different way than if the offering had not been bought. It is the outcome of these intended activities that creates some form of satisfaction for the buyer. This outcome – the effects of the offering – we call 'Net Satisfaction Contribution' (NSC). How much the customer will be prepared to transfer to the seller in the form of price paid depends on the other costs related to the purchase. A sofa 'on sale' at IKEA compared with one in the shop next door needs to be evaluated also in terms of the time to get to/ from IKEA, plus the hassle of transporting and assembling it. Valuing always includes some form of 'opportunity cost', where the alternative uses of resources and time and effort spent on obtaining an offering are taken into account. It is only upon factoring in the full set of required actions and interactions in valuation that one can determine if the desired offering provides competitive 'Net Satisfaction Contribution'.

THE CO-PRODUCTIVE VALUE-CREATION FRAMEWORK[3]

Facilitating *customer value creation* is, within the co-productive point of view, the *raison d'être* for a firm.

This perspective shifts the focus of strategic attention from actor or 'activity' to *interaction*. With this framework, it would for example no longer be 'Electrolux', for instance, that is considered to be competing in the marketplace. Instead, it is a given refrigerator produced by Electrolux, together with its relevant service packages (e.g. installation, warranties) and information (e.g. user's manual, web-site) which will compete against another such offering made by Fagor. What competes is the offering, not the actor.

Offerings are the *output* produced by one (or several) actor(s) creating value – the 'producer' or 'supplier' – that becomes an *input* to another actor (or actors) creating value – the 'customer'.

Offerings compete in a market. Firms collaborate and compete to make competitive offerings available. The way resources and customers interact to co-produce offerings is depicted in Figure 3.1.

Offerings are thus both outputs and inputs. Acknowledging and incorporating the specific *individual* requirements of each customer implies that customers cannot be simply treated *en masse* as anonymous, 'average', de-personalized 'product markets'. Customer requirements can be better understood by knowing how each customer is producing value for themselves and, in turn, for their customers. A company's offerings have value to the degree that customers can use them as inputs to leverage their *own* value creation with their *own* counterparts.

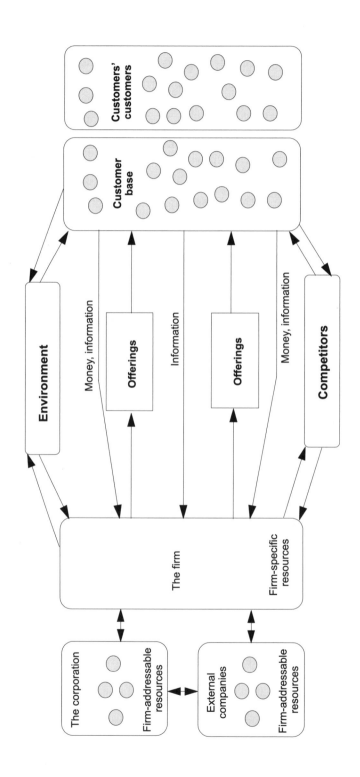

Figure 3.1 The value-creation framework.

Transactional vs. relationship logics

Co-productive value creation for customers can be approached from two distinct perspectives: 'single event'-like *transactions* and 'process'-like *relationships* over time.

The *transaction*-based logic implies that each transaction should cover its own costs plus generate a margin. An example is buying an ice-cream at a road-stop in the middle of the Arizona desert. The ice-cream seller does not expect to do business with the passengers of the car that happened to stop at this particular road stop again, at least for a long time. He does not expect to establish a 'repeat business' with the buyers. All costs incurred in getting the ice-cream to that spot, keeping it cold, advertising, and selling it, must be recovered in the single transaction made.

In the *relationship* logic, customer relationships are seen as extending over time, and are often conceived of in terms of a 'life-cycle'. The relationship logic doesn't solely focus on the profitability of individual transactions. It also focuses on the profitability of all the transactions involving one customer – in other words, all of the transactions that take place during the life of the relationship between supplier and customer. In such relationships, some up front seed investments might be needed to generate later revenues. From the supplier's point of view, one can also assume that current costs can be regarded as investments in higher future returns. An example is selling aircraft engines to airlines. Suppliers often actually sell the engine itself at a loss. But the contract stipulates that the warranty that comes attached to the engine will be honored only if original, certified, spare parts and maker-approved services are used over the life of the engine. The engine itself is a 'loss leader', and the relationship over time that the acquisition entails will provide the profit stream for the engine maker. It is the 'service & spare parts-based' relationship which will guarantee the initial investment (selling the engine below the cost of producing it, at a loss) to be worthwhile.

In the production-centered, mass market industrial era, the transaction logic dominated. More and more relationship-type offerings are appearing in the co-productive era. To explain why, we will use the example of a modern-day offering: an Internet browser.

A new offering: the Netscape navigator

Like Xerox (surveyed in Chapter 2) or the airplane engine seller mentioned above, Netscape took a relationship approach to business development. It did so primarily as a way of acquiring and securing a customer base.

Netscape started its relationship-based attack on the software market in 1994 by introducing its Navigator browser and giving it away to customers for free. An important aspect of this strategy for Netscape to take into account was that the cost accumulation of its business model took place in the initial phase of the browser's life-cycle, while revenues would flow only later. The risk was that the projected later cash flow would not occur, or that it would be distorted by later competitive actions.

Soon after it introduced its Navigator offering, IBM and Microsoft decided that the messaging and group-ware markets were 'strategic', meaning that they were willing to take non-economic returns in these. In other words, entering these markets would be done in the hope that doing so would help them image-wise and/or margin-wise in other businesses. Non-economic returns in a single market are considered good business even if it means that IBM and Microsoft sell their products at prices below costs in that market. The loss is considered an 'investment' in customer relationships, which will pay off in other product categories. Bill Gates called this space 'hyper-competitive' for IBM and Microsoft, and was of the opinion that Netscape had made a huge mistake by focusing on group-ware and messaging.

But by then, Netscape was no longer offering its browser for free.

The Economist drew the following conclusion regarding the browser market in September 1996:

> In less than a year, Microsoft has matched Netscape's software technically, signed up all the biggest Internet service firms to distribute its browser, and is giving its program away for free while Netscape charges $50 for its own. If current trends continue, Microsoft may have passed Netscape in the market by the second half of 1997.[4]

Nine months later it admitted it had been wrong.[5] The Netscape market share still was 60–70 percent.

What happened? How could Netscape maintain market share against a well-known, much bigger rival offering a competing product *for free?*

Let us begin first by looking at how customers value a transaction-based offering, applying this understanding to the example of an Internet browser.

A transaction-based offering includes the following four features:

1 The *customer value* (CV) element (what value the customer perceives he or she will obtain).
2 The *cost* element (the cost of resources required by the supplier to make the offering available to the customer).
3 The *price* element (what the supplier charges the customer for the offering).
4 The *exchange value* (EV) element (what value the supplier perceives they will gain).

Customer value (CV), the value of one transaction, from the customer's point of view, consists of the following elements:

- Net satisfaction contribution (NSC), or how well the offering supports the actual value-creation activities of the customer. In the case of a company, NSC can be measured by assessing the impact on the customer's sales revenues and/or profit. In the case of individual consumers, NSC is often measured in terms of the contribution to the level of customer satisfaction (increasing levels of satisfaction or reducing levels of dissatisfaction, as the case may be).
- The actual purchasing price[6] – the initial cost to the customer (C_1).
- The interface (or handling) cost – the cost for the customer to get the offering from the supplier to his own system (ordering, purchasing, transport, etc.) (C_2).
- The integration cost – the cost for the customer to integrate the offering into the customer's own value-creating system (C_3).
- The life-cycle cost – the projected cost-in-use related to the offering

during its utilization (operating and maintenance, financing, depreciation, disposal costs, etc.) (C_4).

- The relative risk position related to the transaction – the risk that the supplier will go out of business due to bad credit rating or, more subjectively, the perceived risk based on the level of reliability of the supplier or offering[7] (R), which is always – by definition – negative, but can be of different magnitudes.

- The potential learning/information-transfer advantages for the customer, arising from the relationship with the supplier, and enforced by and through the transaction (L), which is either 0, or – by definition – positive, but can be of different magnitudes.

Therefore, the customer value (CV) in transaction-based offerings can be expressed by the formula:

$$CV = NSC - C_1 - C_2 - C_3 - C_4 - R + L$$

When relationship logics win over transactional ones

So what happened with Netscape?

When industrial buyers in 1996 and 1997 made their browser purchases, *all elements* of the customer value equation affected their decision making.

Netscape customers began to download their Navigator browser from the Internet for free, beginning in October 1994.

By the time Windows 95 was released in mid-1995, 6 million copies of Navigator were already in use.

And when Microsoft released its first version of a browser that could claim to work as well as the Navigator in June 1996, many Windows users had already installed and learnt to use Netscape's browser.

The fact that Microsoft's Explorer browser was free represented only one element (C_1) of the customer value equation CV. Netscape, however, had the upper hand (at least for a while) on all the other elements.

The integration costs of components for corporate information systems – loading them into the system in ways that are compatible with existing elements – are often many times larger than the sales price of the individual systems component. Integration costs not only derive from technical integration (C_3), but also include all the learning necessary to get a new system introduced to hundreds or thousands of users (L), as well as the decision-making costs (C_2) that changing from one systems component to another involve.

Microsoft tried to bundle its browser with upgrades for Windows 95 and Windows NT. But this turned out to be counterproductive. As the Microsoft browser was not compatible with older Windows versions, companies still using different versions of Windows 3 were in effect forced to choose Netscape.

In a relationship-driven economy, the relative importance of customer value (CV) elements other than the purchasing price (C_1) increases. By addressing only the purchasing price element (C_1), Microsoft failed to convince Netscape customers to switch to its own browser.

The relationship offering and the supplier's perspective of value

One of the first companies realizing the potential of addressing customers as individuals with whom to establish long relationships was SAS, the airline company.

In the early 1980s Jan Carlzon, the CEO, launched SAS as the 'businessman's airline'. SAS targeted individual business travelers, and developed bundles of services that were much more customized for each individual passenger than anything competitors offered at the time. When making the flight reservation, SAS' offering made it possible simultaneously to reserve one's preferred seat, the hotel room one liked, as well as transport between the airport and the hotel. At the time this was revolutionary. SAS developed new capabilities within its own organization, and links to other organizations, in order to be able to create offerings that would match the individual value-creation logic of its most profitable customers, the businessmen, as closely as possible. Such thinking marked the invention of the 'business class' offering, which has since become as common as Xeroxing. What SAS aimed to do with this configuration was to transform what had been a transaction-based business logic into a relationship-based one.

The changing importance of the price element in establishing value within the context of a relationship-based economy affects how suppliers perceive value, not only the way customers do, as we saw above. The supplier's exchange value (EV) can be defined in a similar way to the customer value (CV). For a supplier, value is established as a function of:

- The selling price[8] (P, identical with C_1 for the customer).
- The resource cost (RC) – the cost to the supplier to access and allocate the resources necessary to provide the customer with the offering.
- The competitive blockage factor (B) – the extent to which the transaction affects the future competitive position of the supplier in relation to its competitors.
- Goodwill (G) – the transaction's customer-relationship-goodwill influence, which can affect later transactions with that particular customer or other customers, in terms of how much marketing is in effect carried out by customers.
- The relative risk position related to the transaction – either quantitatively measured (e.g. the risk that the customer will go out of business due to bad credit rating) or more subjectively evaluated, based on the level of trust in the customer[9] (R), which is always – by definition – negative, but can be of different magnitudes.
- The potential learning/information-transfer advantages arising from the relationship with the customer and enforced by and through the transaction (L), which is either 0, or – by definition – positive, but can be of different magnitudes.

Therefore, supplier's exchange value can be represented by the formula

$$EV = P - RC \pm B \pm G - R + L$$

This second equation helps to understand how Netscape eventually lost the battle to Microsoft.

Creating value in a relationship economy means that the offering's 'leverage value' or 'capability in-use enhancement' for the *buyer* (i.e.

customer value); as well as the *supplier's* exchange value, must both be positive over time.

The supplier's exchange value has to be considered in the context of the total offering set made available to the customer. That is, it must take into account not the single browser offering, but all of the elements which join a supplier and a customer. Microsoft, which also sells operating systems which link it to its customers, holds 'broader' relationships (consisting of a richer offering set, including the operating system and the browser) than those which Netscape could ever obtain through its single, browser, offering. Recall that Microsoft also offers software applications such as Word (for writing documents), Excel (for making calculations and spreadsheet analyses), and PowerPoint (for making overhead presentations).

It was within this context of 'narrow' vs. 'broad' offerings that customers continued to buy Navigators from Netscape, and pay for them, even after Microsoft had started to give away its Explorer browser for free in late 1996. However, for Netscape to keep charging for the browser, it needed continuously to maintain a significant advantage gap in its product compared to Microsoft's. In early 1998 this was no longer possible, for the RCs required to keep the differential with Microsoft's improved offerings became prohibitive. This meant that what had been a significantly positive G element became less marked. As time went by, the L value for Netscape decreased. And so, Netscape was forced to offer its basic browser for free (P) as well, without having Microsoft's advantage of making other offerings subsidize this. While Netscape could charge for some of its more sophisticated browser versions, less than a year later, Netscape joined America Online in a position of relative weakness. Microsoft had captured the browser market in accordance with *The Economist* prediction, but not as rapidly as it had expected.

Both the customer value and exchange value equations can be analyzed from a benefit/cost perspective. All elements of the value equation that have a positive value are benefits, as the elements with a negative value are costs. At least one of the elements has to be a benefit in order for the offering to be pursuable by the actor, as the equation has to have a positive value. As the browser case shows, the total value exchange potential for Microsoft was such that Microsoft could charge a price below cost for its browser, because Microsoft could develop relationship value in which this 'cost leadership' subsidy was more than made up for by other elements of the exchange value equation. Like Carlzon had done 10 years before, as of 1995 Bill Gates proclaimed that Microsoft was shifting its focus from product sales towards creating a stream of repeat business from existing customers.[10]

Other examples of relationship businesses

Arguably, most business is still today based on a transactional perspective, but we can see an increasing amount of relationship-based behavior in which the seller de-emphasizes immediate benefits from a single sale in favor of relationship-building elements.

The overview in Chapter 2 of how Xerox hit on a relationship-based logic early – through a happy set of coincidences! – shows the interest in establishing long-lasting customer relationships. A couple of examples of how this logic is manifested help illustrate our view of its rising interest.

An example of this shift is offered by Browning-Ferris Industries, Inc. It is the number-two trash hauler in the United States. It recognized that even if 86 percent of its customers remained loyal, 7,000 customers were lost every year. To reduce 'customer churn', Browning-Ferris asked customers to describe their service experiences in detail, so that it could learn what could be done to improve service to enhance its customer retention rates. The strategy was a major shift, from a focus on acquiring new customers, to one of retaining current customers as the cornerstone for future growth.[11]

Another case of a relational business logic is the outsourcing arrangement of the national insurance recording system for the Department of Social Security in the UK. The system holds 65 million records covering every UK adult and is crucial to the operation of pensions. This deal was won by Andersen Consulting at a bid of

£45 million to run the project on a seven-year extendible contract. The bid had a price which was about a third of the bids of its rivals, CSC and EDS. The reason for the low bid was that Andersen treated the project as 'an investment'. Andersen decided to put a value on the possibility of structuring the deal to own the intellectual property rights and the ability to use the skills acquired for *future* projects (i.e. learning value *L*). This *L* value enabled them to take a £100 million cut on their bid on the basis that proving that they can design and run this system will provide them with future business (i.e. goodwill *G* and competitive blockage *B*). They will then have a world class reference site to demonstrate what they can deliver.[12]

THE OFFERING AS A MEDIUM FOR VALUE CREATION

From product to offering

At least as early as the 1970s, marketing scholars already looked upon products as a package of benefits the customer receives from a supplier upon completing a transaction. Corey[13] offered the following definition of a product:

> The 'product' is what the product does; it is the total package of benefits the customer receives when he buys. This includes the functional utility of the goods, the service that the manufacturer provides, the technical assistance he may give his customers, and the assurance that the product will be delivered when and where it is needed and in the desired quantities. Another benefit might be the seller's brand-name and reputation; these may help the buyer in his promotional activities.

Theodore Levitt from the Harvard Business School defined a product as a 'complex cluster of value satisfactions'.[14] He emphasized the need to expand the understanding of the product beyond the 'generic' product to include the notions of 'expected', 'augmented', and 'potential' product. He stressed that a product has meaning only from the viewpoint of the buyer or the ultimate user. The view presented in this book, that a given 'product' will have different meanings for different customers, has therefore been supported for a number of years by marketing people.

Combining the views of Corey and Levitt, the *offering* is here defined as 'a limited set of focused human interactions which can, and is intended to, generate positive exchange and customer value.' This definition acknowledges that the offering can provide benefits to the customers not only in the form of physical products, but also in the form of service transactions, and/or usable or new information. Normann and Ramírez[15] argued that in any case, obtaining value from a good always also required the service and information aspects of the offering. No such thing as a 'pure good' exists. Nor is there such a thing as a 'pure' service, which can be valued independent of the use of a good.

Defining the offering as a set of interactions extends the Normann and Ramírez view of an offering to also include access to – or enhancement of – *relationships*. These relationships may be formed in the selling and buying activities, or later, as customers use the offerings with others. Particularly in industrial marketing, such relationships are normally now an explicit part of the 'package of benefits' that the purchaser gets access to upon acquiring an offering.

When applying the value-creation framework (Figure 3.1) for business analysis, it is useful to examine the offering in terms of a three-dimensional activity package (Figure 3.2). The three axes are *hardware* (or the 'physical product content' of the offering), *software* (the 'service and infrastructure content'), and *'peopleware'* (the interpersonal relationship or 'people content').

- The *physical content* of the offering consists of elements such as the core product, the packaging, the quality and dependability of the good and its material components, the product range, etc.
- The *service content* includes distribution, technical support, product modifications, customer training, on-line advice, troubleshooting, warranties and other trust-supporting insurance aspects, information brochures, brand reputation, complaint handling, invoicing, integrated information systems, etc.
- The *people content* covers issues like long-term partnerships, interpersonal trust, reputation, human resource co-development, etc.

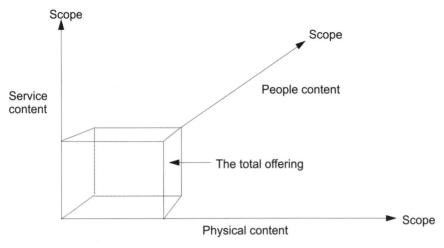

Figure 3.2 The three-dimensional offering.

In keeping with Levitt's[17] view that a product only has meaning from the viewpoint of the customer, different customers will emphasize different axes of the offering.[18]

In co-production terms, the value-creating potential along each of the dimensions of the offering – physical, service, or people content – depends on the value-creating system of the customer. Two customers from the 'same' segment may have completely different value-creation systems, and thus view the elements of the 'same' offering differently. Take, for example, General Motors (GM) and Toyota. Toyota tries to develop long-term partnerships with its suppliers. General Motors has historically been more transaction focused, and long-lasting relationships have not been seen as a worthwhile goal. As customers (of a supplier's offering), GM and Toyota would have radically different measurements on the 'people content' axis, as depicted in Figure 3.3.

From product strategy to value constellation design

Extending the concept of 'product' to one of 'offering' also implies expanding the industrial era perspective of 'product strategy' into a co-productive era one of 'designing value constellations', as is depicted graphically in Figure 3.4.

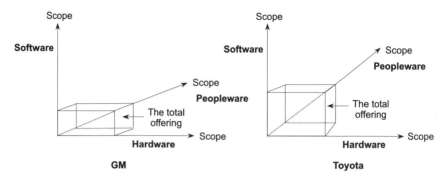

Figure 3.3 Optimized offerings for GM and Toyota respectively.

The axes of Figure 3.4 indicate the level of 'granularity' or 'resolution' applied to the issue. By 'granularity' or 'resolution' we mean the level of detail that is obtained: higher resolution would make trees appear as a relevant unit, lower granularity would mean that the forest as a whole appears. 'Granularity' or 'resolution' thus have to do with how much differentiation a view of something allows for. Our contention is that competition in a co-productive environment requires more resolution than competition in the industrial ones. The greater differentiation of enhanced 'granularity' or 'resolution' is translated, in practical terms, into

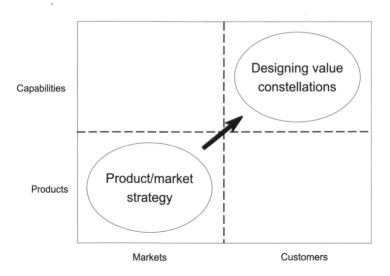

Figure 3.4 From product/market strategy to designing constellations.

greater information. As IT (information technology) becomes widely available, it physically renders it possible for businesses to enhance the granularity/resolution they deal with, by providing them with much more detailed information about each aspect of their businesses. IT thus makes it materially possible to move from a 'product/matrix' business world to the 'value constellations' one which we explore in this book.

In this chapter, and in Chapter 5, we concentrate on the horizontal (market to customer) axis. The vertical (product to capability) one is explored particularly in Chapter 6.

Enhanced 'granularity' or 'resolution' was not present in the traditional, 'industrial' logic. There, supply and demand factors were considered at a fairly aggregated level, as (generic) products and (mass) markets. For example, car manufacturers didn't think of their customers as individuals, but viewed them as a mass of buyers (markets or market segments) who bought the same product.

As the potential for interactivity between the firm and its environment increases, being able to specify the contribution of each individual party participating in value co-production is of great help. Instead of throwing products at undifferentiated market 'sinks', in co-productive situations, companies must decide which of their firm-specific capabilities to deploy for each specific customer.

A car manufacturer's capabilities in aerodynamic design, for example, is what some customers (sports car enthusiasts) will expect from their 'supplier' (the car manufacturer). Other customers will favor the possibility of extended warranties, which the manufacturer can organize for them. The choice of capabilities is derived from the customer's specific value-creation logic. In the first case, the value (to the customer) is being seen in a fancy sports car, or the joy of driving fast. In the second case, the customer wants a hassle-free relationship with the car. IT makes it possible to go beyond the relatively broad (low granularity) 'segments' of the industrial market, which simply catalogued the sinks by 'type'. Instead, we are moving to each individual customer being 'his own' (or her own) market. And so, 'share of customer' is becoming at least as relevant a notion in the co-productive economy as 'market share' was in the industrial one, if not more so. 'Share of customer' relates to how much of a customer's business a supplier has.

Every supplier firm designs a value constellation for its customers. This has always been the case. Today, however, firms are forced to be explicit about which value constellation they design for each customer. We say 'they are forced' because if the suppliers do not do it for their customers, customers will do so for themselves, perhaps with the help of other customers and suppliers. It is not by accident that WalMart claims that it does not 'sell' food, but that it 'buys it' for its customers. Supermarkets are in fact systems which allow the individual customer to tailor WalMart's acquisition into the greater, individual granularity which WalMart is today incapable of offering. Invaders such as PeaPod.com, the Internet-based grocer, are attempting to 'invade' supermarkets by doing the granularity enhancement for the customer, relieving individuals from the hassle of doing so themselves.

Value constellation designs are based on the deployment of appropriate capabilities. These capabilities are put together by a supplier in ways that result in the customer-specific, customer-appropriate value-creating offering which enables these very customers to create value. In the car example above, different capabilities (aerodynamics, insurance) are brought to the offering by the manufacturer, to best fit each individual's value-creation preference.[19]

Based on this we can define value creation as follows:

> *Value creation* is the process of co-producing offerings (i.e. products and services and information and relationships) in a mutually beneficial seller/buyer relationship. This relationship may include other actors such as sub-contractors and the buyers' customers. In this relationship, the parties behave in a symbiotic manner leading to activities that generate positive values for them. The actors brought together to interact in this process of co-producing value form a *value constellation*.

Value constellations are constantly changing. A firm designing or co-designing these must therefore have a management process to take care of its positioning within its value constellations. This constellation management process can be defined as follows:

> *Constellation management* is the management process whereby the firm (explicitly or implicitly) makes decisions on how to create value for itself and for and with customers and other possible actors in the form of offerings. It does this through value constellations. It takes into

consideration time, the larger environment, customers, suppliers, competitors and other stakeholders, as well as other resources. Constellation management requires the firm to gather and interpret data; to make, communicate, implement, monitor, and adjust decisions about tasks and resource allocations; and measure and compensate performance in respect of its present and future offerings.

Xerox, reviewed in Chapter 2, provides a good example of a company that has invented at least two important value constellations: the original photocopying one, which was so successful that it came to be known as 'Xeroxing', and the 'Documenting' one. Below we revert to the Xerox case and look into how the concepts introduced in this chapter can be applied to better address the value-creating opportunities of a firm.

Applying the value-creation framework to Xerox

Applying the value-creation framework to Xerox, we can see some major differences between the new configuration of Xerox as per 'Xerox 2000' (illustrated in Figure 3.5) and the first configuration with which Xerox succeeded.

'Competitors' in the new 'documenting' configuration are much more numerous and diverse than they were in the 'photocopier' one. The relationships with these competitors are much more varied than they were in the first constellation, where Xerox simply 'dominated' them. Xerox's goal still is to dominate other copier makers. With non-copier manufacturers, however, Xerox looks for a variety of collaborative possibilities (strategic alliances and licensing agreements, for example).

The role of the *'suppliers'* category in Figure 3.5 has also changed. A 'vendor certification process' reduced (by half) the suppliers working with Xerox. The goal was to develop better and longer-term relationships between Xerox and its suppliers.

The *distinction* between 'suppliers & vendors' and 'competitors' is increasingly blurred. In most cases, suppliers are also competitors. Xerox has developed collaborative relationships with Microsoft, Sun, Novell, AT&T, Adobe, etc.

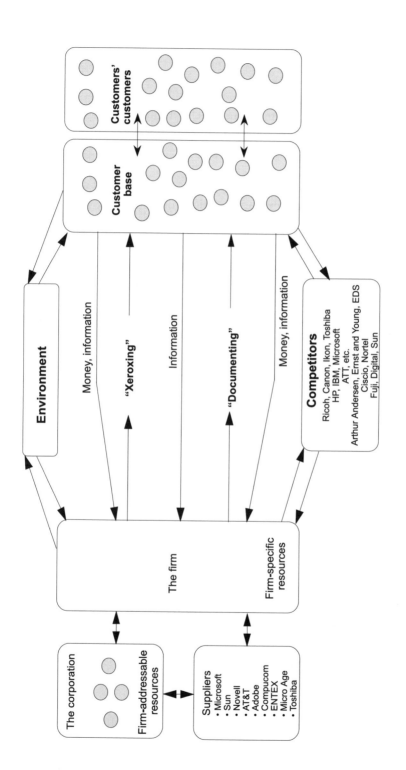

Figure 3.5 Applying the value-creation framework to Xerox.

The interaction with information technology players includes developing standard-definition agreements such as 'the Document Alliance', which offers cross-platform document compatibility. In other words, this alliance allows users to exchange documents on different platforms (PC, Mac, etc.), no matter where those documents were created. There also are different co-development efforts with different industries and activities (for example, the military, and the medical imaging industry).

Incorporating information technology players into its configuration, however, clearly enhanced the difficulties of being a prime mover. The reason: many of the chosen counterparts are standard setters in their own right. Xerox has been careful to keep its degrees of reconfiguration freedom open:

> We have announced and established relationships with a wide range of external companies, but none of them has had a substantial strategic impact. (Roger Levien, Head of Corporate Strategy)[20]

There are also *new actors* involved in this category, namely the *resellers* who sell Xerox personal and small offices products to both smaller and corporate customers. Xerox has developed agreements with these resellers in which Xerox provides them with training, support, and documentation. In exchange, the resellers take on Xerox maintenance and commit to the purchase of Xerox replacement parts. These agreements are often intense and collaborative, taking the form, for example, of strategic alliances, joint maintenance programs, joint development, etc. The 'Document Company' strategy, however, also complicates these arrangements, as the players become both collaborators and competitors. One example: Toshiba is both a Xerox supplier (of engines) and a competitor (in the field of copier manufacturing).

'Customers' have become much more fragmented. Greater granularity translates into a substantial multiplication of customer categories. New categories emerge as the distinction between analog and digital businesses becomes less clear. Xerox copiers are increasingly becoming both imaging machines and electronically connected boxes. As outsourcing

and consulting relationships replace leasing, role conflicts also arise in the customer category. Xerox in effect takes on parts of its customers' activities, and the evaluation of performance must be altered as a consequence. Also, priorities need to be re-examined: is selling boxes better than diminishing the number of boxes a customer will use through more effective documenting – aided by Xerox?

As we saw in Chapter 2, the '*offering*' has become much more strategic for many of Xerox's customers. For them, its function is now to increase client productivity and/or competitiveness.

Hardware has become more digital, and can be more easily customized (programmed). It is also broader, and includes not only individual copiers, faxes, printers, and scanners, but also a combination of this hardware into 'document management' systems.

Software focuses on integration, consistency, and even compatibility (for example, to enable the cross-platform capability described above) with existing devices and competitor's products. Software now also often includes logistics, and supply chain management.

Selling has changed what software – and people – are expected to do. Software is now integrated in different layers of Xerox offerings: operating systems, middle-ware and applications. Software is key to allowing the diversity of a product's functions and its user-friendliness.

Xerox avoided establishing its own standards for operating systems. It adjusted itself to the existing standards. In terms of applications, developed in the X-Soft division, it developed, for example, DOCU SP, which is a print-service software text bridge (a software package that allows users to access their personal computer from any fax machine in the world). Xerox's spin-off, 'Documentum' sells software for document management to pharmaceutical companies.

Many of the *people* at the customer interface are no longer Xerox employees, but rather employees from reseller companies. When Xerox employees do interact with customers, they must make a decision of whether to take the business-as-usual 'box' approach or the 'document' approach. Xerox employees who see themselves working in a 'document' company act differently from photocopier salesmen and service technicians. The very definition of 'service' is substantially different between the two approaches – from the maintenance and repair definition of the box approach to the customer solutions definition of the document approach.

These expanded and redefined 'service' offerings are mainly handled by the Xerox Business Services Division. This 'facilities management' business has existed in various forms for a long time, primarily as part of the US Customer Operations. However, it was not given adequate resources or strategic weight before 'Xerox 2000'. As a result, it did not take off until it was established as a Business Division in its own right in 1992. By 1997, this division became an outsourcing entity managing 4,000 customer locations in 36 countries, and employing 10,000 people worldwide. Nearly 90 percent of these Xerox employees work on customer sites.

Xerox became the industry leader in document outsourcing, a business it was instrumental in configuring. Prior to 1992, outsourcing was growing at 2 percent per year. Thereafter, outsourcing services revenues grew 50 percent per year: $400 million in 1993, $600 million in 1994, $900 million in 1995. XBS has grown faster than the market, which grew at an average rate of 33 percent during this time.

Xerox's initial ('photocopying') business model had been very hardware-centric: it was about selling machines. Then, up to the late 1980s, Xerox expanded its offering to be more service-centered (parts and repair, supplies and financing), which were still areas related to the machines. From the beginning of the 1990s, it moved to a software-centric company (yet still providing the hardware). Xerox then not only offered the hardware but also the connectivity, the integration, and the help to the customer. In 1996, 45 percent of Xerox revenue came from hardware, while 55 percent came from follow-up, 'post sale' revenues.

Xerox was here referred to as an example of a firm that has successfully undergone a business model transformation. Our value-creation framework highlighted how actors come to hold a plurality of simultaneous roles when value constellations, and not simple value chains, become the dominant logic of an industry. Our framework can also be applied prescriptively, to help firms make their business models compatible with emerging business opportunities and challenges to be better and faster. Finnsugar Bioproducts provides an example.

FINNSUGAR BIOPRODUCTS – APPLYING THE VALUE-CREATION FRAMEWORK TO DESIGN VALUE CONSTELLATIONS[21]

Finnsugar Bioproducts (FSB) is the world's largest supplier of betaine, producing natural betaine from mainly sugar beet molasses. Betaine is a molecule present in many living organisms. The main use of betaine is in feed for poultry, both for its impact on the growth and health of animals as well as for its function as a methyl donor. FSB was in 1997 a subsidiary of the Cultor Group, one of the world's leading companies in high-performance nutrition products with sales exceeding $1.5 billion. In 1999 Cultor merged with Danisco, another global player in nutrition products.

In 1996 Cultor introduced what they called their 'corporate value processes', of which one was 'customer orientation'. The role of customer orientation was defined by Björn Mattsson, CEO, in the following way: 'by learning to pinpoint customers' needs and by seeing how to operate better, Cultor is able to create growing amounts of value for its customers' (Cultor, Annual Report 1995).

The value-creation framework (see Figure 3.1) was used by Cultor as the conceptual model for developing customer orientation within the group. FSB was one of the units participating in the first phase of adopting the value-creation framework. The objective was to understand better the value-creation processes of its customers, and to be able to allocate resources to create the highest possible growth for the company in the short and medium term.

The agricultural market is local in its nature. Swings in world market prices of products such as wheat, barley, and corn affect local preferences in relation to ingredients for feed production. In the UK, wheat and barley account for 65 percent and 31 percent of the total grain production, respectively (1995/96). In Spain, wheat and barley account for 31 percent and 43 percent of grain production. The different combinations of feed ingredients also affect the optimum dosage of betaine. For a producer of feed ingredients, the complexity of integrating the feed ingredient into the complex feed mix is a significant challenge. Also, the effects of one particular feed ingredient depend on a combination of factors. The impact of one single ingredient is thus difficult to measure, which again affects the betaine dosage. This means that selling betaine is not only selling hardware, but also selling knowledge applied to this hardware.

FSB launched its customer-orientation pilot project in autumn 1996 to understand better the value constellations pertaining to customers in some selected markets. For these markets FSB wanted to establish the specific value-creation processes of a number of individual customers to see if there were significant differences among them. In addition FSB wanted to see if the results from the first two steps could be used better to guide decision making on (a) resource allocation, including co-operation with distributors, product support and sales activities, and (b) resource development.

Figure 3.6 offers a graphic presentation of results from one of the selected markets, the UK market for broiler production, using the value-creation framework presented in Figure 3.1 on page 48.

The analysis of these results included detailed information about the volumes and market shares of each player, at each step of the 'feed and food chain'. It also included an assessment of the relative importance of push and pull factors within the industry. This for instance included comparing the influence of each producer on other members of the producer community, as well as on members of – say – the retailing community; and vice versa. The point of this exercise was to determine the various 'referent' organizations in the UK broiler industry value constellation.

Broiler production activity is very concentrated in the UK. The FSB study made in-depth analyses of its most important feed and meat producers. The producers were in general willing to co-operate and share their views of their perception of FSB as a supplier.

The concept of the three-dimensional offering (Figure 3.2) was used to structure interviews and discussions. Specific attributes relevant for FSB had been developed and established in separate brainstorming sessions,

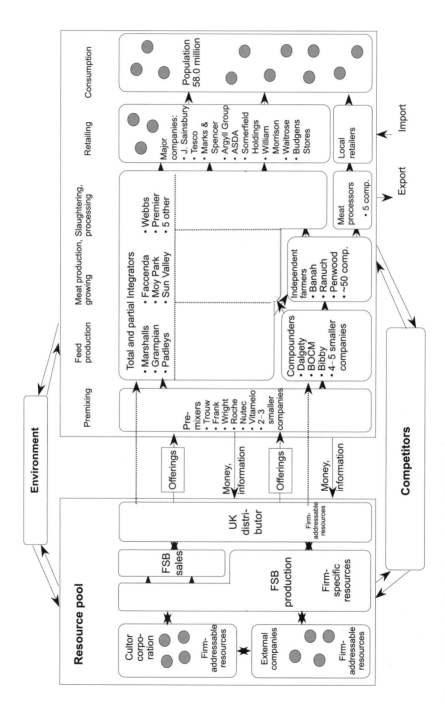

Figure 3.6 The broiler industry in the UK 1996.

and customers could therefore provide detailed views on the physical product, the services and the personal relationship elements relating to the FSB offering. Customers were asked to specify which offering elements they considered most significant in their relationship with FSB.

What FSB learned

The results of the study were somewhat surprising for FSB. The level of customer complexity was much greater than FSB originally anticipated. In other words, the granularity or resolution that was required to understand the value constellation was much greater than had been assumed previously. The analysis further demonstrated the need to understand better the relationships among the different actors within the value constellation.

Let us begin with the UK. At the strategic level, customers expressed intentions both towards integration and disintegration.

- Some broiler producers stated that they followed a low-cost strategy. This implied a desire to reduce or eliminate middlemen such as distributors, pre-mixers and feed producers. By establishing large integrated operations, they expected to reduce costs through better economies of scale and scope.
- Other producers followed an output-focused strategy, identifying and stressing their competence as meat producers and stating that they need not have all the expertise (such as nutrition) in-house. Therefore they saw the role of feed formulation as a non-strategic activity that they out-sourced to pre-mixers.

The complexity which the analysis unearthed did not end there. Even if customers shared the same strategy, they had divergent opinions and expectations in relation to FSB's offering.

- One customer, a large integrator, strongly signaled that he was primarily interested in only the core offering of improved feed conversion ratio (that is, how well the animal can absorb the energy of the feed). He was thus also interested in lower price per ton of feed, as well as better meat yield, that would lead to increases in the value of the further processed product. Service issues were seen as a given. Basic service was taken for granted. The producer was quite skeptical regarding discussions about more in-depth co-operation between the integrator and FSB. It would make sense only if the partnership would improve the value of the physical feed product, otherwise each party would do best in concentrating on his own business. In sum, this customer focused on the hardware dimension of FSB's offering.

- A second customer, also a large integrator, viewed the people element as the most significant FSB resource advantage. The competence of FSB professionals, their trustworthiness and readiness to co-operate in different trials (with new feed formulae) were regarded as very important elements of the FSB offering.

The example of the second customer highlights one of the strengths of FSB's offering: the 'people' dimension. FSB was operating in the UK through a distributor. From the point of view of the customer, the combination of the distributor and FSB was perceived as a single joint entity providing the offering. FSB was, in other words, operating through a so-called 'composite channel' business model, whereby FSB *and* the distributor had divided the execution of the channel functions. The UK broiler market was quite mature in respect of penetration of betaine, and the relationship between FSB and the distributor seemed to work fairly well, and had created confidence also among the customers.

In addition to the UK, another geographical market was selected for the customer-orientation project analysis. This market was less mature than the UK's. Betaine as a feed additive had not yet been adopted. Still, FSB operated through the same type of 'composite channel' business model here, but with mixed results. Some in-depth customer interviews in this market revealed that the challenge of integrating betaine into the local feed formulas was much more demanding than in the UK. For example, some feed ingredients were suspected of disturbing the impact of betaine in the feed formula. Solving this dispute scientifically proved more complicated than expected, and the local distributor did not generate a good turnover or margin. This in turn led to reduced and limited support to customers in terms of time and capabilities. Yet, potential customers expressed the need for full commitment of FSB and the distributor to address the emerging needs of the market.

The analyses of the two markets showed that FSB needed to design its offerings, and its constellations, not only on a market-by-market basis, but in 'advanced' markets, also on a customer-by-customer one. Market segmentation would simply not do the job in such situations – it did not have high enough granularity, or resolution. Thus, further efforts to redesign the offerings based on the above-surveyed analyses led to the development of a preliminary hypothesis by the management of FSB. This hypothesis was that in emerging markets, resolution could remain relatively low. A 'market segment' approach would do. Here, where betaine was not yet fully recognized as a feed additive, the focus of the offering would be on the core 'hardware' elements of the offering. Yet the key to success would not be the selling price, but the integration cost and the net satisfaction contribution. This is because, as feed formulae and their production economics are fairly complex, the introduction of the product requires substantial scientific knowledge. Therefore, the capability requirements in terms of scientific product knowledge are much higher in emerging markets, than in more advanced ones, when the 'proof of concept' is already established.

As markets mature, and betaine gets established, customers tend to require more fine-tuning (more granularity or resolution) of the value-creation process, and work sharing between themselves and the supplier becomes more customer-specific. As we saw in the second UK customer example above, representing a mature market, the people dimension can play a vital role if the customer wants to see the supplier as a genuine co-producer. In such tailor-made situations, it is important to become a supplier that can be trusted to support the developmental activities of the customer. We saw that the same logic applies to Xerox's 'documenting' offerings.

The above preliminary hypothesis was tested by FSB through additional interviews, and was well received both externally and internally. It had a significant impact on the FSB strategy, and was later 'borrowed' by other divisions of the Cultor Group.

Seppo Ruikka, Managing Director of Finnsugar Bioproducts and Antero Nyyssönen, President of Cultor Nutrition's Suomen Rehu Division commented on the redesigned value-creation framework as follows:

> An integral part of Cultor's approach today has also been to shift from thinking in terms of linear value chains, such as those linking companies involved in simply producing a product for example, to thinking in terms of broader 'value networks'.
>
> We wanted to open up how we looked at creating value, and bring more resources and ideas into play that would enable us to be more than just another raw material supplier. That's why we want to involve farmers, consumers, consumer organizations, health issues, environmental issues, and quality issues in our business. The quality of food on people's tables is very much a common goal for all of us in the 'food production network'.[22]

DYNAMIC VALUE CONSTELLATIONS

Using the value-creation framework to analyze the business logic of their main customers on different markets helped FSB to realize the importance of having the *right* capabilities deployed. These were able to provide the necessary offering elements for each *individual* customer. Customers that did not yet fully know FSB and betaine as a product were much more concerned about the immediate benefits, and costs, related to the product. And as they did not yet know the effects of betaine, they were also more risk averse than customers that already had used betaine for a long time.

More experienced customers on the other hand developed in two directions. Some of them saw FSB as a partner that could help them on a consultative basis, whereas others wanted FSB to provide a low-cost solution. The insights derived from these analyses enabled FSB to adjust its previous production and marketing focus towards greater emphasis on individual customers. In the same way, Xerox found that its 'Documenting' logic requires much more tailoring than what the 'business as usual' characteristics of leasing photocopiers required. One outsourcing deal is different from the next: in one you take over people employed by the customer and manage them, in the next you bring in your own – or a sub-contractors' – employees. In rapidly developing businesses, these solutions have to be co-developed and re-invented at a rather fast pace; it is only after the 'steeper' part of a learning curve has been left behind, that such experiences can be grouped, standardized, and finally catalogued as predesigned offerings.

In sum, as both the Xerox and FSB examples illustrate, from a supplier's point of view, a value constellation features a supplier targeting a range of different customers with a range of different offerings. Customers have different priorities in their value creation, and offerings targeted at them reflect these. The characteristics of the offerings can include low-risk solutions; low-cost solutions; broad relationship-based offerings, co-produced with a distributor or not; co-learning initiatives; facility of integration into customer systems; and so on. As customers' value creation conditions evolve, the offerings – and thus the capabilities brought in to make them possible, must be altered. The dynamism of value constellations depend on how well prime movers (established constellation designers) can make their constellation evolve to fit and anticipate customer value-creation logics, and on how many new entrants challenge their position. The more the types of 'fit', the more granularity or resolution is required, also with respect to capabilities.

From a customer's point of view, a value constellation has an architecture designed around each individual customer, with many suppliers targeting this customer with different offerings. The logic is the same: offering architecture will be judged in terms of 'fit' with customer value creation. A good purchaser (like Xerox) will establish a value constellation among suppliers, as well as one for customers, and will find itself co-designing both in relation to each other.

An Emerging Architecture for Value Creation $\quad$ 4

Previously we analyzed the way value is perceived, and the mechanisms of exchange which form the foundation for value creation. In this chapter we further expand our perspective to explore the business and management context in which value creating takes place.

Here we:

- Show how companies define a *business model* which answers the question: 'What value do we want to create and for, and with, whom?' An in-depth case study at the beginning of the chapter illustrates the different factors that guide organizations as they define and, most importantly, change their business models.

- Introduce an *open system model of the firm* which includes both business and management processes (and the resources used by those processes). In turn, both business and management processes intervene to develop the business model for value creation. We refer to this developing of the business model as *interactive business modeling*.

- Present *four alternative business modeling priorities* for creating value. These four priorities are: customer orientation (explored in depth in Chapter 5), capability focus (explored in depth in Chapter 6), lean management (explored in both Chapter 6 and Chapter 7), and market making (explored in depth in Chapters 7, 8, and 9).

- Thus is structured the remainder of the book.

THE BUSINESS MODEL

As shown in the previous chapter, a company must deploy the right capabilities to co-produce – with customers, suppliers, and other partners – a value-creating offering for and with the customer. However, a number of questions arise:

- Which capabilities should be deployed?
- Which co-production partners should be involved and how?
- Which offerings should be co-produced?
- Which customers should be targeted?

All of these questions are in effect 'answered', or 'contained' in the business model of the firm. All firms in effect have 'business models', but many do not explicitly question the one they have. This chapter provides a conceptual framework with which the current business model can be surfaced, rendered explicit, and tested in terms of its viability and robustness.

An explicit business model represents what the firm is trying to accomplish. An effective one represents what the firm actually does.

Over time, the business model has to change in order to evolve with, or anticipate, and even create from scratch, new value-creation possibilities and challenges. How a firm adapts its business model effectively determines its success.

The business model can be defined as follows:

> The business model of a firm defines value-creation priorities in respect to the utilization of both internal and external resources. It defines how the firm relates with stakeholders, such as actual and potential customers, employees, unions, suppliers, competitors, and other interest groups. It takes account of situations where its activities may (a) affect the business environment and its own business in ways that could create conflicting interests, or impose risks on the firm, or (b) develop new, previously unpredicted ways of creating value. The business model is in itself subject to continual review subject to actual and possible changes in perceived business conditions.

An example of how this works was offered by the Xerox history surveyed in Chapter 2. The story showed:

- how Xerox got into serious trouble by not changing its established business model when it should have changed it,
- how it then reinterpreted changes in perceived business conditions, first by attacking its quality and cost problems, and then rethinking the very fundamentals of its business model, and
- how when it did this, it created a new set of value-creating offerings based on the Documenting perspective, which involved its having created a new business model.

Changes in the business model will be triggered by causes catalogued as 'internal', 'external', or 'values-related' developments.

An internal development might be the naming of a new CEO, who wants to set new priorities.

An external development might be a perceived substantial transformation in customer demands, a technical breakthrough by a supplier, the end of a patent, or a new product from a competitor. The Xerox case is a good example of such a development.

A values-based development might be a shift in the values or culture of the corporation, for example following an important environmental incident. Shell, for example, decided that the whole company would 'go dry' following the Exxon Valdez ship accident. This change did not affect the business model, but it did change the way important visitors would be treated at lunch! A more fundamental change occurred for Shell after the Nigerian human rights scandal and the difficulties it encountered with environmental groups upon its wanting to sink the North Sea exploration platform 'Brent Spar'. It decided it would be much more proactive in its relationship with stakeholders to whom it had not paid enough attention in the preceding business model.

In many actual business model changes, a combination of at least two of these factors is involved. In some cases, as in the case of ABB Fläkt described below, all three 'triggers' are involved when the business model is changed.

ABB FLÄKT: THE DYNAMICS OF THE BUSINESS MODEL[1]

In 1990 Percy Barnevik, CEO of ABB Group, initiated a corporate-wide effort in ABB called 'Customer Focus'. The message he gave when introducing this program was:

> We know the key to our long-term success and profitability: the unconditional and total satisfaction of our customers with every contact they experience and every product or service they receive from us. Whatever we do must be aimed at satisfying their needs and expectations at an even higher level. We have to be aware that this is a moving target, because their needs and expectations change. We must welcome such changes as opportunities for adding more and new values for our customers.
>
> To install this uncompromising customer-driven attitude throughout our Group, we have started a process called 'Customer Focus'. To me, it is one of the most important processes that we have embarked on in our company. Quality and cycle time are vital elements of this process since improvement of both offers a huge potential for increasing customer satisfaction.[2]

In 1990, when customer focus was initiated, ABB had revenues of $26.7 billion and employed 215,000 people worldwide. At that time the ABB Group was made up of eight business segments which together contained 65 business areas and 1,300 companies.

One business segment, environmental control, was entirely contained in one subsidiary, the ABB Fläkt Group, which boasted revenues of SEK20.8 billion (about $2.5 billion) and had 21,000 employees.

The customer focus process in the Finnish part of the ABB Fläkt Group started within its industrial division in October 1991 through a project called 'Customer Base Management'. At that time, the industrial division, headed by Antero Hietaluoma, employed 75 people and had a turnover of $40 million (1991). The industrial division's offerings related to air pollution control systems, pulp and paper dryers, industrial fans, and service contracts relating to these installations.

By the mid-1990s, Barnevik's customer focus initiative had changed the core business models of both the industrial division of ABB Fläkt and the ABB Fläkt Group as a whole.

Here's how.

PROJECT NUMBER ONE: THE INDUSTRIAL DIVISION OF ABB FLÄKT

The first step of the 'Customer Base Management' project was a customer base analysis which studied the buying behavior of the 30 largest (defined in terms of cumulative ABB Fläkt sales over the three previous years) customers for the period 1988–91.

The results of this analysis were considered in a November 1991 seminar held to define the goals of the customer base management project in greater detail. The seminar participants (the 15 most senior sales people of the industrial division) were asked to present their views on the business potential for three customer segments:

- Domestic customers
- East European customers
- Other export customers

Specifically, participants were asked to rate on a scale from 1 to 5 their views on business volume development (decrease, status quo or increase) within the coming 3–5 years for these three segments.

The results were unexpected. Participants considered the business potential for the domestic market to be far poorer than existing budgets and plans (the 'official' business model) indicated. On the other hand, participants saw the potential of the Eastern Europe segment to be much more promising than that reflected in existing corporate plans and budgets. Finally, considerable Western export potential was also identified.

These results would be confirmed in follow-up interviews with customers.

The implications of these unexpected results were clear: The allocation of the industrial division's resources had been focused on serving domestic customers. These resources were misallocated, and the business model needed to be rethought.

What happened?

The concept of a customer's *value-creation logics*, introduced in earlier chapters, helps to explain the roots of the industrial division's problems. The industrial division's principal customers were drawn from the Finnish construction business. By 1991, Finnish exports to the Soviet Union had collapsed. As a result, domestic spending by Finnish industry dropped dramatically. When spending drops, one of the hardest hit industries is new construction. Thus, the industrial division's customers (the construction industry) suffered from the problems of the customers' customers (Finnish industry).

However, managers at the ABB Fläkt Group were misled by optimistic forecasts – based on past performance – of Finnish economic development (see Figure 4.1). As a result, they were not fully up to date about what was happening to the industrial division's customers (and the customers' customers).

It wasn't until the customer base analysis and follow-up seminar in November 1991 that management clearly understood the value creation logic of its various customers' segments. Understanding this value creation logic and how changes elsewhere affected it helped the firm to

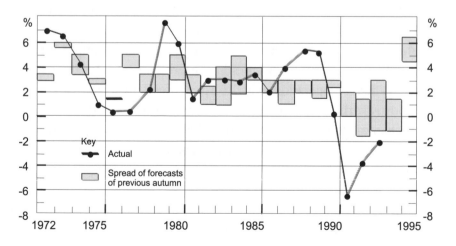

Figure 4.1 Gap between next-year GDP forecasts and the actual GDP growth in Finland (Source: ETLA, The Finnish Institute for Economic Research).

redeploy resources and redesign offerings to shift its strategic focus from existing to new customers.

A new business model

In February1992, ABB Fläkt's top management changed the industrial division's strategic goals. Specifically, it radically redeployed resources to develop business opportunities in Eastern Europe, as well as to focus more on export projects abroad.

Following the value-creation framework introduced in Chapter 3 (see Figure 3.1), three categories of key resources were identified:

1 *The internal resources of ABB Fläkt* (e.g. technical and commercial know-how of key employees).
2 *'Addressable' resources within the ABB Group[3] (including product development, marketing, and finance functions).* By 'addressable', we here mean resources that can be accessed by the industrial division (see Note 3 for further discussion). For example, in 1992, the ABB Group made available special funds for developing businesses in Eastern Europe. Antero Hietaluoma applied for some of these funds. In May 1992 the industrial division was granted corporate funds to further develop the activities of the division in Russia and the Ukraine.
3 *Addressable resources outside the ABB Group.* For example, in addition to the efforts to increase activities in Eastern Europe, Hietaluoma also intensified co-operation with third parties specializing in project exports in the pulp and paper industry. Alliances with the Finnish mechanical engineering companies Ahlström and Tampella resulted in significant orders from pulp and paper companies in Indonesia, Thailand, and South Africa.

The industrial division based its export efforts on two areas, where it had developed a strong technological competence in its domestic market: air pollution control for certain industrial applications, and industrial know-how of pulp and paper processes. Both of these competences had been developed in close co-operation with Finnish industrial companies engaged in these activities, domestically and abroad. The industrial division was, in competence terms, addressing external resources both from customers (like Outokumpu and Kymmene) and from suppliers providing complementary products (like Ahlström and Tampella) to strengthen its own capabilities. In this way the industrial division was part of a value constellation which it designed and developed, where the focus of each member was on capability building.

In conclusion

In general terms, the industrial division's customer base management project was originally an initiative intended to focus on *existing* customers. However, the information it generated revealed that the purchasing power of current customers was not sufficient to secure the profit objectives of the division. As a result of this information, efforts were made to find *new* customers for existing offerings instead of focusing on existing customers.

Since the information that sparked this shift was based on customer feedback, analyzed in the November 1991 seminar, customers were co-producers of the industrial division's new goals. Based on the rephrased goals, the business model was altered to use existing capabilities to look for new customers and provide these customers with existing or slightly modified offerings.

PROJECT NUMBER TWO: THE ENTIRE ABB FLÄKT GROUP IN FINLAND

Step one: developing closer relationships with customers

The customer focus initiative was expanded to include the entire Finnish section of the ABB Fläkt Group in the first half of 1993. The ABB Fläkt Group's project was called 'Key Account Management'. Once again, the goal was to develop closer relationships with existing customers.

Specifically, the project objectives were:

- To adapt key account management to ABB Fläkt's current situation in order to support sales activities – in other words, to transform the existing business model.
- To gather information on important customers in order to be able to develop further customer-oriented priorities and to create customer-specific action plans.
- To classify and analyze customer base management activities: what to do, how to do it, how to group customers.

In other words, the overall objective of the key account management project was to understand better the value creation processes of customers in order to develop customer-specific priorities and action plans. In June 1993, based on the proposals from relevant managers, top management of ABB Fläkt nominated 21 customers as corporate key accounts. More resources, for example the appointment of key account managers, would be deployed for these 21 customers than for the others.

In Chapter 3, we introduced the concept of the three-dimensional offering based on the physical, service, and people aspects of the offering. This concept was applied in the ABB Fläkt project to help separate the 21 key customers from the rest of the customer base.

Here's how it worked.

ABB Fläkt had built up a close customer relationship with most of its customers over many years. Thus, engineers, sales people, and management had an in-depth understanding of the value-creating processes of the most important customers. They knew where the opportunities to strengthen the offering on all three dimensions (physical, service, and people content) existed.

However, ABB Fläkt knew that moving all (or even most) customers into a strategic partnership[4] with the company – making them key accounts, for example – was not economically justifiable. The people content of an offering is often very costly. A seller has to be very careful about where to deploy these resources in order not to risk the profitability of the customer relationship.

Profitability was not the only issue. The overall goal of ABB's customer focus initiative was that every customer should see ABB as a responsive and reliable supplier. However, not all customers want or need strategic partnerships with suppliers for ABB-type products (including products from the ABB Fläkt Group). Thus, ABB developed 'preferred supplier' or 'strategic partnerships' with a certain number of chosen customers with whom it was prepared to further develop all three dimensions of the offering. At the ABB Fläkt level, this was done through the key account management project.

In sum, ABB Fläkt developed strategic partnerships with 21 key accounts because those partnerships were (a) profitable for ABB Fläkt and (b) desirable for the customer.

Step two: a new reorganization

As noted above, the key account management project was expected to change the ABB Fläkt Group's business model. But these changes went far beyond simply shifting to key account management. In the end, the group – and its business model – would be drastically reorganized.

The extent of the change that was required became evident when the key account management project identified the extent of customer dissatisfaction with ABB's organization. From the customer's point of view, ABB Fläkt was very product-oriented. On a customer's construction site, for example, there could be several different ABB units represented: one ABB unit providing air-conditioning installations, another ABB unit taking care of electrical installations, and a third providing service for existing equipment.

Customer concerns brought to the attention through ABB Fläkt's project supported the decision of ABB's top management to redefine the business areas and business segments of the corporation. The goal: to regroup capabilities in a way that would better fit customer value-creating requirements. The ABB Fläkt project results reinforced this need to redefine not only a single business idea, but to do so for various business segments.

At the end of 1993, due partly to the results of the key account management project, a radical reorganization took place. The three units mentioned above were combined into a new company: ABB Installations.

Only the genuine product selling units (industrial products, ducts, ventilation products, and air terminal units) remained within ABB Fläkt, which thus was substantially reduced in size. At the same time the former industrial division of ABB Fläkt became a separate unit, ABB Environmental Systems.

Reflections on the ABB Fläkt case

When the first ABB Fläkt customer base management project started in September 1991 the goals of ABB Fläkt were driven by perceptions of product cash flow generating potential based on existing forecasts. In retrospect, as Figure 4.1 indicates, these perceptions had been unreliable for several years. Yet in 1991 management faced a larger gap between incoming results and forecasts than had been seen for 20 years. This was due to the collapse of Finnish exports to the Soviet Union and the subsequent dramatic drop in domestic spending. The construction industry, which was a main customer segment of ABB Fläkt was particularly hit by this recession.

The November 1991 seminar created the first deep doubts about the outlook for 1992 that the then-existing business model implied. These doubts were further confirmed through the in-depth interviews. It became evident that 1992 objectives would be unattainable if ABB Fläkt management continued to concentrate resources on providing present domestic customers with existing or new products, instead of redeploying resources to developing export business.

Understanding the value creation logic of different types of customers helped ABB Fläkt to redeploy resources and redesign offerings to shift its strategic focus, from existing to new customers. In February 1992 the industrial division decided to deploy more resources for exports, and at the end of 1993 the reorganization took place.

Final results

When asked, in August 1995, what had changed between 1992 and 1995, Antero Hietaluoma, the head of the industrial division of ABB Fläkt in

Finland answered: 'outsourcing'. In 1995 the former industrial division employed fewer people than in 1992, but used much more subcontracting. The focus on business unit performance was however still very strong. The ambition to increase cross-divisional activities had been attained only to a limited extent. External firm-addressable resources were still often more attractive than corporate resources.

As we saw, one of the effects of the key account management project was a complete reorganization. This reorganization can be attributed to three factors.

1 The business climate worsened considerably in the beginning of the 1990s, and the downturn of the construction industry hit ABB severely. In other words, the existing business model was affected both by changes in the customer base of ABB in Finland and by contextual changes in the wider business environment. This is similar to Xerox realizing that its previously successful business model would not do well in light of Asian price-cutting competition.

2 A corporate customer focus initiative was launched. Top management wanted it adapted at the local level (in this case ABB Finland). The changes caused by the internal customer focus initiative thus fulfilled two objectives: they improved ABB Fläkt's internal efficiency, which was necessary due to the recession on the local markets. At the same time, it was a way to increase customer orientation, which was a corporate goal.

3 The whole ABB Group was globally reorganized. In 1994 the revenues of ABB amounted to $31.8 billion (up $5 billion from 1990) but ABB only employed 208,000 people (down 7,000 from 1990). The number of business segments had been reduced from eight to five. The previous semi-independent ABB Fläkt Group was now to be a part of the industrial and building systems business segment, the single biggest ABB business segment with revenues of $12.8 billion. During the same period the revenues of the Finnish ABB units had increased by more than 10 percent in spite of reduced domestic sales. The reason being a doubling of exports between 1990 and 1994, from $300 million to $600 million.

In sum, the industrial division changed its business model, redeploying resources to find new customers instead of focusing on existing customers. The new business model for the ABB Fläkt Group had two important effects in practice. First, it meant that closer relationships with customers through key account management would be established. Second, it meant a drastic reorganizing of its structure. The ultimate reasoning behind all of these changes was the following: How can we redeploy our firm's resources – and those we can address elsewhere – best to create value for the customer?

THE FIRM AS AN OPEN SYSTEM[5]

When the resources which a firm owns, or addresses, are linked with customers' actions, in ways that customers value, value co-production takes place. A firm's management processes (ABB Fläkt's key account organization, for example) support its business processes (for instance, ABB Fläkt's bringing in resources from Ahlström and Tampella to enhance the effectiveness of its own customers' value creation). In other words, management makes it possible for the business to deploy the right resources to be effective so that this deployment actually does help customers to create value.

Strategic management thus consists of finding effective *links* between resources and customers' value creation.

The remainder of this chapter explores in more detail a firm's business and management processes, and how they are represented in the business model.

To do so, we first introduce a model of the firm as an 'open system' (see Figure 4.2). As shown in the illustration, two major aspects of the firm as an open system are: co-ordination and business modeling. Since the values of the society the firm is embedded in, and the values of its owners, managers, employees, customers, and other stakeholders, play an important role in shaping how the firm determines its business model, culturing is discussed as an important element that influences business modeling. We treat each in turn (the notions of transactional and contextual environments which are found in Figure 4.2 are dealt with in Chapter 7):

The border of the firm

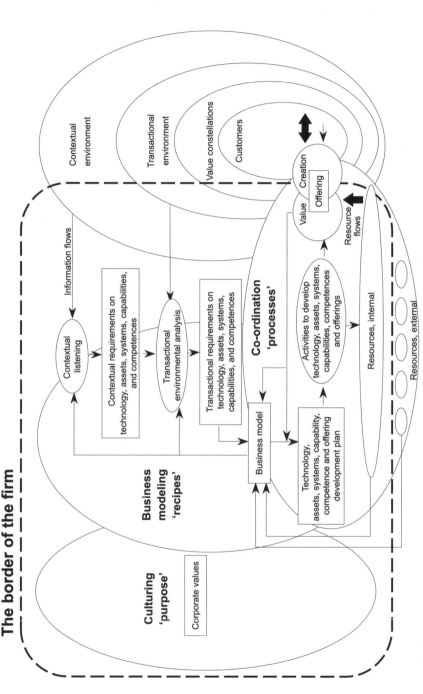

Figure 4.2 The firm as an open system.

Co-ordination

To be able to provide value to customers, the firm has to develop and deliver offerings. These require its developing or accessing resources, including technology, physical assets, systems, capabilities, and competences. The firm's 'business processes' develop or access resources and co-ordinate the deployment of these resources with customers to deliver value-creating offerings.

For example, FSB (described in Chapter 3) had value-creating business processes which included the following, among other elements:

- the scientific development of betaine,
- the packaging of betaine into the right format to be provided as a feed ingredient to be sold to poultry farmers,
- established distribution partnerships,
- persons with technical knowledge supporting the farmers' value creation, and
- actual delivery of the offerings, together with the distributors.

Business modeling

A firm must make decisions about which resources to develop or access and deploy. These decisions are influenced by external and internal environmental factors, including the desires or actions of customers, competitors, and other stakeholders. Therefore, business-intelligence activities – getting information about, and feedback from, the firm's business environment – support, and are often key elements in, making the right decisions.

Business intelligence and decision making form the business modeling process. Good business modeling also includes creative reinterpretation of the information so gathered. In addition, as we see below, business modeling is strongly influenced by values. The result of the business modeling process is the business model.

As shown through the Xerox and ABB examples, the business model has to be re-evaluated often (if not continuously). It has now become acceptable to think of the environment in which a firm exists to be continuously changing, although each of the elements constituting the environment does not change all of the time.

In the ABB Fläkt industrial division case, the situation it faced in 1991 in which most of its customers, due to the local recession, drastically reduced their spending, meant that their changes would be immediately felt by the firm. In effect, customers are often the most immediate, regular contact a firm has with its external environment. The change in its customers' situation was the decisive element in helping the industrial division rapidly to redefine its business model. In Xerox, although signals regarding competitors were abundant, it was again the significant loss of market share (the migration of established customers to competitors) that finally prompted the company to change its model.

Culturing

As covered more fully below (on pages 97–101, 'Involving stakeholders' values in goal setting'), corporate culture plays an important role in the business modeling process of a company.

A business model sets forth the business goals of the company and how it plans to achieve those goals. In our terms, it sets forth the value-creating priorities of the company – specifically, what value will be created in its offerings, for (and with) whom those offerings will be created, and what resources will be used to create those offerings. The answers to these questions are rooted in the corporate culture of the company.

For example, a company whose culture emphasizes the short-term pursuit of wealth will produce different value in its offering than a company whose culture emphasizes learning. ABB's customer focus initiative reflected a switch in corporate culture from short-term wealth to long-term learning (specifically, learning more about the customer in order to provide better value for the customer). The business model, as we see in the next section, had to be changed accordingly.

In sum, *culturing* involves defining and developing and 'explicating' the corporate values of the organization. We adopt the notion of 'explication' which physicist David Bohm[6] introduced, and which involves rendering the implicit explicit. Culturing provides the foundation for an organization's ultimate business model.

Note that culturing not only refers to defining an organization's overall values, but also to defining the values of the individuals within that organization – not always an easy task. As the top managers of ABB discovered, individuals can be tenacious in holding on to their old values and ignoring the new ones urged by management.

BUSINESS MODELS AND THE GOALS OF THE FIRM

Russel Ackoff[7] defined 'objectives' as desired states or desired outcomes. Goals can be seen as a set of interrelated 'gap-closing' measures to reach objectives. Goals are an important element in shaping a firm's decision making, and thus in shaping its business modeling.

In the case of Xerox, after new entrants came in, its goal was to *escape a cost-leadership war*. A critical element in determining this goal was that Xerox's objective was to return to a differentiated situation in which it could avoid the commoditization in which it had now found itself. The culturing it had been involved in for decades was one of being a successful original business model designer; not one of being a 'me too' actor in an undifferentiated playing field.

In the case of the industrial division within ABB Fläkt, achieving *yearly profit* objectives was the dominant goal. A critical question in determining such a goal is to what extent a gap presented only in budgetary terms can be clearly identified and communicated. A 'corollary' goal presented to ABB's units, including ABB Fläkt, was the one of *'customer focus'*. Because of the profit-driven entrepreneurial culture of ABB, it was unclear to many in the company how this goal was to be achieved, especially if it threatened (was inconsistent with) the profit goal. Many people saw the two goals as at least partly conflicting. The two ABB goals, profit and customer focus, highlight two fundamentally different approaches to how goals are set, and what they are meant to achieve.

Two broad approaches for setting goals

The first, most traditional, approach for setting goals is to define clearly objectives that depict desired future states of the firm's system elements. Such objectives are often formulated numerically. Year-end profit targets, which manifest profitability objectives, are typical examples of this type of goal setting. To meet the goals, cost-cutting and/or revenue-enhancing processes are defined, so as to make it possible to reach these 'future' states.

There are two problems with this approach. First, in practice, it is often very difficult when setting goals to define realistically what the desired state of the firm's system elements should be in the future. This is particularly the case in environments which change in unprecedented ways, in which forecasting is unhelpful (we further discuss these environments in Chapter 7). For example, in 1985, AT&T projected — as it turned out, erroneously — that the number of US cellular phone users in 1995 would be 900,000. Based on this (wrong) forecast, the company buried its young cellular program. However, the number of US cellular subscribers in 1994 turned out to be 20 million. To correct this mistaken projection, AT&T acquired McCaw that year ... at a cost of $12 billion.

Above we saw another example of this danger: the 1992 sales budget of ABB Fläkt's industrial division, which also involved a false projection (but in this case in the form of a substantial overestimation of demand).

A second, and more fundamental, problem with the traditional goal-definition approach is that predetermined goals have a nasty tendency to become 'cast in concrete', and often do not allow any room for learning. As the firm is an open system, it interacts with its environment. In so doing, it gains knowledge which, if well exploited, can be used to adapt and adjust its goals to that knowledge. The existence of predetermined ('yearly') goals prevents this from happening — particularly as important bonuses are attached to reaching these goals. People will 'reinterpret' information coming in to them, that impacts on the realism of these goals, so as to prevent them from learning. The story of Xerox surveyed in Chapter 2 shows how difficult it is for managers to 'read' signs which change the goals early enough. In the same way, Kees van der Heijden has documented the eight-year time lag which the oil industry exhibited between registering the fall in demand which the 1973 'oil crisis' produced and actually decreasing production capacity. The decrease in demand had been the first, and only, such decrease since World War II.[8]

This is important. If the ambition of the firm is to learn new things, a completely clear future state, expressed in terms of absolutely clear objectives, cannot be explicitly predetermined, much less communicated and acted upon. Put simply, with this type of goal setting, you don't know what you could – and should – be learning.

Therefore, firms facing unpredictable business conditions find that goals can only be expressed as inquiry processes that will deliver outcomes in the form of new knowledge. Goals become dynamic, testable, and contestable. This second type of goal setting also has disadvantages, particularly if expectations of the role of management are kept as if the first type of goal setting was still in place! The type of organizing this demands requires a different type of management, and expectations among employees, than that which the 'cast-in-stone' version of goal setting calls for.

In many workplaces organized according to this first type of goal setting, lower-level employees, who are less 'employable' than highly trained professionals often state that they prefer to stay with 'fixed' goals. The ever-moving ones that senior (and highly employable) managers and expert professionals do well with can, from their point of view, within established organizational forms, 'corrode their character', as sociologist Richard Sennet put it.[9] In effect, for many non-mobile workers, fluid goals are experienced as violent attacks on the more-or-less stable world they have managed to forge through life-long effort.

Recognizing the growing importance of questioning established knowledge, and of obtaining new knowledge – of 'learning a living' individually and as a firm – goal setting as an ongoing process is becoming more accepted among senior managers. For example, 'customer focus' was a goal that reflected an ongoing, adaptive process. This was recognized by the ABB Executive vice-president Gerhard Schulmeyer, who stated that customer focus would require a complex, and slow, process of cultural change. Organizing in ways that allow lower-level and/or not very 're-employable' employees to 'find their way' with dignity and in economically attractive ways remains an important challenge.

When fluid goals are incompatible with more fixed ones, getting an organization to accept to live according to both as a legitimate business process becomes difficult. This also was recognized by Mr Schulmeyer, when in his new position as CEO of Nixdorf Information Systems, he noticed that

> Restructuring into decentralized business units is the easy part. Senior managers are happy. But when you tell them they have to work together and network together, that's when it begins to fall apart ... The shift from entrepreneurial competitive, to entrepreneurial co-operative is the issue – and it's painful.[10]

The 'corrosion of character' dangers mentioned above will lead most members of an organization designed to meet only the first type of goal setting to favor the shorter-term, 'fixed' one. Thus, for example, lower-level managers in ABB felt that the 'safe way' was to focus primarily on the traditional goals of short-term profits. They would then accept reallocating any remaining available resources to the issue of customer orientation. Unfortunately – hardly a surprise! – these resources could seldom be found. The institutionalization of the first type of goal setting explains why many good companies take so very long to react to fundamental changes in their environment.

Involving stakeholders in dynamic goal setting

If the goals of the firm can be defined as processes which generate new knowledge, which in turn affect goal setting, then one conclusion is that external stakeholders must be participants in the goal-setting process of the firm, explicitly or implicitly.

For example, customers of the industrial division helped divisional management recognize its misinterpretation of the market before the company's official 'prognosticators'. Some of the practical implications of this are discussed below.

The first implication is that the choice of which external stakeholders the firm interacts with here becomes a crucial issue; not only in its present value creating, but also for the quality with which it will determine its future ones. The company's growth and knowledge development will be directly impacted by this choice.

Customer feedback from the industrial division's largest customers revealed flaws in the division's strategic goals. This experience prompted the parent company, ABB Fläkt Group, to launch a process that would more closely connect the group to its most important customers – and thus improve the group's knowledge development. *Customer contacts are thus the 'R&D' of the co-productive economy.* Finding out which are one's most sophisticated customers – the ones one can learn most with – is thus a crucial piece of information. We examine this in more detail in Chapter 6.

As the firm takes a more adaptive process approach to goal setting, a question arises: Who sets the direction for the firm's processes and activities based on the developed knowledge?

The issue is crucial. As knowledge develops in the interface between the firm and its environment (for example, through customer feedback), it becomes difficult to evaluate how relevant this knowledge is, how relevant it will be, and how and when to apply the new knowledge. Compounding the problem is the fact that new knowledge acquired during an ongoing process is typically not received directly by top management. Instead, such knowledge tends to be a fuzzy combination of scattered observations involving multiple individuals, which is not properly configured for decision making.

For the firm to react effectively to new knowledge, for it to adapt its behavior and priorities, management must ensure that the staff – the multiple individuals receiving this knowledge – have the authority and confidence:

- to question established truths;
- to, where appropriate, make a decision based on new insights; and
- thus, to act rapidly.

In 1999 Finland had the most Internet connections per capita in the world, partly because the management of some of its leading telecom firms exhibit this type of behavior. The idea of offering easy Internet connections to the public was suggested by an astute marketing manager of Telecom Finland (now Sonera) in 1994. Top management has a tradition of tolerating innovation, which has helped the firm to become one of the most successful incumbent phone operators in the world. So in spite of some initial skepticism, the Internet offering was launched in March 1995.

Involving stakeholders' values in goal setting

In the process approach to goal setting, goals must be aligned as much as possible with the values not only of the organization as a whole, but also with values of others inside and outside its borders. Inside, it includes the values of stakeholders of the units within the organization, right up to the individuals within the units. For when goals conflict with values, goals will lose out (as demonstrated by the example of ABB's managers ignoring the customer orientation goal, when it conflicted with immediate profit making, which was perceived to represent the highest prioritized value of ABB).

Thus, the adaptive approach requires a more complete understanding of the dynamics of values. Some authors have done this by attempting to understand how 'values' and 'needs' interact. Ackoff[11] studied how values relate to needs and their satisfaction, how changes in needs produce changes in values, and what produces changes in needs.

To connect the goal formulation of the firm with the values of different stakeholders, we use the following definition of the values of the firm:

- *Corporate values* are generalized, relatively enduring and consistent priorities of what the firm considers itself to be, and wants to be.
- Corporate values address two basic questions:
  - Who are the main stakeholders of the firm, and in which order shall they be served?
  - How shall each stakeholder be served with respect to each element of the corporate values?

The Swedish sociologist Hans Zetterberg[12] identified six cardinal socio-logical values, four of which are directly relevant in business:

- Pursuit of wealth.
- Search for knowledge.
- Civic virtue.
- Beauty (or 'aesthetics').

To these can be added two additional values, which are arguably of a more biological and psychological nature:

- Survival (which here is understood as relating to the survival of the firm).
- A sense of belonging – which we take as particularly relevant for employees, but also applies to every stakeholder in a value constellation.

A firm's six cardinal values are thus: pursuit of wealth, search for knowledge, civic virtue, beauty, survival, and belonging. An important step in formulating process-type goals is to rank the values of a firm's major stakeholders on the basis of these six cardinal values. The matrix below (Figure 4.3) offers a framework for this comparison. One decision managers must make when formulating goals in light of values is to consider whether all of these stakeholders are important to the process, at the time they are considering reformulating their goals.

In the late 1990s there has been an ongoing debate about the shareholder versus stakeholder approach. American companies are seen as following a shareholder value philosophy in which the value of the firm is focused on creating shareholder wealth. In contrast, European and Japanese companies have been seen as adopting a stakeholder perspective in which employees and customers have a larger say. The serious trouble that many Japanese companies were experiencing by the second half of the 1990s has increased the support for the shareholder value proponents. The huge sums that US and UK pension funds can invest has also encouraged an increasing number of European

Values Stakeholders	Wealth	Knowledge	Civic virtue	Aesthetics	Survival	Belonging
The company itself						
Owners						
Customers						
Employees						
Society (= other stakeholders)						

Figure 4.3 A matrix for understanding the values in a value-creating system.[13]

continent-based corporations to adopt the shareholder value perspective.

However, there are companies like Volkswagen and Nokia (classed by the *Financial Times* in June 1999 as the European company having created the most shareholder wealth in the last five years) which beg to differ, at least somewhat. They recognize a link between creating value for shareholders and creating value for other stakeholders, in particular customers and employees:

> The ultimate goal for any company's existence is to generate value for its shareholders. In today's open and global world, where active interaction with the environment is the essential requirement for success, improvement in shareholder value stems from customer care and dedicated personnel. (Jorma Ollila, CEO, Nokia, 1997 Annual Report)

Corporate values both reflect the surrounding cultural environment and affect how the firm relates to society. This is why, for example, many Japanese companies advocate a holistic approach to creating value, that includes not only shareholders, customers, and employees; but also the community in which the firm operates. Shoichiro Toyoda, Chairman of

Toyota and Hiroshi Okuda, President, explicitly addressed this issue in the 1998 annual report:

> We maximize shareholder value over the long term by harmonizing the interests of all our stakeholders: customers, suppliers, employees, and members of the community at large, as well as shareholders. At the same time, we are stepping up our efforts to address the special expectations of shareholders.

In sum, national culture and other social affiliations (religions, interest groups, etc.) provide positive and negative valences which become manifested in brands and communication.

Let us take the example of Virgin, whose music business represents a strong link to young customers. The adventurous image of Richard Branson himself, the main owner and CEO, strengthens the Virgin brand. Based on these values, Virgin can negotiate a 50/50 agreement with a perfume manufacturer, who in exchange for the Virgin brand (50 percent of the value) will put all the R&D, the manufacturing and packaging facilities, the actual perfume molecules, the distribution agreement, and the advertising expenses. As we show in Chapter 10, personal values are related to the values of the culture in which the individuals live, and are modified by the values of valued counterparts as well as by individual life situations. Branson and Virgin have proved to be a very successful combination in this respect.

The balance between the first two values identified in Figure 4.3 – pursuit of wealth and search for knowledge – influences to what extent the goal setting of the company is short or long term, and whether goals are stated in terms of future states or processes. In the case of ABB Fläkt the original goals were very outcome focused: deliver the annual profit target. As the market situation deteriorated, the industrial division had, at least temporarily, to shift to a more process-focused approach. To answer the question 'what do you do when the original goal is no longer attainable?', the industrial division entered an open process that ultimately resulted in the reformulation of the business model.

Today, as we saw above, defining goals in financial terms appreciated by shareholders is the prevailing goal-setting model. Arie de Geus[14] called companies that exhibit this model 'economic companies'. However, there is an increasing interest in the notion of the learning organization[15] as an alternative model to the 'economic company'. The following quotation from BMW's 1997 annual report illustrates this:

> The prerequisites for a learning organization are: thinking in context, individual abilities, mental models, a shared vision, and the ability to learn as a team. This perception of an actively contributing workforce is BMW's best guarantee for future success.

Corporate values in learning organizations take the form of a somewhat broad, long-term direction, providing coherence, specially in a large organization. (*Customer focus*, for example, is a 'broader' goal than a profit target). Such broad, or 'umbrella', goals refer to a (higher-order) purpose of a corporation and the domain in which this purpose is to be realized. The major aim of this 'umbrella' is not to direct the firm's priority towards a predetermined outcome. It guides the motivation of participants whose contribution in the strategic actions is needed[16] and; most importantly, distinguishes what is considered possible from what is considered impossible.[17]

TRANSFORMING THE FIRM WITH AN OPEN-SYSTEMS PERSPECTIVE

As we saw above, goals set a framework for the firm's value creation, both in the present and in the future.

Achieving the goals in practice requires manifesting them in terms of action. The 'recipe' that allows goals to be enacted involves what we call *interactive business modeling*.

As we have seen, a business model defines the way resources are developed and accessed to design, produce, and deliver value-creating offerings with customers. To enact the offering, which manifests the business model commercially, one needs not only ideas, but also 'implementation'. 'Idea' and 'implementation' are two faces of the same coin – not separate phases – in interactive business modeling.

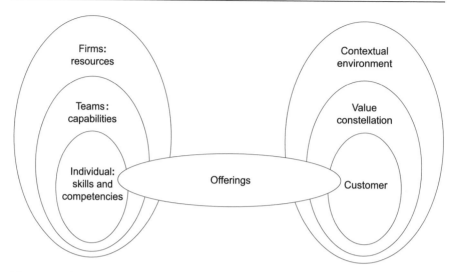

Figure 4.4 Skills, capabilities and resources as building blocks for value creation.

Interactive business modeling, and the actual value creation it permits, is best explained by examining the firm in terms of the open systems perspective. Figure 4.4 offers an extract from the previous illustration of the firm as an open system (Figure 4.2) with the specific purpose of highlighting the building blocks for value creation.

We begin this description by defining the different components of our open systems perspective of the firm. Note that the environment – an essential aspect of this perspective – is analyzed further in Chapters 7–9, and is therefore not elaborated in this section. The remaining definitions are based on definitions originally suggested by authors writing on the competence-based view of the firm.[18]

Definitions of the components of the firm as an open system

As Figure 4.4 illustrates, the basis for the open system perspective is the *interaction* between the resources of the firm and the potential to create value for and with customers in the form of offerings. We thus start by defining resources, and different sub-categories of resources.

> *Resources* are assets that are available and useful in detecting and responding to customer value creation opportunities or threats.

Resources include capabilities, as well as other assets, such as physical ones.

At Xerox, resources include many patents (on the mechanics of paper handling, the chemistry of ink fixing, optics, electronics, etc.), as well as know-how on lease-based relationship management, R&D skills and capabilities, sales-force and repairman management, outsourcing, and so on.

For FSB, key resources include the access to the sugar beet producing community in Finland, the scientific know-how related to developing betaine into feed additives, and a worldwide distribution network built up over the years.

For the Finnish ABB Fläkt Group, resources include production facilities, a local distribution network covering the whole of Finland, a multitude of patented ventilation products, and high-level engineering know-how related to a vast field of applications concerning air pollution control, ventilation, and drying.

Firm resources can be firm-specific or firm-addressable. Firm-specific resources are those which a firm owns or tightly controls, such as Xerox's R&D laboratories in Palo Alto, California (PARC), Grenoble (France), and Cambridge (UK). For FSB these resources include those related to the production of betaine from sugar beet molasses. Firm-addressable resources are those which a firm does not own or tightly control, but which it can access and use from time to time, such as those of suppliers, or the distributors – for example, FSB's representatives in the UK.

Capabilities are repeatable patterns of action in the use of resources to create, produce, and deliver offerings.[19]

For Xerox, mastering the integration of digital information management with the physics and chemistry of high-speed scanning and printing is a capability. For FSB, producing natural betaine from sugar beet molasses is a capability. The industrial division of ABB Fläkt has the capability to build systems to clean flue gas for coal-fired power stations, which is key in rendering ABB's offerings competitive in the air pollution control project business.

A *skill* is a specific form of capability useful in relation to the use of resources.

Xerox is skillful in retaining customers. It is also skillful in its advertising and positioning. In FSB, the production of betaine includes several steps in the production process that ask for specific skills among the workers. In the same way the building of air pollution control systems requires engineering, electrical, and assembly skills at ABB.

Matching capabilities and customer's value creation

Focusing our discussion on capabilities, rather than resources or skills, is helpful for understanding the value creation of a firm. Skillful individuals and groups, who exercise and develop their capabilities effectively, actually link resources to the value creation of customers. As we saw earlier, this link is manifested in terms of offerings.

The business model provides the 'recipe' for enacting value creation. If resources, capabilities, and skills are the building blocks of value creation, the business model will define *which* resources, capabilities, and skills are to be actually deployed. In effect, if it is to be useful, the business model is not only the 'espoused' theory of value creation, as Chris Argyris and Donald Schön called believed realities, but also its 'theory in use', or actual reality.[20] Whether the business model is changed explicitly by management directive, or implicitly through changes in internal behavior, it both reflects actual value creation and guides it.

In Chapter 2, we surveyed in detail how Xerox changed its business model from 'photocopying' to 'documenting'. FSB and ABB Fläkt both shifted from a focus on the physical dimension of the offering to strengthen the service and people ones. Since different types of value creation require different capability mixes, a shift in how value is created means that the priorities for each capability have to be adjusted.

We have seen that gathering information on customer value creation is helpful to explicate the current business model. It also helps in exploring alternatives to the existing business model. Noticing that photocopying was but one aspect of the broader documenting cycles which customers' value creation involves helped to reposition Xerox's business. Understanding the organization of the UK broiler producing community as depicted in Figure 3.6 provided the grounds for the revised business model of FSB. For ABB Fläkt, understanding the relevant Finnish value constellation of Fläkt customers and customers' customers helped clarify the limitations of potential value creation within the constellation.

In practice, business model development includes both a reinterpretation of the role, and of the importance, of capabilities, based on a reinterpretation of how they support customer value creation.

For the purposes of analytical clarity, we examine customers as the main focus of transforming value creation in Chapter 5. In Chapter 6 we examine how capabilities can be leveraged. In Chapters 7, 8, and 9 we focus on how addressing both simultaneously opens up important spaces for business development.

FOUR DISTINCT PRIORITIES IN INTERACTIVE BUSINESS MODELING

Chapter 2 surveyed how different the destiny of Xerox would have been if CEO David Kearns had chosen something other than the 'modified Boeing' priority which he happily (!) decided upon. The chosen priority focused on reinterpreting the existing links between several capabilities in which Xerox had for a long time been a leader, to its established customer base. Kearns' choice was entirely consistent with the argument developed in this book, for the reinterpretation was crystallized in reinterpreting the offering – even to the extent that new wording was required to manifest it.

Had Kearns and his team gone for the so-called 'Chrysler' priority, it would have meant, in effect, abandoning the leadership position in many key capabilities which had been developed over decades. The 'Sears' Priority meant even further concentration on the customer relationship as an asset, almost completely ignoring the capability end of the equation. Finally, Xerox's 'BMW' priority involved reinterpreting what had been a successful relationship-centered business model into a transactional-centered business model.

The ABB example also shows that a firm has at its disposal different alternatives upon developing its business model. The industrial division started its customer base management project with the goal of strengthening its joint value-creating processes with its *existing* customers. This would have involved building or acquiring further capabilities to serve its existing customer base. However, by heavily involving its customers in the goal-formulation process, it became evident that there was a much bigger value-creating potential if ABB instead used existing capabilities for value creation with *new* customers. These capability-leveraging activities became the major ingredient of the new business model chosen by the industrial division during spring 1992.

In this section we 'catalogue' choices such as those which Xerox and ABB faced in terms of four distinct possible 'business modeling' priorities. When developing a business model, the company can emphasize one of four alternative priorities, depending on how its managers determine priorities between capability and customers' value creation. This is graphically summarized in Figure 4.5, and explained below.

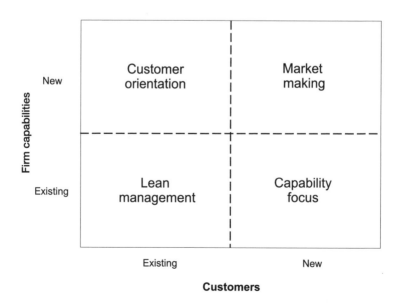

Figure 4.5 The four alternative business model priorities.

A first possible choice to consider, in business modeling, concerns a preference towards that which we call *customer orientation.*

Developing a customer-oriented business model means that the firm tries to rethink its current business model starting from a focus on how to best retain and develop its existing customer relationships. To this effect, the firm reconsiders its capabilities: it may want to get rid of some, develop others, acquire a few new ones.

The 'Chrysler' and 'Sears' priorities for Xerox which Kearns and colleagues considered were two versions of this position. ABB's 'key account management' meant to shift the company's attention from a strong emphasis on technology and products toward more emphasis on important individual customers. This is a typical example of customer orientation.[21]

We look at this approach in more detail in Chapter 5.

A second business modeling priority, based on reinforcing the value-creation potential of established capabilities, is what we call *capability focus.*

A capability focus involves retaining and developing the existing resource base as the main driver for developing new business. Capability focus looks to develop new applications and offerings based on the existing capabilities of the firm.

The 'pure', original 'Boeing' priority suggested at Xerox involved this type of reasoning. Recall that it meant building on Xerox's established (capability-based) excellence at making and selling copiers, to 'push through' the idea that paper-based documenting would retain its 'part' in what we can call the 'office document market share' against digital documenting.

This was also a route taken by the industrial division of ABB. As the pulp and paper industry in South East Asia was in a very buoyant mode, the industrial division was able to leverage its capabilities and sell them to new buyers in this area, limiting the need to develop new capabilities. We look at this approach in more detail in Chapter 6.

In that same chapter we will look at the third priority, *lean management,* which is also based on reinforcing the value-creation potential of established capabilities. The difference between the two strategies is that *lean management* focuses on leveraging existing capabilities for *existing* customers while the capability focus priority is directed toward new customers.

A fourth business modeling priority is to engage in business development by jointly growing new capabilities and new customer relationships. This type of business model we call *market making.*

We have borrowed this notion of 'market making' from Nokia.[22] They believe it is the right priority to use for business modeling when markets feature

- very rapid growth and turbulence, in an environment with
- highly competitive and also co-operative (the mix is now sometimes called 'co-opetitive') behavior of companies that
- are aiming at creating new businesses, when
- product life-cycles are very short, and there is
- strong standardization- and technology-based competition.

These tendencies emphasize the importance of

- right timing, as well as
- speed in bringing innovations into the global market place.

The 'modified Boeing' priority which Xerox pursued, and which led to its Document Company repositioning, illustrates this approach. Based on capabilities manifested as new technology (digital print-on-demand) Xerox successfully approached new customers. Recall that with their publishing offerings, Xerox entered the reprographic departments of large organizations, and printers. They had never approached this kind of customer before. But today, the printers represent 80 percent of Xerox's publishing market.

We look at three different versions of the market-making priority in more detail in Chapters 7, 8, and 9. Each of the three represents a different way of positioning market making within the context of the firm.

It is possible for a firm to develop both new capabilities and to serve new customers, creating what is *for that firm* a new offering. If the offering so provided is similar to offerings made available by some competing firms, the situation is not one of 'market making', but of *imitation*. As this book explores how to fundamentally transform businesses – as its focus is on business innovation – we do not here further explore this (arguably, fifth type of priority, which we can call 'imitation') alternative.

Lean management (in terms of cost effectiveness and customer retention) is paramount for any business model. This holds true irrespective of whether the focus is on one of the three other elements or not. For any company pursuing business modeling, combining development efforts with lean management becomes a critical success factor.

As we saw above, in the end the development of the ABB Fläkt Group in Finland was very much influenced by lean management preoccupations, as one of the main drivers for reorganizing the group was to improve cost efficiency. Lean management was also the major reasoning behind the so-called TB50 project within ABB (obtaining cycle time reductions of 50 percent). And despite its documenting preference, much of Xerox also has to continue the lean management imperative which its Japanese competitors impose upon the 'business as usual' box-part of its business.

BUSINESS MODELING IN PRACTICE

The four business modeling priorities depicted in Figure 4.5 are present – in different businesses, in relation to different customers – in any company at any one time.

But any *one* business development effort is *always* oriented mainly onto only *one* of the priorities, graphically depicted as quadrants in Figure 4.5.

Companies wanting to reconfigure their business will typically attempt to pursue an alternative priority to the one which they observe is being taken by companies they consider to be their competitors, and which together with them form their 'industry'. True prime movers will be those that find a *market-making* possibility that others – in their 'industry' or another – have failed to see, to articulate, or to make work.

'Strategic groups', groups of individual companies that determine priority in relation to the companies they classify as key competitors, typically demonstrate a common behavior that corresponds to one of the four priorities in Figure 4.5. For example, many leading car companies have in the 1990s appeared to concentrate their attention on *lean management,* improving cost efficiency through mergers and consolidation. Some of these, and others, also exhibit *capability leveraging,* opening new factories to attract new customers, such as Fiat and Ford in Brazil or Toyota in France.

Single firms change their business model priority over time. In the beginning of the 1900s, Ford could be described as a genuine *market-making* company. The automobile clearly changed the way society worked, and Ford drove this change. As the 'industry' which its market making created matured, car manufacturers around the world began consolidating (from over 350 groups to a dozen by the beginning of the twenty-first century), and became more and more alike in how they operated, giving way to the lean management focus we see today. The Smart initiative by Daimler-Chrysler is a first effort – not yet having met unquestionable success at the time of writing – to re-enter the market-making mode – something we can expect to see more of as leading players attempt to exit the cost wars which lean management brings about. The 'Smart' is the first attempt at doing to cars what Xerox did with its 'documenting' to the lean-management orientation which 'photocopying' exhibited between 1975 and 1985.

Firms exploring alternative priorities within their business model will benefit from the suggestion in Chapter 3 of enhancing the 'granularity or resolution' of their value constellations. Firms have to not merely look at products and markets, but instead more carefully examine the capabilities and the value-creating processes of individual customers. It is this enhanced granularity which can provide managers with more information, allowing them to position each business in terms of the four priorities which our business modeling framework offers. As the car industry illustration shows, each firm has a multitude of alternative priorities available, even if the industry as a low-resolution aggregate may appear to be commoditizing.

CONCLUSION

In this chapter, we introduced the notion of business model, which manifests the value-creation logic of a firm within its context. The business model is to the actual business which a firm pursues what an architectural model is to an actual building. The business model articulates the emerging architecture for value creation which companies must understand and use to design their viability today and tomorrow.

We explained the firm as being 'open' to the environment in which it is, and with which it evolves.

In working through the model of the firm as an open system, we saw how using combinations of – on the one hand – new and existing capabilities, and on the other – new and existing customer relations, a firm's business model will give priority to one of four priorities. These four distinct priorities are:

- Customer orientation.
- Capability focus.
- Lean management.
- Market making.

The following chapters examine each in turn. Chapter 5 thus analyzes customer orientation, Chapter 6 the leveraging of capabilities (capability focus and lean management) and Chapters 7, 8, and 9 review three different types of market making.

Customer Orientation: Aligning the Value-Creation Logics of the Firm with the Value-Creation Logics of *Existing* Customers

5

Exploring customer orientation is one of the four priorities of the business model.

As we saw in Chapter 5, a customer-oriented business model is based on aligning the value-creating logic of the firm with the value-creating logic of its *existing* customers. Specifically, this chapter:

- Identifies *three criteria* that define key customers: profitability; their roles as standard-setting or 'referent' organizations; and/or their knowledge and expectations, or potential as co-learning partners.
- Shows how to *identify the value-creating logic* of customers based on the interaction between customers and their own counterparts.
- Shows how to *match the value-creating logics* of a company and its customers by focusing on both the *value* of the offering and on aligning the *values* of both the supplier and its customers.
- Offers an in-depth case study of *Caterpillar* as a sterling example of a customer-oriented firm.

ROOTS OF OUR UNDERSTANDING

The classical argument for customer orientation was first fully presented in 1960 by Theodore Levitt, in his seminal article 'Marketing Myopia'. Levitt proposed that American railroads were in trouble because they were too product-oriented instead of being customer-oriented. The railroads, he argued, assumed themselves to be in the railroad business rather than in the transportation business.

A group of researchers, whom we can call the 'service management school', developed Levitt's insights into what came to be known as 'relationship marketing'. One definition of marketing from that school is a good example of the underlying premises for customer orientation:

> Marketing is to establish, maintain, and enhance (usually, but not necessarily, long-term) relationships with customers and other partners, at a profit, so that the objectives of the parties involved are met. This is achieved by a mutual exchange and fulfillment of promises.[1]

Industrial marketing discovered the importance of relationships. Today we understand that in the co-productive economy, a given relationship has different functions (and economic consequences) for each actor. Outcomes of different relationships become very interdependent. So any one actor just *has* to be concerned about other actors to be successful.[2] And any one relationship must take into account how it relates to other relationships.

CUSTOMER ORIENTATION VS. MARKETING ORIENTATION

As we saw in the two previous chapters, the 'higher resolution' involved in dealing with *customers* provides business development possibilities which cannot be obtained with the 'lower resolution' notion of *markets*. It follows from this discussion that today the notions of marketing orientation and customer orientation have different connotations. The major differences are listed in Table 5.1.

An example of how a firm sees customer orientation is offered by Hewlett Packard's view:

> Knowing customers' needs is not enough. To have what we (Hewlett Packard) call a truly imaginative understanding of user needs, we must know customers so well that we fully comprehend both their spoken and unspoken needs – now and in the future. We need to know what new products, features, and services will surprise and delight them. We need to

Table 5.1 Differences between marketing orientation and customer orientation

Marketing orientation	Customer orientation
Purpose of marketing is to make a sale	Purpose of marketing is to create a customer
Sale is result and the measure of success	Sale is beginning of relationship; profit is measure of success
Business is defined by its products and factories	Business is defined by customer relationships
Price is determined by competitive market forces; price is an input	Price is determined by negotiation and joint decision making; price is an outcome
Communications are aimed at aggregates of customers	Communications are targeted and tailored to individuals
Marketer is valued for its products and prices	Marketer is valued for his or her present and future problem-solving capability
Objective: to make the next sale; find the next customer, enhancing market share	Objective: to satisfy the customer you have by delivering superior value, enhancing share of customer

Source: Webster, 1993.

understand their world so well that we can bring new technology to problems that customers may not yet truly realize they have. Our ultimate goal is this deeper, richer level of understanding.[3]

Customer orientation links the value-creation process of each individual customer, the value-creation potential of the total portfolio of customers, and the firm's set of own or addressable capabilities. Each of these three elements is dynamic and interdependent. Thus, value creation is, over time, a systemic and dynamic reconciliation, and where possible, an optimization, task.

The basic assumptions behind customer orientation, as we define them in this book, are:

- Long-term customer relationships can be economically beneficial if managed properly.
- The cost of maintaining and upgrading existing customer relationships is cheaper than spending to develop new ones.
- The cost of maintaining and upgrading customer relationships to prevent defection is cheaper than spending to recuperate customers who have defected.

- Each customer relationship is a manageable variable from the point of view of the supplier, which means that suppliers are (partly) responsible for how customers behave.
- Customer relationships need to be managed as a portfolio of relationships which relate to each other.
- Adopting a systemic approach which treats customers, offerings, and capabilities holistically will provide the firm with both short-term benefits in the form of better resource allocation, and long-term benefits in the form of learning and business development.

In many business situations, the profitability of customer relationships improves over time. On the one hand, joint learning, increased trust (less need to check each other out), and mutual knowledge reduce 'transaction'-related costs. On the other hand, as customers get to know their suppliers and become more effective buyers, they receive greater value from the relationship. Furthermore, often these customers spread positive word-of-mouth messages about their relationship with the supplier, in effect acting as the supplier's marketers. For example, in Europe, one IKEA catalogue is typically passed around to 15 different households. This provides the customers with valuable, experience-based, additional information to the one provided by IKEA itself. So for both IKEA and its customers, costs decline and value increases over time: a win-win relationship is developed.

LEARNING WITH CUSTOMERS

Customer orientation emphasizes learning from and with customers. The supplier, considering his exchange value objectives (see Chapter 3), has to

- understand the value-creation processes of the customer, including how these are manifested at the interface between one's own customers and the customers' own counterparts or customers;
- define the appropriate offering;
- design the processes with which to more effectively co-produce the offering with the customer, and

- efficiently access, develop, and allocate necessary resources and capabilities.

When allocating the necessary resources and capabilities for learning, the supplier must combine mutual learning about/with the customers (L in the exchange value equation) with the relevant risk factors (R). For example, a supplier can allocate resources to visit customers regularly, even if there is no new offering to sell to them. This allows the supplier to both learn (of any developing customer need, for example) and reduce risk (visits strengthen the customer–supplier relationship, thus reducing the risk of the customer bolting to another supplier). Thus, customer visits and other 'learning enhancement/risk-reduction' practices help a firm to become customer-oriented.

Of course, not all customers are alike in terms of learning potential. One very important criterion for 'segmenting' customers in co-productive businesses is the potential for learning what different customer groups offer. A related criterion is what customer relationships offer the most significant business development potential.

Learning with key customers

Customer orientation as explained above means that the firm explicitly tries to adapt its own value-creating system to align it with the individual value-creating systems of its most valuable customers. This alignment process requires a creative understanding of customers' value-creating processes. Three specific steps make it possible:

1   identifying key customers,
2   identifying key counterparts of key customers, their values and their co-producing logic, and
3   realigning value-creating activities to fit the logic of the interfaces between key customers and their counterparts.

We deal with each of these in turn.

Identifying key customers

Three basic reasons to classify a customer as 'key' exist. They are based on the exchange value equation. If a customer qualifies on more than one criterion, its importance for the supplier is further enhanced.

The first criterion of key customers are those that provide a disproportional part of the *profitability* of the firm (measured by yearly sales less than the costs of goods sold). Such customers are typically big customers. It should be noticed that among the biggest customers one will also find those that produce the biggest losses! The key to calculating customer profitability, is to calculate the actual resource consumption per customer.

In other words, to be able to fully grasp the profitability of customers, it is necessary to go beyond traditional margin-based calculations, since the decisive elements of customer profitability are to be found in so-called variable costs. Examples of such costs are those contributed to by sales, marketing, technical support, warranties, after-sales service, entertainment, and discounts. In addition, indirect (including, or also known as, 'average', 'back office', 'support', 'sunk') costs have to be allocated to each customer as much as possible. In a number of analyses conducted by our SMG colleagues in different companies, as many as 40 percent of the customers were unprofitable, and as few as 5 percent of the customers can bring in over 360 percent of net profits.

Since most companies do not have a customer-based accounting system, and instead have product-based ones, they do not know how profitable a given customer is. As they do not know which customers are profitable and which are not, they cannot determine which ones are 'key' according to this criterion.

As product lines produce different profit levels, what is considered to be an 'internal' cross-subsidization among product lines (with things such as 'loss leaders') will often end up as an external cross-subsidization among customers. The reason in such cases is that different customers do not buy the same mix of product line packages. Some customers will buy a bigger proportion of low profit products, while others will buy a bigger proportion of high profit ones. So many companies discover that they, unintentionally, have become machines enabling some customers to subsidize others.

It is important to note that customers are 'key' according to profitability not because they were born that way, but because of how their suppliers have managed them, consciously or unconsciously. A 'difficult' customer is difficult because the way the supplier has organized the relationship invites the customer rationally to act in the difficult way in order to obtain whatever he requires.

In the same way, unprofitable customers are 'unprofitable' because the supplier has determined that it is better to lose money on them than to lose them altogether. This judgment may be correct – particularly if the customers in question fit at least one of the other two criteria for being key customers.

The second criterion for determining key customers concerns identifying the customers who in effect set the rules for others. This is most often not because of formal agreements among the customers. Instead, it is simply due to the pre-eminence of one customer in relation to others. As we saw in Chapter 1, we call such customers '*referent*' ones.

Referent customers may be big or important customers, but there may also be other reasons for their influence. If, for example, Wimbledon accepts a new automatic device to detect if tennis serves fall within the court, it is likely that other important tennis championships, such as the US Open, or Roland Garros, will accept this new device as well. If so, Wimbledon acts as a 'referent' organization in the adoption of this new device in tennis competitions. Wimbledon would therefore be 'key' not primarily because of its direct profitability contribution, but because Wimbledon would provide substantial value through either one or both of 'competitive blockage' and 'goodwill' elements of the exchange value equation.

According to our experience most companies ignore who their referent organization clients are. Finding out who these were was one of the advantages of the Cultor/FSB activities we described in Chapter 3.

It becomes evident from the discussion on the pages above, that *a third criterion* of being a key customer is to provide important *learning* opportunities to the supplier. The Department of Social Security in the

UK provided its supplier with this value as well as goodwill value, as was described in Chapter 3. The Department could benefit from this value for the supplier and get a price quotation much lower than the actual cost of the offering.

Not all customers are good (actual or potential) learning partners. In most businesses, the best learning partners happen to be the most *sophisticated* customers. By 'sophisticated' we mean three interrelated things:

1   they are *knowledgeable* not only of their own business, but also of their suppliers' – in particular knowing how to help the supplier develop offerings that help *them*;
2   they like to be in the 'driver's seat' when in discussion with counterparts (they want to set the agenda of what is to be discussed); and
3   they are considered to play something of a 'referent' role by others, particularly those that consider them competitors.

The sophistication of customers is depicted in Figure 5.1. As the figure shows, there is an overall behavioral trend towards the 'north-east' quadrant of the diagram. In company after company, industry after industry, and market after market, suppliers consider that customers are continuously becoming more informed, educated, sophisticated, and demanding.

This trend is evident not only in relation to the customer's past sophistication, but also to the supplier's sophistication. In other words, customers are not only becoming more informed and educated than they were in the past, but often they are also becoming more informed and educated relative to their suppliers! In effect, the customer is acquiring the means with which to outconfigure the supplier.

What drives this north-east trend? In part it is the pervasiveness of enhanced access to information, helped by media (television, radio, the press, the Internet). Today customers access information, which was previously not available to them, with unprecedented ease.

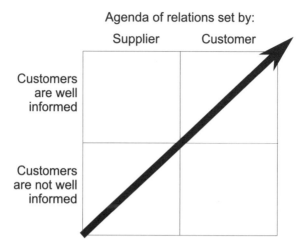

Figure 5.1 A matrix showing the segmentation of customers according to their sophistication.

In France, with the help of a de-jargonized guide to medicines, customers can now check if the prescription their doctor gave them can be better served by a generic drug costing less than the branded one prescribed.

US customers can now create 'on-line' groups of potential buyers, joining forces to decrease the unit costs of items they buy (like cars or household appliances) from single supplier outlets that give volume discounts. In effect, the Internet allows customers quickly to organize into buying co-operatives, enabling them to enhance their buying power. Retailers are finding themselves competing against buying co-operatives which they do not control directly, and which can cherry pick (through arbitrage), preventing the retailers from using loss-leading cross-subsidies to bring in customers.

Higher levels of formal education (at least, in most OECD countries) also make customers increasingly knowledgeable. Finally, the so-called 'consumer' movement, helped by the courts (particularly in the United States), has rendered customers relatively more powerful. Since Ralph Nader started to popularize the movement, consumer magazines, consumer groups, consumer pressure groups, and juries defending consumer interests have provided consumers with enhanced power and recognition. From the Ford Pinto, whose gas tanks exploded, to many cases in which consumers have brought companies to trial for dangerous or low quality goods, the consumer has become 'king'.[4]

As a result of such forces, as Figure 5.1 suggests, customers are moving, at different rates of speed, towards being better informed, and/ or more capable of setting the agenda of the relationship they want to establish with prospective suppliers. In short, they are becoming more sophisticated.

Most companies, and most businesses (there are exceptions[5]) make more money out of relatively uninformed, less-demanding customers than they make on 'sophisticated' ones.

Plotting one's customers positions on Figure 5.1 helps the firm assess the current sophistication of its customer base. For example, if all of one's customer base is in the south-west corner, then cash flow from these customers is *at the moment* positive, customers say they are satisfied, and business is doing well or very well. However, with no customers in the north-east quadrant, the current happy state may not be viable for very long. This is because of the overall north-east trend, and because of the reconfigurability of existing offerings and value constellations.

Conversely, if all of one's customers are located in the north-east quadrant of the figure, the price/earning ratio of the company is likely very high, it is considered a 'darling' of the stock-market and the industry, and it is considered to have a brilliant future, although cash flow may be negative.

An example of such a company, at the time of writing, is Amazon.com. In the same way, one could say that Dell intelligently adapted to the value-creating logics of its more sophisticated customers, by offering them the opportunity to design the computer themselves, and guaranteeing rapid delivery. In radically redefining its offering, it repositioned itself so as to co-learn with the more sophisticated customers, allowing the lessons to be applied to less sophisticated and/or demanding ones as well.

Another way of using Figure 5.1 is to compare one's customers not statically, but dynamically. This allows one to segment customers not by their current sophistication, but also according to their *potential* sophistication

An example of this type of comparison concerns a supplier of engines to the civilian airline industry. Executives from the supplier put British Airways in the north-east corner, and Virgin Atlantic in the south-east one. Virgin was very demanding, although relatively less well informed than British Airways. However, in the view of these executives, Virgin Atlantic was moving north – was becoming ever-better informed – faster than British Airways was moving north-east. Using the diagram in Figure 5.1 allowed the executives to determine that in many respects Virgin was a better 'learning' partner, because its dynamic learning incited one to learn with them as fast as they themselves learned.

Another demonstration of this chart involves a steel company with customers located everywhere in Europe. A hot debate on where to place Fiat on the chart ensued within the steel company between an executive from the company's world headquarters and the executive in the company's Italian branch. The headquarters' executive plotted Fiat's position much further south and west than the Italian executive did. As a result, the Italian executive realized that it was what he considered the headquarters' executive's misperception of the position of Fiat on this map that had led to past erroneous strategies from HQ on how to develop business with Fiat.

'Manufacturing' sophisticated customers is one version of what Prahalad and Hamel (1994) called 'stretch'. An example of 'creating' sophisticated customers follows:

In the mid-1960s, a Philadelphia-based company called ARA decided that in order to be a leading player in its business, which was providing restaurant services to large institutions, it had to have at least one customer that was located further north-east than any customer in its existing customer base. After a brainstorming session, the company's managers realized that the most 'difficult' (most demanding, most informed) customer the company could have in its business was the Olympic Games. So they set up a task force to obtain a contract in this business, which led to a restaurant service contract for the Montreal Olympic Games. The company figured that if it could

- set up a kitchen and a dining room out of a parking lot, from scratch,
- feed 100-meter runners, 1500-meter swimmers, javelin throwers, journalists, marathon runners, and the public, in ways that each of them considered appropriate;
- take down the kitchen and the dining facilities after the event, leaving behind only the parking lot,

then they would be able to do 'anything' in their business. They would be able to serve the most demanding customers they could find. The Montreal Games contract was a success, and the company now has a division which regularly supplies large-scale sporting events.

The lesson of this story is that one may have to 'create' one's own 'sophisticated' customers, to have them be the firm's 'business R&D'.

Identifying the co-producing logics of key customers

The actualization of the value of the offering takes place in the interface between the customers and their counterparts. Thus, the relationship that the key customer has with these counterparts also affects the value-creating potential of the key customer for the supplier.

We return to Wimbledon to illustrate this. Except for the surface (grass), tennis is played no differently at Wimbledon than at other tournaments. What sets Wimbledon apart (and makes it a 'key' customer) is its historical traditions, which are highly appreciated by the general public, the press, and the professional tennis community – including other championships which would buy whatever Wimbledon buys. If the decision makers at Wimbledon consider automation as a dangerous step away from these historical traditions, then the question of acquiring an automatic device that judges whether a tennis serve was in or out involves more than pure objective cost/benefit considerations. Instead it becomes one where the (historical, traditional) values of the *referent* customer have to be aligned with the (new technology-based) values embodied in the supplier's offering.

The historical *values* of Wimbledon are a key component of the *value* that Wimbledon offers its customers. Therefore, suppliers who have Wimbledon as a customer must align the values embodied in their offering with the values embodied in Wimbledon's offerings to its counterparts: the general public, the press, the professional tennis community.

In certain cases, customers feel that their offering embodies not only the value which their suppliers' *offering* helps them to create, but also embodies the very values of the supplier. These values will be interpreted not only by the purchasing function of the customer, but will also influence the customer in a much broader way. In such cases, the customer looks for alignment of its own values with those of its suppliers', and even the suppliers' suppliers.

Thus, Motorola publicly announces that it looks for supply partners that share its values. Motorola sharpens the skills of these partners by teaching them its own Total Quality Management techniques, even requiring them to take courses in cycle time reduction, customer satisfaction, and so on at an education program it calls Motorola University.

IKEA has typically done the same in relation to suppliers, in some cases 'manufacturing' these suppliers, virtually from scratch, by finding suppliers with related activities with whom it shared its values. A Czech shirt maker thus became a chair cushion maker for IKEA, and a window maker was helped by IKEA to manufacture glass table-tops.

When in 1986 Honda picked Donnelly Corp. to make all the mirrors for its US-manufactured cars, Honda managers knew that the company, based in Holland, Michigan, had never made exterior mirrors and had no factory for making them. But Honda managers had known Donnelly for many years as an interior-mirror supplier, and they liked what they had seen. They knew that Donnelly's values and culture squared perfectly with Honda's. And with only a handshake to mark the birth of the new deal, Donnelly built an entirely new plant to make Honda's exterior mirrors.[6]

The above illustrations are examples where the customers – Motorola, IKEA, and Honda – considered their chosen supplier's values as Net Satisfaction-increasing elements of the offering.

Values are also brought to the forefront when customers oppose the exposed values of the firm. Nike (because of its Asian sub-contractors using child labor) and Shell (because of its alleged anti-environmental disposal plans for its Brent Spar oil platform in 1995) faced a significant number of their customers – and other stakeholders – objecting to the values attached to these activities. Subsequently both companies had to change their way of working: Nike announced new practices for supply management, whereas Shell transformed how it would dispose of Brent Spar, dismantling it instead of sinking it.

Other companies, like Levi Strauss and the Body Shop, have tried pro-actively to increase the awareness of their firm's 'good' values among potential customers and suppliers, and to position themselves as role models for companies adhering to these values.

The values in the interface between the key customer and its counterparts (between Wimbledon and the general public, or Shell and its angry pro-environment customers, for example) must therefore be consciously managed. By 'manage', we mean

- understanding these interfaces and their dynamics,
- finding a valued role within them, and
- co-developing them with the customers.

Customer values are thus as important to manage as the value-creating activities of one's own employees. Ultimately this means that we may choose not to interact with certain customers, because of the values they (or their counterparts) represent. In the same way, customers may refuse to deal with a supplier because of the supplier's values; or on the contrary, seek out the supplier because of them. As we further examine in Chapter 10, we have to accept and realize that we have to manage both economic value, non-economic values, and the relationship between them.

An example can illustrate the advantage of extending the normal, *singular*, business notion of 'value', to the *plural* one of 'values' which we advocate. Ford's acquisition of Volvo cars in the beginning of 1999 raised the following questions:

- To what extent would the technical characteristics of Volvo vehicles be similar to those of Ford cars? Too much similarity would be interpreted as having the acquisition cannibalize Ford's established market.
- To what extent would typical 'market segmentation' characteristics (socio-economic, demographic) of Volvo buyers be similar to those of buyers of Ford's 'premium' brand cars, such as the Lincoln? Too much similarity would also be interpreted as having the acquisition cannibalize Lincoln's established market.

But if in addition to such 'product/market matrix' questions, one adds higher-resolution, enhanced granularity 'value constellation' ones (see Figure 3.4 on page 60), the envisioned impact of the acquisition on business potential becomes very different. A question of this type, relating to values (in the plural) is:

- How are the values of Volvo buyers, and the way these are articulated with their counterparts, different from the values of Ford buyers, and the way these values are articulated with *their* counterparts?

If the values the Volvo and Ford car buyers exhibit in relation to their valued counterparts turned out to be sufficiently different, then segmenting customers based on these would be more helpful than traditional product/market segmentation. A segmentation based on values may reveal, for example, that Lincoln Town Car or Ford Taurus buyers have different values from, say, Volvo S-70 buyers, even if the cars from both manufacturers were to be considered technically similar, and the socio-economic and demographic characteristics of the buying populations were also similar.

ADAPTING INTERNAL VALUE-CREATING ACTIVITIES TO STRENGTHEN 'KEY' CUSTOMER RELATIONSHIPS

We have seen that while designing relationships with each key customer is important in a co-productive economy, it is also important to deal with all customer relationships as a portfolio.

While unprofitable customers who are considered to have no 'key' role potential may become the objects of less resource allocation or price increases, there may be other unprofitable customers that 'should' remain in the supplier's portfolio for good reason.

Some customers may be unprofitable today, but may be captured early in their life (for example, a retail bank signing on business school students) on the expectation that the relationship with them will turn out to be profitable. Others may be unprofitable for life, but may play such an important 'referent' role, that the losses they occasion are extremely lucrative marketing investments.

Once such decisions are taken, measures to convert a (low resolution) industrial customer relationship architecture – based on 'average' and anonymous customers – into a (high resolution) 'co-productive' one must be taken.

> One pharmaceutical company working with institutional buyers in a European country identified that it had 600 actual and potential customers in that country. It carried out an analysis of which ones were 'key' customers, and determined 300 of the 600 fit the criteria. It then allocated 100 out of its 103 sales staff to the 300 key customers (3 customers/sales person), and the other 3 sales staff to the 300 non-key customers (100 customers/sales person), finding this reallocation to be extremely profitable.

This may appear to be an extreme case, but in our view it is not. Adapting the internal structures inherited from an industrial era to a co-productive business environment is bound to produce profound changes. Companies to an increasing degree have to adapt to the radical value creation changes in their environments.

ARM Ltd emerged in 1990 as a spin-out from Acorn Computers in Cambridge, UK. As far back as 1983, Acorn was involved in RISC ('Reduced Instruction Set Computing') chip design, essentially a streamlined approach to microprocessor design.

The semiconductor industry in which ARM considers itself to be can be described as hypercompetitive. This means short opportunity windows for new products, a fast pace of change, and rapidly changing competitive criteria. As a small supplier of RISC chip technology, ARM chose partnering with its major customers as its business model. ARM enters into contractual licensing agreements with its customers, but the key to the success of ARM's partnerships, however, is not so much contained in these contracts. Rather, success is due to the 'structure and culture' of the teams involved at the interface, or boundary, between the firms. The power/control base of the relationship between ARM and its customers is 'expertise'. Thus ARM's expertise helps to ensure that ARM, the smaller partner, does not cede control to the larger customer-partners.

Like the pharmaceutical company, ARM has adapted its structure based on its relationships with its customers. Specifically, ARM made the relevant interdependencies of its alliances with each customer the central design criterion of its organizational architecture. This means that ARM has become an ongoing organizational 'compromise' of the relationships it has with each and every one of its customers, shifting and changing its structure and activities with each of these interactions.

The co-productive permeability at the firm's boundaries are facilitated by the constant interaction of boundary-spanning individuals. These interactions constantly reshape the firm's members' perceptions of their own competences. They also update their knowledge of useful assets and capabilities, and suggest new ways of organizing and co-ordinating, all of which contribute to a process of continuous alliance-based competence building and leveraging.[7]

One of the best examples of a customer-oriented company that we are aware of is Caterpillar. We examine this in the next section of this chapter.

CATERPILLAR: A CUSTOMER-ORIENTED COMPANY

Introducing the company and the business

Caterpillar had 1998 revenues of $21 billion, net profits of $1.51 billion, and over 65,000 employees. Caterpillar's business is capital intensive. The financing support for dealers and customers is considerable. The profitable years of 1993–98 re-established the financial strength that Caterpillar had had prior to the losses in 1991–92.

Caterpillar is by sales the world's #1 maker of earthmoving machinery. The industry is global and commoditized. While some product features may be customized, such as the operator's cab or the paint job, the standard product can be sold virtually unchanged throughout the world.

Caterpillar operates in three principal business segments:

1 Machinery (construction, mining, and agricultural) with 64 percent of sales (in 1998),
2 Engines (31 percent), and
3 Financial products (5 percent).

Historically, Caterpillar's first product family, the track-type tractor, is the best known branded heavy equipment product worldwide. Other Caterpillar machines are excavators, loaders, scrapers, mining shovels, motor graders, engines, compacts, solar turbines, and paving products.

The main customer industries are transportation (24 percent), mining (16 percent), commercial and industrial construction[8] (15 percent), housing and forest products (14 percent), and energy (12 percent).

The number of US distributors of construction and mining equipment is slightly less than 3,000. Caterpillar arranges its distribution through independent dealers, of which there are 64 in the US.

The volume of the equipment rental industry is approximately $16 billion.[9] Of this, construction equipment rentals total approximately $4.2 billion divided 50/50 between rental chains and equipment dealers. The trend is that leasing is used as a major channel for distribution.

The move from owning to leasing is a major trend in the industry. The main reasons for the growing leasing business are:

- Leasing offers better fiscal benefits than ownership.
- Management philosophy has led companies to outsource ownership and service, and concentrate on the 'core' business.
- The number of large construction projects has decreased, causing contractors to take on a greater number of smaller, more specialized jobs in order to meet multiple deadlines, which require specialized equipment.
- The growing pressure to conserve capital and cash.

The volume of the construction and mining equipment manufacturing in the US was approximately $16 billion in 1993. Of this volume $14.5 billion was the construction part and mining accounted for $1.5 billion. The industry employed 88,000 people in about 1,100 firms. Caterpillar is by far the biggest player in this industry in the US. The main competitor worldwide, Komatsu, comes in second in the US, with estimated US sales of $1.735 billion in 1998. Other important competitors are Deere & Company, Terex Corporation (including Clark), Harnischfeger Industries (including Joy Industries), Case, Navistar, Ingersoll-Rand, Hitachi, and Kubota. The product mixes of these competitors (Komatsu excluded) overlap Caterpillar's only in part. Therefore a direct market share analysis is less relevant as some of the players define their markets more narrowly .

Applying the value-creation framework to Caterpillar helps to understand how it is conducting its value-creating activities in relation to a multitude of customers, and in different constellations. To illustrate this, Caterpillar's 1996 position is depicted in Figure 5.2.

A traditional 'industrial' perspective of Caterpillar, that is, a perspective which analyzes and defines an 'industry' according to the 'value chain' and the physical goods it produces, would primarily focus on which moves Caterpillar should make in relation to its competitors. As Caterpillar is selling its machines to dealers, another issue which an industrial perspective would consider is the possibility of repositioning Caterpillar

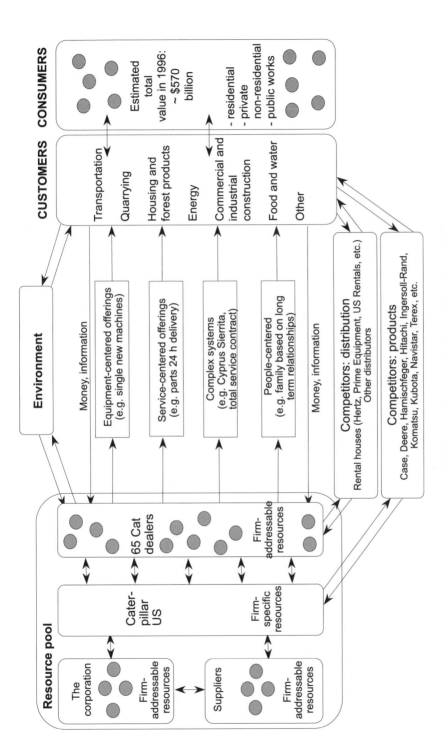

Figure 5.2 Caterpillar's value-creation system, 1996 figures (Source: Wallin and Ramírez, 1996).

within the value chain though vertical integration by acquiring dealers. This would be a viable option if the analysis concluded that the distribution industry was attractive. For an industrialist, the two central issues would be: the attractiveness of the industry for long-term profitability, and the determinants of relative competitive position within the industry.

Analyzing Caterpillar from a co-productive perspective takes into account not only the industrial characteristics, but also – and centrally – the relationships that Caterpillar possesses within its value constellations, in its industry and outside it, and the roles it plays there. The following quotations from the 1995 and 1998 annual reports indicate how Caterpillar treats these relationships:

> Good priorities, well-planned and well-executed. Without them, we would not have achieved the record-setting sales, profits and world-wide market share ... Key to that success is our decentralized corporate organization, put in place at the beginning of the decade. With it we've developed a keen focus on two synergistic priorities – the customer and the bottom line ... Anticipating what our customers want and responding to their needs encourages long-lasting relationships ...
>
> Those long-term commitments, in term, help keep sales strong (more than 80 percent of our sales are from repeat customers) and improve results.
>
> Our new product introduction (NPI) process has cut development time by 25 to 30 percent. And in the last four years we've revamped every product family. In doing so, we've served both priorities. Streamlining how we introduce new products is cutting costs, bringing new technology to the marketplace sooner and improving sales. At the same time, we're far more responsive to changes in customers' needs while achieving a better ROA. (Caterpillar, Annual Report 1995)

And:

> Cutting edge. State of the art. Sophisticated. Caterpillar manufacturing is all three. We spent $1.8 billion to modernize our factories in the late '80s and '90s – and we continue to invest to keep our competitive edge.

Customers are reaping the benefits, getting new and better products
sooner . . .

We spent $838 million on research and engineering in 1998 (4.0
percent of total sales and revenues), introducing 44 new or improved
products with countless technological changes – changes that gave
customers a successful edge.

There is a team culture at Caterpillar. Most product development is
handled by New Product Introduction (NPI) teams – multifunctional
groups that ensure that customers' wishes for a new product are carried
out efficiently. We put ourselves in the customers' places, working to
improve their bottom lines. Our ultimate goal: our customers'
successes. By helping them succeed, we succeed. We believe that's the
way it should be. (Caterpillar, Annual Report 1998)

The quotes above highlight the processes matching the resources of
Caterpillar with the value-creation potential of its customers. Caterpillar
uses the words 'long-lasting relationships' and 'long-term commitments',
'putting ourselves in the customers' places', which manifest a view of
priority as an interactive process, not just as a positioning game within
an industry. 'Commitment' in the sense that Caterpillar uses it is quite
different from the use of the same word by Porter.[10] Porter talks about
communicating commitment to pursue a move, or retaliate against, a
competitor's action. Caterpillar's commitment seems to be customer,
not competitor, focused:

The construction business is changing all the time. It has to. Same with
mining. And power generation. It's true of all the industries we serve . . .

So the people in those businesses who buy our machines and engines
– our customers – expect us to more than keep pace. To supply them
with products and services that allow them to serve their customers
better. We're doing it . . .

We've set up a decentralized corporate structure based on products
and geography. Individual divisions make their own product and sales
decisions that reflect the special needs of their customers and the nature
of their products . . .

Because each division knows its customers best – and can respond to
them quickly and meaningfully. (Caterpillar, Annual Report 1995)

Fulfilling commitments to customers

How does Caterpillar fulfill its commitments? In other words, how does Caterpillar help its customers create value with its offerings?

In Chapter 3, we introduced the 'three dimensional' offering description, made up of hardware, software and peopleware dimensions. In the hardware-based construction equipment business in which Caterpillar's origins lie, the physical product is the offering's historic core. It is upon this core that software and peopleware have been added to enable the customer better to create value.

Caterpillar stresses the importance of its physical product line in the following manner:

> As we've become more responsive to customers, they've increasingly invested in our products. That has translated into even greater participation in the world-wide market ... For example, we're now number two in the world in the back-hoe loader business even though we introduced our first machine just 10 years ago ... (Caterpillar, Annual Report 1995)

Three years later, the pace continues:

> We've got the best product line we've ever had. We have the widest engine and turbine product portfolio in the world. (We) introduced 244 new or improved products to our customers in the last five years ... (Caterpillar, Annual Report 1998)

From this strong hardware foundation in the product line, the importance of the software element (distribution and services) is described as follows:

> Unparalleled Distribution System. It's the best in our industry. And it makes us truly a global company. 186 dealers serving 197 countries, with an average of more than 50 years service as a Cat dealer ... Independent, most locally owned, they are in tune with what their customers need. They have state-of-the-art facilities and more employees collectively than Caterpillar. Dealers are teamed with 25 Cat

parts distribution facilities – with 10 million square feet of warehouse space – design, manufacture, market, finance, and provide support for Cat machines and engines. (Caterpillar, Annual Report 1995)

Three years later:

Unparalleled Distribution System. It's the best in our industry. And it makes us truly a global company. 195 dealers serving nearly 200 countries, with an average of more than 50 years service as a Cat dealer ...They are the best in our industry. They know the business and they know it from their customers' point of view. They understand customers' needs and are equipped to deal with them ...

Our dealers have opened Cat rental stores in many locations on three continents ...

Customers know there's significant value in the Cat machine or engine they own – beyond the quality, reliability and durability they've purchased. They know they can quickly get the product and service support they need – faster and more competently than anyone else in our business can provide. (Caterpillar, Annual Report 1998)

The peopleware aspects of the offering is at the core of a *Harvard Business Review* article[11] in which Donald V. Fites, Chairman and CEO of Caterpillar Inc., describes the relationship between Caterpillar and its dealers as follows :

People – employees and dealers – design, manufacture, market, finance and provide support for Cat machines and engines ...

- we don't gouge our dealers
- we give our dealers extraordinary support
- we ensure that our dealerships are well run
- we communicate fully, frequently, and honestly
- we believe strong business relationships are personal
- we strive to keep dealerships in the family.

Donald Fites claims that the biggest reason for Caterpillar's success has been its system of distribution and product support, and the close customer relationships it fosters.

The quoted statements from the annual reports show that Caterpillar has ensured that all three offering elements are taken care of. Building these types of relationships differentiate the firm in the marketplace, providing it maintains its hardware strengths.

The relationships, when well managed, are subject to increasing returns, as we show in Chapter 8. Because of this, with time it becomes ever more difficult for competitors to create offerings which match the worldwide dealer network containing relationships averaging more than 50 years! The duration of such relationships provides a competitive advantage which one can term to be 'timeware'. Timeware complements each of the three dimensions of the offerings in an increasing returns logic. Timeware relates to the durability of Caterpillar's equipment, to the reliability of its services, and to the responsiveness and trustworthiness of its people. It is because of this that about 80 percent of Caterpillar's business originates from repeat customers.

The way the different offering elements come together and form the comprehensive bundle of benefits that constitute a customer-oriented offering is depicted in Figure 5.3. Crucial elements for making customer orientation a feasible priority for Caterpillar are:

- as a significant part of the business is repeat business, fitting one's own development with existing customers' business development is thus crucial;
- the products last long, and thus stay in service for many years. The software, peopleware, and 'timeware' dimensions of the offering on top of the hardware core need to be managed systematically as an integrated offering;
- the value-creating processes of individual customers vary substantially, even if from a 'SIC-code' perspective, the customers appear to belong to one homogenous segment. Dealers take care of the differences for Caterpillar, supported by Caterpillar;
- the economic actors in the value constellation depicted in Figure 5.2 interact in different ways with Caterpillar. Catepillar's organization facilitates its having very different relations with such actors, who hold different roles, simultaneously, in relation to Caterpillar. For

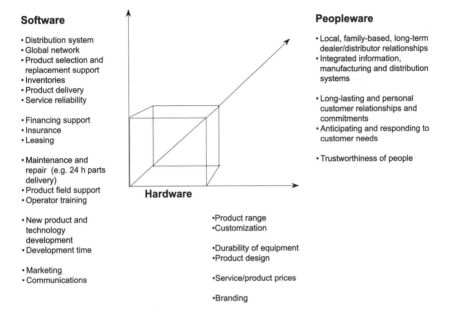

Software

- Distribution system
- Global network
- Product selection and replacement support
- Inventories
- Product delivery
- Service reliability

- Financing support
- Insurance
- Leasing

- Maintenance and repair (e.g. 24 h parts delivery)
- Product field support
- Operator training

- New product and technology development
- Development time

- Marketing
- Communications

Hardware

•Product range
•Customization

•Durability of equipment
•Product design

•Service/product prices

•Branding

Peopleware

- Local, family-based, long-term dealer/distributor relationships
- Integrated information, manufacturing and distribution systems

- Long-lasting and personal customer relationships and commitments
- Anticipating and responding to customer needs

- Trustworthiness of people

Figure 5.3 The Caterpillar offering.

example, Tamrock, a global mining equipment company, buys engines from Caterpillar for its equipment, sells rock excavation hammers to Caterpillar as an OEM manufacturer, and has signed on a Caterpillar dealer in South East Asia as its distributor;

- Donald Fites gives the independent but exclusive dealers credit for the developments that allowed Caterpillar to become one of the leading players in back-hoe loaders. The dealers invested sizeable sums in rental fleets when it became clear that many small contractors preferred to rent, rather than buy, the machines. In addition, they aggressively added salespeople to call on these smaller customers, with whom Caterpillar hadn't traditionally had much contact. This illustrates how important changes in business logics can be detected earlier by understanding that the value is co-produced with customers: both dealers and their customers, the users, alike. These parties serve as 'early warning systems' that signal opportunities and threats in a complementary way to classic competitive analyses carried out by studying market research, industry, and other aggregated competitive information;

- learning by both customers and suppliers is important to jointly develop the business.

Caterpillar's reliance on dealers is summarized by Donald Fites as follows:

- local dealers, who are long-established members of their communities, can get closer to customers than a global company can on its own;
- to tap the full potential of such dealers, a company must forge extremely close ties with them, and integrate them into its critical business systems;
- dealers can serve as proxies for customers, as consultants, and as problem solvers;
- dealers play a vital role in product design and delivery, service and field support, and management of replacement-part inventories;
- dealers provide a wide range of services before and after the sale, including advice on the selection of a product, financing, insurance, operator training, maintenance, and repair, and help in deciding when it makes economic sense to replace machines.

Donald Fites concludes by saying that 'the global winners over the next 10 to 20 years are going to be the companies with the best distribution organizations that also provide superb customer support'.

The Caterpillar dealers' combined net worth in 1998 was about $6 billion, or about 20 percent more than Caterpillar's stockholders' equity. The biggest dealers have annual revenues in the neighborhood of $1 billion. The relationships between Caterpillar and its dealers gives the company unequaled capacity to register and interpret market signals which for others remain weak, and to relate them to each other in ways that other organizations cannot match. This allows Caterpillar and its dealers to adjust their own developmental activities. In other words, intelligence gathered from dealers and customers is fed back so that it benefits new product development and enhancements in service.

This is done on a very systematic basis. Caterpillar works with dealers to survey every purchaser of a Cat machine at least three times during the first two years after the sale. In addition, Caterpillar sends out nearly 90,000 surveys each year, and as a measure of performance of its relationship capabilities, it obtains a remarkable score of about 40 percent response rate, which is as clear an indication of the company's superior relationship capabilities as any.

The range of customers Caterpillar serves is very broad, extending from the Freeport-McMoRan mine in Indonesia, which uses more than 500 pieces of Caterpillar equipment worth several hundred million dollars, to the small-business owner whose livelihood depends on a $50,000, 79-horsepower back-hoe loader. This variety requires superb capabilities in designing offerings that fit the specific value-creation logic of each one of these vastly different customers. Caterpillar considers its new product introduction process, which reflects Caterpillar's offering design capabilities, to be largely responsible for its return to profitability.

The integrated manufacturing and distribution systems are designed so that a part in any machine anywhere in the world can be replaced within 48 hours. Caterpillar ships more than 99 percent of the parts that a dealer does not have on hand the same day the order is placed. Competitors cannot match this kind of consistent performance, according to Donald Fites.

Caterpillar's philosophy of customer orientation can be summarized in the following quote from the aforementioned *Harvard Business Review* article written by Donald Fites: 'We'd sooner cut off our right arm than sell directly to customers and bypass our dealers.' Furthermore, Mr Fites states:

'We've developed a computer-based parts-ordering system so a dealer's technician can use a laptop computer to order parts from the field. Customers know there's significant value in the Cat machine or engine they own – beyond the quality, reliability, and durability they've purchased. They know ... the company and our network of dealers are committed to making the customer's acquisition of a Caterpillar product the best value that money can buy. So we'll provide the necessary service – from the needs of a single product owner to large customers who have a fleet of Cat equipment. Replacement parts are available almost immediately or are on their way within 12 hours. We'll help a customer successfully plan the use of equipment – on the most economical time to repair before failure – on rent–lease–purchase options. For larger customers, we'll assign employees to a work site to help maintain their Cat machines.

Caterpillar only sells directly to customers in the formerly Communist countries, to original equipment manufacturers, and to the US government. The trust between Caterpillar and its dealers has been built up over generations. The dealership agreements are documents that run just a few pages. They have no expiration date, and either party can terminate without cause on 90 days' notice. But dealer turnover is rare because both parties recognize that they are in this together, that they are integrated into one common business logic of jointly creating value with and for customers. The way the dealers together with Caterpillar conquered the back-hoe loader market is an example. The significance of this close relationship between Caterpillar and its dealers is illustrated by the fact that the final decision to terminate or to appoint a new Cat dealer rests with the CEO of the company. No one else at Caterpillar can make that decision.

ADDRESSING THE RISKS OF BECOMING 'OBSESSED' WITH CUSTOMERS

When the study of business became popular, management thinkers counseled against the proliferation of products, and even such an influential writer as Lyndall Urwick warned that the temptation to respond to customers' demands could be ruinous:

> To allow the individual idiosyncrasies of a wide range of customers to drive administration away from the principles on which it can manufacture most economically is suicidal – the kind of good intention with which the road to hell or bankruptcy is proverbially paved.[12]

Even today, not everyone considers customer orientation to be what their company should focus on. Akihiro Wada, executive vice-president in charge of research and development at Toyota states: 'I like people not to be too concentrated on the voice of the market.'[13] However, some researchers argue that customer orientation is paramount:

The leverageable base of most companies' core competencies is in service activities. These in turn usually rest on some special knowledge-based or intellectual skills ... With this must come a management shift from short-term, product-oriented, inwardly focused priorities toward longer-term, people-centered, service-oriented, knowledge-based, and customer-focused priorities.[14]

In our view, customer orientation does not automatically mean that the firm must maximize the breadth of the offering's content by including as many features on its products as possible. As Figure 5.4 depicts, there are different possible views on how offerings and customer relationships affect each other.

One could argue, for example, that the car industry in the early 1900s was 'customer-oriented' just from its focus on producing more and cheaper cars. At this stage, the customer was so amazed by the new possibility of individualized transportation, that the mere fact of having an alternative to the horse carriage was indeed considered as something highly customer-oriented. As we know, in the 1920s customer

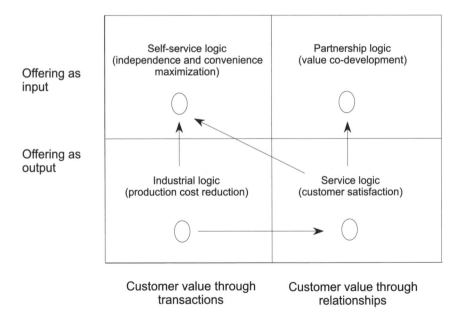

Figure 5.4 Alternative views on how offerings and customer relationships interact.

perceptions changed, and customers wanted more than just transportation from their cars. The car also became a status symbol, in which such elements as the color of the car became important.

For Henry Ford this change was an unpleasant attack on his own business model, which focused on the utility, not the aesthetic value, of the car. Not until General Motors almost forced Ford out of business did Ford also adopt this new perspective on what the offering has to contain in order to create value for the customers. What General Motors *de facto* did was to take the car industry from the *industrial logic* (customer value through transactions) to a *service logic* (customer value through relationships). It did so by offering different 'models' that best fit the value-creating logics of each phase of its customer's life-cycle, allowing it to retain the customers as they changed their car preferences over time.

From then on, the car industry has seen a constant fight between the two major elements of customer value within the business model: (a) cost-efficient transportation, and (b) status-symbol enhancing self-esteem. For many customers, offering a status symbol is a more effective way of keeping their loyalty than offering them a cost-effective ('good') deal. This is important. Every car supplier seems to aim for strong and enduring customer relationships, since loyal customers have been estimated to bring some $200,000 to car suppliers over their individual lifetimes. Thus, car producers have extensively examined the question how to achieve cost efficiency, but at the same time enhance a buyer's changing definition of status.[15]

Customer orientation has to be considered in the context of the firm's business modeling. For Caterpillar, this context is immediately centered around Caterpillar and its dealers, and its focus is on enabling the dealers to be effective in helping their customers create value with their own customers. In such a situation, customer orientation means developing close personal relationships with the dealers, helping these do well in their own business – including preparing young family members of established dealers to take on managerial responsibilities for a given dealership. But this does not mean that Caterpillar should not also be prepared to change its dealership structure, or its business model, if the world around it is changing.

There is an increasing tendency among farmers to use the Internet as a means to gather and exchange information. Caterpillar and the dealers have to design carefully how they will meet this challenge. Caterpillar will not be as easily outconfigured as a PC manufacturer, as the hardware content of the offering lasts longer and is more difficult to replace. But the increased information flows among all actors within Caterpillar's value constellations will ultimately strengthen the power of the customers.

CUSTOMER ORIENTATION AND OFFERING DESIGN

Customer orientation does *not* mean providing every customer with a comprehensive offering, including a broad range of services, as Lyndall Urwick suggested. For example, the business model of IKEA, which is based on providing *less* services to customers (for example, you have to pick up the furniture and assemble it yourself) is still very customer-oriented.

For IKEA, the value-creating process of the customer means that the ideal offering is one that provides maximum value within a certain price bracket. Ingvar Kampard, the founder of IKEA, wanted his company to accomplish the following task: 'We shall offer a wide range of furnishing items of good design and function, at prices so low that the majority of people can afford to buy them.'

Since it sells most of its products as do-it-yourself packages, IKEA reduces purchasing costs, but (according to the customer value equation) increases the buyer's integration costs. IKEA customers, however, are happy to do the assembly work themselves, as for many of them the alternative value of their free time is zero (which means that integration costs are zero). And some of them even consider the assembly of the furniture fun.

Another aspect transforming established truths about customer orientation is e-commerce, or doing business on the web. Amazon.com. was established in 1995 with 1998 revenues of $610 million. In March 1999 it was valued at $22 billion. In comparison, Caterpillar had a market capitalization of $16 billion with 1998 revenues of $21 billion.

Amazon.com has been able to reconfigure book selling by matching its own capabilities with the value-creating processes of its individual customers, creating an innovative set of offerings. Amazon's offerings hold two advantages for its customers.

First, as a first mover, it was able to build up a very large customer base, which, in turn, allows Amazon.com to reap scale advantages in supply management. In essence, it acts as a huge buying co-operative. This advantage is passed on to customers in the form of competitive prices, which, in turn, enhances the advantage – in other words, more customers mean lower prices which mean more customers and so forth.

Second, it has invested considerably in information technology to be able to benefit from the information generated through on-line transactions. This information is used to define user profiles according to actual and espoused value-creating preferences, which enables Amazon to segment more intelligently, and respond to, customers each time they contact Amazon.com. Thus, another virtuous cycle is created: customer visits generate resolution-enhancing information that allows better service that encourage more visits that generate more information and so forth!

As a result, the Amazon.com customer gets the impression of dealing with an organization that is genuinely concerned with the specifics of what he or she wants. This is the opposite of the feeling many of us have when filling out forms with detailed personal information as we check into hotels belonging to chains that we have visited tens of times before.

Internet/web technology is also beginning to reconfigure established 'industrial' businesses such as the automobile industry. Car manufacturers have always been at the forefront of incorporating new technology into the hardware part of the offering.[16] In the same way, many *services* have also been added to the hardware part of the offering.[17] But the Internet provides other ways to change the relationship between the car buyer and the seller. One effect that has come to the fore is that the position of the car dealer is under increasing threat by the customer's enhanced ability to access information about the car. The Internet provides customers with the possibility of moving from the service logic into one of self-service (see Figure 5.4), thus improving the efficiency of the transaction – an improvement they expect to see reflected in the form of lower purchasing prices.

Car manufacturers recognize that there is a fundamental and permanent change within the industry. The role of price as an offering element has become more important. This pressure on price is compounded by rapid consolidation, which paves the way for intensified competition. At the same time, car producers face a dilemma: how to relate to their dealers. Like Caterpillar, many car manufacturers have had very strong relationships with their dealers, and thus stayed clear of retailing activities. However, with increasing price pressure, distribution costs are being scrutinized. Large dealer network groups have started to appear. Previous trust-based relationships between car manufacturers and car dealers are eroding, from both sides.

Auto makers could, like Amazon, use technology to understand more deeply the value-creating potential in each individual customer relationship, and to provide a continuous and optimized service. This partnership between the car manufacturer and customer would redefine established offerings and roles. The emphasis of the car makers' offerings would no longer be on the existing physical car but rather on a complex bundle of mobility, status, and interactive (with the customer) value-creation attributes. Mercedes' attempt in this direction (without commercial success at the time of this writing) with the 'Smart' offering represents such an exploration. The idea behind the 'Smart' offering is to provide the customer with a new form of individual mobility.

The 'Smart' offering seeks to enhance the circulation of individuals in urban areas, but also creating a link to other transport services. The offering aims to appeal to environmentally conscious customers, and to become an organizer of a constellation of actors that could best enhance the quality and effectiveness of their mobility.

Like Amazon, the offering introduced by Smart would build up a database of the mobility needs of its customers. It is still too early at the time of this writing to tell whether the formula will work or not – cars are more multi-functional offerings than books or back-hoes, rendering Smart's approach much more difficult to put into practice.

CONCLUSION

In this chapter, we considered the business modeling priority of customer orientation, which is based on *reconsidering* the firm's capabilities to create a better fit with existing customers' value-creating logics. In the following chapter we will consider two other business modeling priorities, capability focus and lean management, which are based on exploiting existing capabilities with new and existing customers respectively.

Capability Focus and Lean 6
Management: Leveraging the
Existing Capabilities of the Firm
to Create *New* Offerings

Here we discuss the two priorities of the business model – lean management and capability focus – related to the exploitation of existing capabilities to create new offerings. Specifically, this chapter:

- Defines the various components of the two basic types of capabilities involved in a business model: *business and managerial capabilities.*
- Pinpoints, based on the value-creation framework, the *two sources for existing capabilities* – relations with the customer, and the firm's own unexploited capabilities – that are the basis of new offerings.
- Uses the case study of a French overnight delivery service, *Port-Express*, to demonstrate, specifically and in detail, how a firm can identify a radically new business model redeploying its existing capabilities, and acquiring new ones, to enact that model.

CAPABILITIES IN THE BUSINESS MODEL

In this chapter we discuss the priorities of the business model introduced in Chapter 4 which are related to the exploitation of existing capabilities.

Existing capabilities are mostly manifested in existing offerings, which can be provided to new customers as well as existing ones. Thus, existing capabilities are typically organized in combinations defined by the offering. This means that there is a potential for recombining existing capabilities, in other words, allowing *new offerings* to be made available to new or existing customers from the existing set of capabilities. Existing capabilities can also be provided to existing customers, in *customized offerings* created by reallocating the capability–customer relationship for every individual customer. This is made possible by the 'higher resolution' logic of co-productive business which we introduced in Chapters 3 and 4.

In our presentation of the different priorities of the business model, we defined 'lean management' and 'capability focus' as the two priorities related to the leveraging of capabilities. We choose here to treat both of these priorities together because, from the supplier's point of view, many of the elements are similar. This is so whether the capabilities are provided to an existing customer (as in the case of lean management), or to a new customer (as in capability focus).

Recall that in Chapter 4 we defined capabilities as 'repeatable patterns of action in the use of assets to create, produce, and deliver offerings'. Two broad types of capabilities exist:

- Business capabilities
- Managerial capabilities.

Business capabilities are those which directly reflect the business processes whereby resources and the customers' value creation are brought together to create value. These involve:

- Accessing, developing, and maintaining of resources.
- Designing and developing offerings.
- The actual creation of offerings (manufacture, assembly, enabling of customer self-service).
- Rendering the offering accessible to customers (e.g. advertising, retailing, delivery).
- Developing and maintaining customer relationships.
- Developing relations with both external and internal stakeholders of the firm.

Management capabilities support business ones. They include

- Determining what is possible[1] (or what is impossible), desirable or undesirable, and acceptable or unacceptable, and ensuring that these determinations are effectively shared.
- Defining, following up, sanctioning and rewarding business performance.
- Preparing, making, and communicating decisions about tasks and resource allocations, including organizing accountabilities and responsibilities.
- Enhancing the quality of dialogue.

We look at each in turn.

BUSINESS CAPABILITIES

We have identified four major types of business capabilities.[2] The four categories are defined according to two sets of criteria. The first is whether the capability relates mostly to *resources* or to *customers*, following the value-creation framework shown in Figure 3.1. The second criterion concerns whether the capability relates more to value creation carried out *inside the supplying firm* or to value creation carried out *outside the supplying firm,* or *co-produced between the supplying firm and outside counterparts*.

The four categories of business capabilities are

1 Relationship.
2 Transformative.
3 Generative.
4 Integrative.

Relationship capabilities concern the capabilities involved in developing and maintaining relationships with customers.

It includes two parts: *customer intelligence* and *customer linking*. Customer intelligence involves the processes for gathering, interpreting, and using market information. The customer interviews conducted within both FSB and ABB Fläkt are examples of customer-intelligence activities.

Customer linking includes the procedures and systems that a firm uses to achieve collaborative customer relationships over time, such as loyalty programs – or in the case of Xerox, its lease-renewal process. Recall that the formalized key account management procedures adopted within ABB Fläkt in the summer of 1993 also developed customer-linking capabilities.

Transformative capabilities refer to the capabilities related to the design and development of offerings that help customers create value.

Strategically, the most crucial transformative capability is arguably *offering design and development*,[3] which involves putting resources together, and determining which party – including customers – will do what in the value-creation formula so devised. This must also take into account which risks the offering involves, how they will be addressed, and by whom. The way the industrial division within ABB Fläkt combined its resources with other export companies, such as Ahlström and Tampella, to provide turnkey solutions for international tenders is an example of offering design. Another example is Xerox's reinterpretation and gathering of internal and external resources, and generative, relational, and integrative capabilities to devise a new and original value constellation which could transform offerings from 'photocopying' to 'documenting' ones.

Generative capabilities involve the ability to imagine entirely new kinds of offering possibilities 'from scratch'. They include both *innovation* and *execution*.

Innovation is the creative process leading to, for example, Xeroxing. Some results of generative capabilities are patentable, others – particularly certain types of 'service' innovations – are not, unless they include software packages that are.

Execution refers to the capability of conducting business processes effectively, according to objectives identified through innovation. The swift shift in emphasis from local customers to increased attention on export possibilities was an example of execution capability within the industrial division of ABB Fläkt.

Integrative capabilities make it possible to deploy resources both inside and outside the boundaries of the firm/business unit. They comprise both *internal integration* and *external integration*.

ABB's industrial division showed strong integrative capabilities when developing its export business. It was able to attract corporate financial

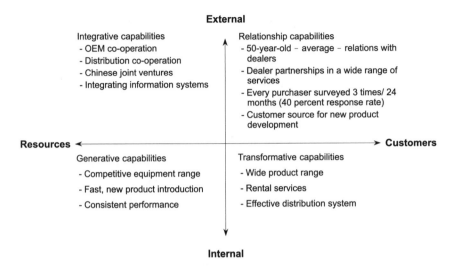

Figure 6.1 Mapping capabilities at Caterpillar.

support, use international distribution strengths, and co-produce with other Finnish export companies, even reorganizing the whole business to fit better with customers' value-creating logics.

To illustrate how this business capabilities framework clarifies the 'left side' of the 'value-creation framework' we presented in Chapter 3, and which we illustrated in Figure 3.1, we return to the Caterpillar case presented in the previous chapter.

For Caterpillar, its emphasis on 'customer orientation' requires the continuous development of new capabilities, for instance installing on-board electronics on tractors, in order to be able to serve customers with a flow of new offerings. As discussed in the previous chapter, Caterpillar is highly focused on its product-development process. Its product-development efforts would not be possible without a versatile, dynamic capability base. Figure 6.1 provides an illustration of what types of business capabilities Caterpillar utilizes to develop continuously its versatile range of offerings.

MANAGEMENT CAPABILITIES

Management capabilities shape:

- How a firm structures, develops, and allocates its human, information, and financial resources; as well as its business capabilities.
- How meaning and significance are built and changed.
- How it interprets and acts in relation to time.

The category of management capabilities which have been studied most we call *activity management*. These capabilities typically involve 'breaking down' the firm into units defined as tasks or 'activities', and understanding how best to manage, as well as integrate, them.[4] Excelling in such capabilities is the primary focus of the 'lean management' position in business modeling (see Figure 4.5).

Beyond this first category of management capabilities, we have identified three other major capability types. These are:

- co-ordination,
- business modeling, and
- culturing.

Co-ordination capabilities consist of:

- change management,
- constellation management, and
- internal co-ordination.

Change management entails making it possible for an organization to actually change from one business model to another. The way the industrial division shifted its attention from its existing Finnish customers to new export customers, and the transformation of parts of Xerox from photocopying to documenting are examples.

Constellation management involves (co-)deciding with whom to create value; (co-)determining the roles each actor will play in value constellations, including allocating accountabilities and responsibilities; and managing these relations as a coherent system. It includes the explicit formulation of goals. Arranging and maintaining Xerox's relationships with Microsoft, Sun, Novell, AT&T, and Adobe is an example of this capability. In the same way, once ABB's industrial division had decided to change its business model, it had to decide how and with whom to create value. Choosing the export alliance partners Ahlström and Tampella and developing its working relationships with these companies was part of its constellation management process.

One very useful method of crystallizing constellation management capabilities is 'accountability and responsibility' charting.[5] It can be deployed to

- find out what each economic actor within a firm (a department, or person) or within a constellation of firms is doing, and/or
- co-design what each *should* be doing;
- develop roles for units (firms, business units) and/or individual job descriptions;
- identify what is now delegated to subordinates,
- or/and co-design what *should* be so delegated;
- sort out inter-departmental, inter-organizational, supplier–producer, or producer–client interfaces;
- design appropriate 'work sharing' formulae.

Internal co-ordination renders the day-to-day management of the business possible. It includes 'functions', which can be positioned as 'staff' units and/or out-sourced, such as invoicing, human resource development, payment, legal or information support, marketing (product-centered), or accounting and control. Finance may be considered as belonging here, or may be a part of change management.

Internal co-ordination capabilities are today 'under fire' as the requirements of 'lean management' come to impact them.

For example, managers of the human resource function of a world-class insurance firm suddenly saw that experts and senior managers were becoming much more sophisticated, much faster, in their demands for internal co-ordination capabilities than the back-office line managers who 'bought' most of human resource function's offerings. This was dangerous for their survival as internal suppliers of human resource offerings. The more sophisticated experts and senior managers were setting a higher standard of demand on capabilities than did their established 'captive customers'. The more sophisticated customers could – and were beginning to – buy services from external parties. A discussion ensued as to how the human resource function could best enable the less sophisticated line managers to become as sophisticated as the more influential clients, to prevent the outsourcing of the capabilities offered by the human resource function.

The third category of management capabilities we call *business modeling*. Business modeling capabilities make it possible to actually shape the firm's business model. They consist of:

- *absorptive capacity,*[6]
- *conceptualizing,* and
- *timing.*

Absorptive capacity is close to the notion of foresight which Hamel and Prahalad described as follows:

> Foresight is based on deep insights into the trends in technology, demographics, regulation, and lifestyles that can be harnessed to rewrite industry rules and create new competitive space. [It is] the capability of management to recognize changes in the business environment and identify gaps between existing and future capabilities.[7]

The problem with insights is that they will only be recognized as valuable *ex-post*. Potential 'insights' which at one moment of time looked right and promising, may later prove to be wrong and disappointing. One such example is the case of NEC, which in the early 1990s was praised for insightful behavior. In the year 1999 the financial press reported that NEC had suffered extensive losses, and considerable management changes had taken place.

Absorptive capacity is the ability of firms to recognize the value of new, often 'external' information, and to add it to their own knowledge base. The capabilities relating to the processing of external information are the key element of absorptive capacity.

The fears regarding the future role of paper, which Xerox experienced in the 1980s, gave rise to a number of initiatives which performed well thanks to Xerox's then-excellent absorptive-capacity capabilities. However, when 10 or 15 years earlier, Xerox misread the implications that losing their patent exclusivity would bring to them demonstrated that these capabilities had at that time been underdeveloped.

In ABB Fläkt, the project done during the autumn of 1991 strengthened their absorptive capacity.

Conceptualizing refers to the capabilities of transforming the insights derived from absorptive capacities into actionable activities. Through conceptualizing, management develops actual business opportunities that exploit new ways to create value. Metaphors, analogues, and scenario techniques are examples of tools for conceptualizing.

For the industrial division at ABB, the vision of the new business model was initially conceptualized as 'Eastern Europe'; for Xerox it was 'documenting'.

Timing in many businesses is crucial: too early or too late will kill what otherwise would be a superb new business configuration.

The introduction of the Newton hand-held computer by Apple has been considered a product launch that came too early.

Nokia, which we study in more detail in Chapter 7, considers timing as one of the cornerstones of 'excellence in execution'.

For the industrial division of ABB Fläkt, timing in 1992 was equal to speed: the faster resources could be allocated to export activities, the better.

The fourth and last category of management capabilities recognize, articulate, and shape values and culture within the value constellation. We call this category of capabilities *culturing*.

In Chapter 4, we stated that

> Corporate *values* are generalized but relatively enduring and consistent priorities of what the firm considers itself to be, and wants to be. They address two basic questions:

1   Who are the main stakeholders of the firm, and in which order shall they be served?
2   How shall each stakeholder be served in respect of each element of the corporate values?

Culture has been defined by Edgar Schein as:

A set of basic tacit assumptions about how the world is and ought to be that a group of people share and that determines their perceptions, thoughts, feelings, and to some degree, their overt behavior. Culture manifests itself at three levels:

1   the level of deep tacit assumptions that are the essence of the culture,
2   the level of espoused values that often reflect what a group wishes ideally to be and the way it wants to present itself publicly, and
3   the day-to-day behavior that represents a complex compromise among the espoused values, the deeper assumptions, and the immediate requirements of the situation.

The culture of a group is a pattern of shared basic assumptions that the group learned as it solved its problems of external adaptation and internal integration, that has worked well enough to be considered valid and, therefore, to be taught to new members as the correct way to perceive, think, and feel in relation to those problems.[8]

Culturing capabilities can be broken down into *socialization* and *role modeling*.

Socialization refers to the process of 'teaching' and sharing, or 'passing over' values and culture to the members of the organization and of the value constellation. It includes transferring knowledge from one individual or a group to become knowledge for another individual or group.[9]

Nonaka and Takeushi[10] give an example of an R&D team at Matsushita which is developing a bread-making machine. To see why existing machinery did not produce 'good' bread ('good' in comparison with bread produced by master bakers), the team apprenticed under a master baker. The tacit knowledge of the master craftsman was learnt by apprentices as tacit knowledge through a process they called 'socialization'. In 'socialization', this internalized tacit knowledge is externalized with the help of a metaphor. The Matsushita team thus discovered that the master baker not only 'stretched', but also 'twisted' the dough. This 'twisting' metaphor externalized tacit knowledge by rendering it explicit.

Xerox claims that 90–95 percent of the information of companies is in documentary form, be it analog (paper) or digital (visible on screen). It is information which renders knowledge – even the tacit knowledge about values and culture which is not found in documents – actually shareable, and shared. Bateson[11] famously said information was 'the difference which makes a difference'. Information enables values and culture knowledge to become organizational, rather than only individual, thus allowing these capabilities to survive the departure of an employee.

At ABB Fläkt industrial division socialization was evident when the divisional manager, Mr Hietaluoma, involved salespeople in the process of improving customer orientation. The need to involve the sales personnel became especially paramount when the initial findings in November 1991 revealed that the operational context of the firm was changing. The customer orientation seminars were organized as two-day events, allowing for social activities in the evening of the first day, during which less formalized views could be aired in an atmosphere of genuine problem solving and searching for new innovative solutions. Mr Hietaluoma encouraged open and spontaneous discussions, and supported initiatives to further deepen the analysis of the changing context.

In a rare interview with the *Financial Times*, the CEO of McKinsey mentioned socialization as 'the' most important factor defining the size and growth rate of the firm.[12]

Role modeling involves how referent actors demonstrate values and culture through their own behavior.[13] Analyses on the way structural aspects of organizations are embedded in actual (as opposed to espoused) role behavior show that much actual behavior in the context of organizations obeys not causal but correlative knowledge.[14]

We illustrate role modeling in our discussion of Nokia's CEO, Jorma Ollila, in Chapter 7.

CAPABILITY DEVELOPMENT

If a firm has defined the priority of its business model as 'lean management', it competes on the basis of superior operational efficiency. Its exchange value equation[15] will favor the single transaction and immediate cash flow outcomes. Such a firm will engage in only very limited capability development.

As we saw in examining Caterpillar, if the firm has given customer-orientation the highest priority in its business model, it will build new capabilities and deploy these in existing relationships in innovative ways. It may also seek to acquire or develop capabilities it does not (yet) have access to, but which would help it in this regard.

In the same way, if the firm chooses to give greatest priority to capabilities in its business model, it will concentrate its efforts on maintaining and 'leveraging' these by combining them into offerings for new customers.

Firms have great difficulties in pursuing all three capability development activities – maintaining, leveraging, and building – simultaneously. A study of Formula One racing showed that success was based on all three, but any one of the three predominated the other two at any one point in time of the team's development.[16] When a racing team was being successful (maintaining) it was unable simultaneously to absorb enough new knowledge to redefine (leverage, build) its success over a longer period. Over the period 1960–98, the three most successful Formula One teams – McLaren, Ferrari, and Williams – went through team-specific cycle phases in which either maintaining, or leveraging, or building their capabilities took precedence. This same difficulty to excel at each of the three activities simultaneously may account for Xerox's inability to see the end of its success formula until its market share dramatically signaled the need to reactivate its insight capabilities.

As Professor James March[17] suggested in his now classic distinction between 'exploration' and 'exploitation', any firm has to accomplish two interrelated tasks. On the one hand it has to manage its current operations effectively, and on the other it must be able to change these operations, to meet continually shifting future demands. In managing this dilemma, the firm, in its decision on the business model, has to consider immediate value creation for customers, which primarily asks for capability focus and lean management; but at the same time, it must engage in more long-term resource development, where capability building is a central element.

The choice of the future business model depends on the decision-making philosophy of the firm, the present business model, the competitive environment, the resources available for the firm, and the firm's values and objectives.

Depending on the decision-making style of the firm, it may come up with different outcomes even if the inputs to the decision are similar. It is also possible that situational and context-specific factors will guide the decision makers in different directions at different times. The rapidly changing environment has increased the number of firms capable of adopting the adaptive mode for setting goals which we saw in Chapter 4.

Following the adaptive approach means that the business modeling process constantly updates its perspective on the environment and the future. Plans are updated and re-evaluated when necessary, to the extent that 'plan' becomes a verb more than a noun. In leveraging capabilities, planning thus consists of two elements:

1 identifying whether there is a need to develop new capabilities, and if so
2 defining what capabilities are to be developed and how to do it.

We treat each in turn.

The need to develop the capabilities of the firm can be caused by perceived gaps between the existing, and some future state, of the firm. Sometimes, such perceptions are expressed in very broad form, such as 'we need to become more customer oriented', or, 'we should look into what possibilities the Web holds for us'.

Identifying which capabilities to develop can be approached from two perspectives, which correspond to the two ends of Figure 3.1, reproduced here as Figure 6.2.

The first perspective, begins from the 'customer end' at the right of the diagram, involves thinking about how to relate to customers in the

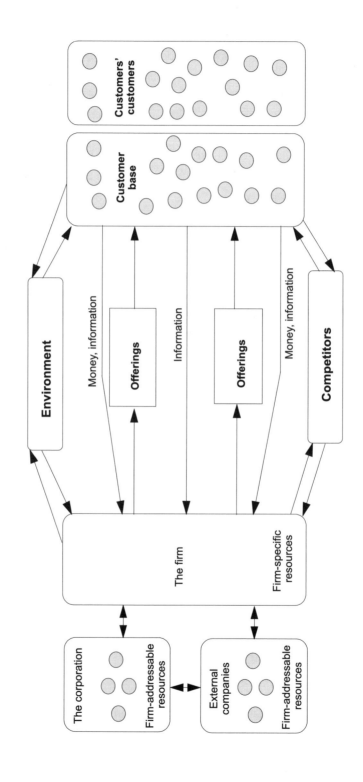

Figure 6.2 The value-creation framework.

future. This means that the development requirement is first apprehended as a need to redesign the offering based on perceptions about non-exploited value-creating potential among customers.

The new offering, in turn, will require the redesign of business processes, which may or may not require the redesign of management processes. The new processes will thus transform the capability base of the firm accordingly. The case of Port-Express presented later in this chapter is an example of such a transformation process.

The second perspective starts from the other (left) end of Figure 6.2. Following this approach, one systematically looks for existing capabilities that have not yet been fully exploited in the marketplace; perhaps because they have only been combined with a limited set of other existing capabilities.

The reasons for such a situation are multiple. It may be that the capabilities have primarily served internal processes, and their use in an external context has never been explicitly considered.

For instance, the first wave of IT-outsourcing was characterized by an increasing number of previously completely internal electronic data processing (EDP) departments starting to offer services to third parties. Once this proved to be successful, many companies decided to spin out these departments into separate legal entities. Some of these spun-off businesses thereafter developed their own commercial role and gradually became less and less tied to their original parent. Others bundled other 'back-office' activities with the original IT-based ones. For example, Shell Services International (SSI) became a 1-billion dollar company initially offering Shell companies around the world anything from window cleaning, car rental, and office cleaning; to sophisticated operation-enhancement services such as re-engineering and IT-based systems integration.

Another reason may concern capabilities built for a specific customer relationship. These may have been kept after the relationship was terminated – for instance keeping an expert brought in for a specific project within a specialized engineering firm.

A third reason may involve capabilities built for a specific technology being kept after the technology becomes obsolete. For instance, the Italian State railways, Ferrovie dello Stato, still has on its books a vast network of aqueducts that used to feed their steam locomotives decades ago!

Irrespectively of which path is taken – starting from either the right end (future customer relationships) or the left end (un-exploited capabilities) of Figure 6.2 – the firm will end up with a vision of what the future customer offerings would look like, and which capabilities are needed to be able to provide these. These insights provide the blueprint for a capability development plan. Whether or not this plan is implemented has to be considered and decided upon separately.

PORT-EXPRESS:[18] CAPABILITY PRIORITY IN PRACTICE

We use here an example of a firm providing express mail and package delivery to illustrate business modeling with a capability focus. A change from an original business model to a very different one, better responding to more effective competitors, is surveyed.

Port-Express was established in the 1960s as a private courier in southeastern France. The company successfully grew its business and became an alternative to the French postal authorities in the express delivery of small parcels. In 1996 the company employed 2,400 people, and reached a turnover of 2 billion French francs.

The original concept of Port-Express was to deliver small parcels, throughout France, overnight. It saw its role as that of designing and organizing pick-up, transport, and delivery; sub-contracting actual transport to national and local carriers.

The three dimensional figure, which we first introduced as Figure 3.2, is here adapted (Figure 6.3) to describe Port-Express' offerings. The three dimensions of the initial offering of Port-Express was basically reduced to only two dimensions (hardware and software), as the peopleware was practically unimportant for most Port-Express customers. The offering was transaction-centered, as the customer would normally not be treated as a relationship, and most often the individual customer remained anonymous for Port-Express.

The hardware in the original Port-Express business model involved trucks, order forms, invoices, and supporting technologies such as phones, computers, and so on. With this hardware the customer could, prior to deciding to use Port-Express, evaluate the speed and reliability

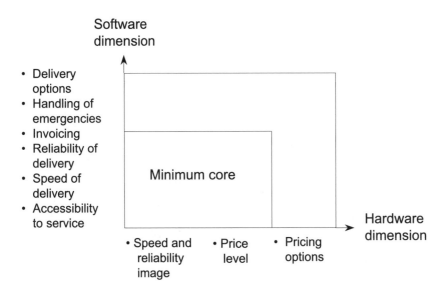

Figure 6.3 The original Port-Express offering 'Express Parcel Delivery'.

image of the service, and could also choose between different options. Ultimately the price would mirror the configuration chosen by the customer.

The original Port-Express offering was fairly simple. The focus was on cost-efficient execution of the delivery process. People and software were basically considered costs in this original, production-oriented, mode. From the customer's point of view, the software dimension presented only four options: time of delivery, handling of emergencies, type of invoicing, and speed. From the point of view of Port-Express the activity package can be described as a circular sequence of service activities, as depicted in Figure 6.4.

Delivery services, like phone companies, deploy technologies to provide offerings, which link customers to each other.[19] In such configurations, it is the other customer, rather than the supplier, which is of value for a given customer. 'Ideally' the customer would like the supplier to be invisible! And when the supplier does its job 'right', the supplier *is* virtually invisible. The only connections the supplier has with the customer are:

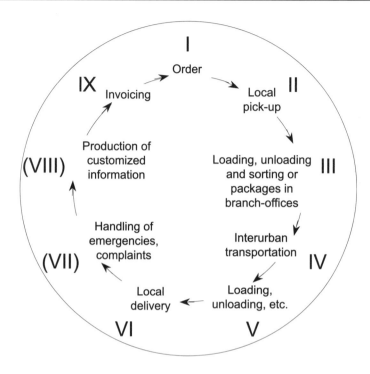

Note: numbers I–IX are referred to in Figures 6.5 and 6.6.

Figure 6.4 The activities forming the original Port-Express offering.

- one phone call (or fax, telex, or e-mail) message to present the order;
- someone picking up a package, and leaving a signed slip; and,
- at the end of the month, the arrival of an invoice to be paid.

These three or four 'moments of truth'[20] – the phone call, the pick up of the parcel and the slip signature, (and possibly the customer's counterpart signing another slip at reception), and an invoice – is all the contact there is between supplier and client if things run well.

Figure 6.5 below adapts the value-creation framework we presented earlier to separate the different flows within the value-creating activities: the material, information, and money flows. In the figure, a customer of Port-Express 'supplies' its own counterpart or 'customer', who is not necessarily a Port-Express customer, but who depends on Port-Express to link it with the 'supplying' customer:

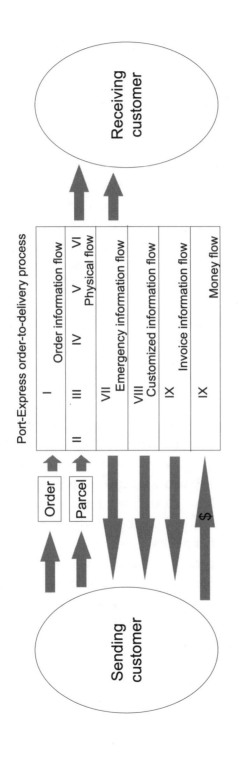

Note: items numbered I–IX appeared in Figure 6.4 and also appear in Figure 6.6.

Figure 6.5 Port-Express' business processes: linking customers to their counterparts.

The execution of the business processes in this business model, which had 'lean management' as its priority, required considerable managerial capabilities, which are depicted in Figure 6.6.

The business capabilities enabling Port-Express to enact its original business model are depicted in Figure 6.7.

In the second half of the 1990s, the competitive situation of Port-Express changed. Pressure from foreign firms (especially DHL) increased. Subsidiaries of the Post Office and the French railways became active in Port-Express' markets. Express delivery use in France grew considerably, which also transformed the perceptions of the services which Port-Express had been offering, from that of 'premium' service to that of 'commodity'. Exceptional performance was no longer sufficient to maintain a price premium.

At the same time, re-engineering and cost cutting among members of the main customer segment of Port-Express, big corporate customers, affected their established buying policy. Reliability was often sacrificed for lower costs. The consequence of all this was that the profit margins of Port-Express declined, and the company was forced to rethink its business model.

When redesigning its business model, Port-Express examined the capabilities behind its existing value-creating activities. It found that for the basic express delivery service which customers now wanted, its existing value-creating system was actually 'too good' (or too 'luxurious' in the French vocabulary). At the same time, it recognized that this also meant that Port-Express had capabilities that the competing, low-cost service providers did not possess.

A thorough remapping of the existing capabilities was therefore undertaken to understand what the underlying resources for the new business model could be. This exercise could be called the 'explication' of what had up to now been an implicit capability map. This is illustrated in Figure 6.8.

Taking the existing capabilities as the starting point for the new business model underlined that Port-Express had five distinctive capabilities that could be considered as the cornerstones of Port-Express' competitiveness:

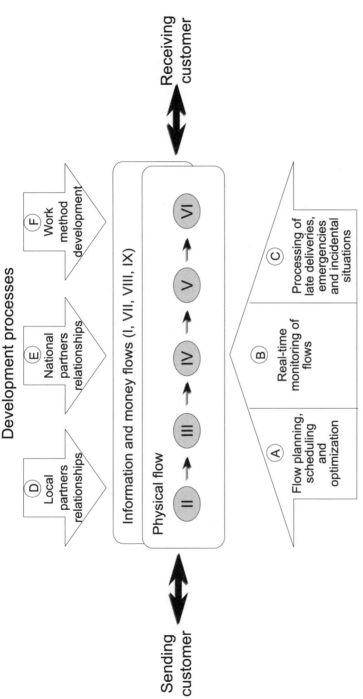

Note: numbers I–IX refer to items in Figures 6.4 and 6.5; letters A–F are referred to in Figure 6.9.

Figure 6.6 Port-Express' management processes: supporting value creation.

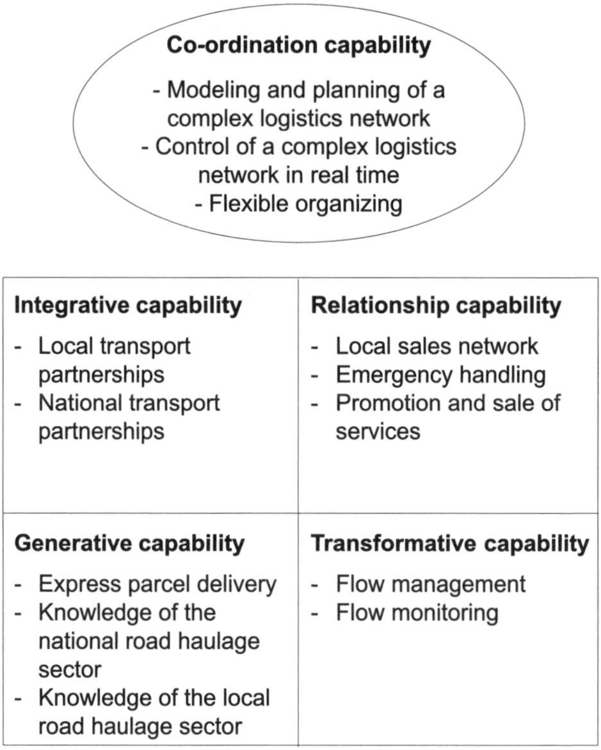

Note: the quadrants depict business capabilities; the circle managerial ones.

Figure 6.7 Key Port-Express capabilities in the original business model.

1 Flow planning, scheduling and optimization.
2 Real-time monitoring of flows.
3 Processing of late deliveries and emergencies.
4 Institutional and personal relationships with national carriers, including the knowledge of the national road haulage sector.
5 Institutional and personal relationships with local carriers and related knowledge.

Using these capabilities as a basis for the redesign of its business model, Port-Express identified the possibility of aiming for a 'premium service' offering concept, compared to what by now had become a 'standard express delivery service' offering. If it were to implement this 'premium service' offering, Port-Express would in effect be changing its own

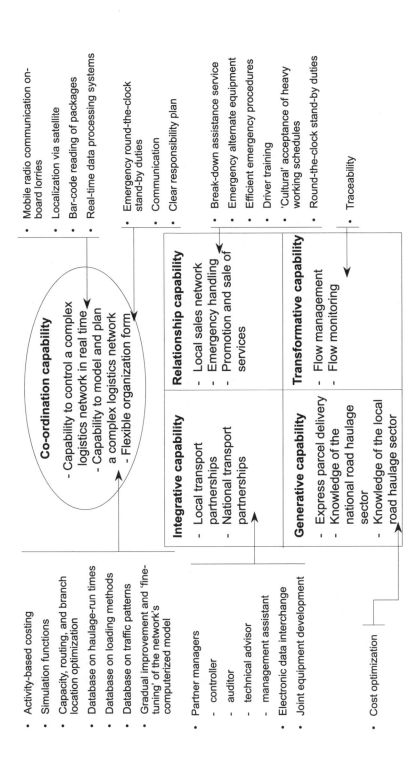

Figure 6.8 Explicated map of Port-Express capabilities before changing the business model (see Figure 6.7).

business model from a production-oriented one into a more customer-oriented one.

The new Port-Express business model would imply a different offering. Instead of the previous *standardized* package of express parcel delivery, Port-Express now would have a *modular*-offering architecture,[21] enabling the company to offer an unparalleled variety of service options to its customers. The new offering would be 'capability-driven and customer-oriented'.

At the heart of the modular offering design were the above-mentioned five capabilities. They included three business capabilities – processing of late deliveries and superior relationships with both local and national carriers – and two management capabilities – flow planning and flow monitoring – plus the additional management capability of designing work methods for the handling of material flows, which was not previously regarded as very important. Based on these capabilities, Port-Express would still have to maintain its basic express delivery service, as it would be the backbone of the new offering. Outside the core offering, Port-Express would then develop a whole array of new, additional offering options.

Some of these would be just add-ons to the basic core offering, such as exceptional delivery by taxi or motorcycle, specific labeling, customized use of storing areas, or improved information services. The major shift however was to take place in offerings for specific customers or customer groups. These would aim at substantially redefining the co-production logic between Port-Express and its individual customers, as Port-Express would offer each customer the possibility of taking care of that customer's total logistics management function. To become focused on this particular strategy, Port-Express formed four specific subsidiaries (which in the study we have mentioned were called 'GERLOG', 'SPIDE', 'SILOG', and 'TREFLE'[22]), each aimed at a specific type of customer, with a tailor-made outsourcing offering for each.

Port-Express managers realized that each of the subsidiaries needed managerial capabilities that could be shared among them, such as activity-based costing, optimization of flows, inventory management, and cost driver measurement. Sharing such capabilities among subsidiaries rendered each more cost effective. The lean management priority of its new business

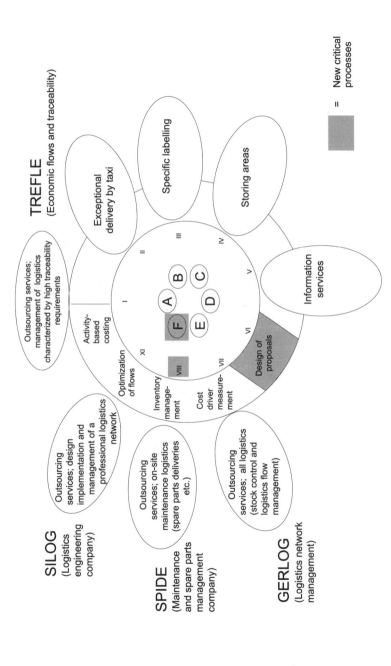

Note: the numbers I–IX are from Figures 6.4 and 6.5; the letters A–F are from Figure 6.6.

Figure 6.9 The new modular offering design structure for Port-Express.

model was to remain important, as the original cause for change was increased pressure on margins. But the new business model also had another priority: capabilities. So in addition, Port-Express realized that providing outsourcing services required the specific capability of developing tailor-made proposals and contracts, an important part of the order-to-delivery process for big institutional clients. This would be required for Port-Express to be able to solicit the logistics business of these clients. This was a capability that Port-Express had not needed before. It addressed it by deploying its new modular organizational architecture, so that capabilities could easily be allocated and reallocated according to specific customer value-creation profiles.

The new modular structure of the Port-Express offering, and resulting business model, is illustrated in Figure 6.9.

For Port-Express, the need to reconsider its capabilities was initiated by perceived changes in the competitive environment. The recognition of existing capabilities as a possible source of future competitive advantage provided Port-Express with the option to address the new competitive

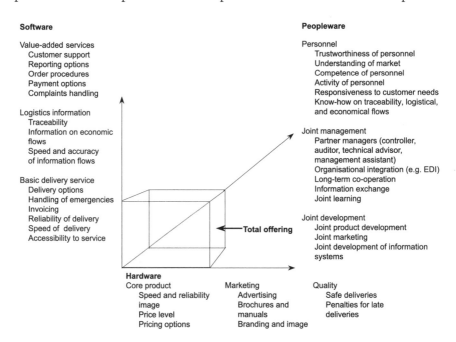

Figure 6.10 The offering of one of the new Port-Express subsidiaries.

situation with a new set of offerings. The way the offerings in this new situation would be different from the original express delivery one is shown in Figure 6.10.

The new offerings Port-Express developed had three (full) dimensions, as opposed to the two dimensions of the original one. The importance of the peopleware dimension increased, as the logistics services that Port-Express offers required in-depth expertise and consultative services from Port-Express.

INTERACTIVE RESOURCE PLANNING

'Lean management' and 'capability leveraging'-oriented business models such as that of Port-Express hold a new connotation in the rapidly changing environment that many firms are facing today. Traditionally, quality management and re-engineering efforts could be implemented over considerable periods of time. Now, the firm is often required to adapt rapidly and often, or it will see competitors move ahead of them, with the risk that these competitors' dynamics will make *them* prime movers, preventing anyone from ever catching up with them.

This type of competitive landscape requires an interactive approach to the issue of resource planning. We can define such a system as an *Interactive Resource Planning (IRP)* system. An IRP system integrates sales, marketing, and production planning, and it is by definition customer-driven. The planning system, and the routines around it, are built on the interactions between the firm and its customers. The primary function of the IRP system is to make sure that the lean management part of the business model is fully competitive under such conditions.

In an IRP system, customers are segmented based on standardized service requirements, purchasing volumes, and profitability. The pricing for each customer is based on this segmentation, and production efficiency is monitored by comparing actual and standard costs.

The IRP system supports decision making, both in production and sales, by offering unified information, which is stored in a data warehouse. A data warehouse is a common database enabling co-ordinated and flexible access to relevant information about the whole organization. Integration of the IRP system with other systems in the firm enables optimization of production and sales across division borders.

A traditional resource-planning philosophy could be characterized as an inside-out process. Such resource planning started from production and sales (1). These two functions created the offering (2) that was more or less customized for different market areas (3), usually based on a geographical segmentation. The registration of information from the customer into the resource planning system was limited to the sales ledger. The main objectives for the company were production efficiency and meeting predetermined sales targets.

In contrast, an interactive planning perspective is customer driven (1). The customers are segmented depending on their own, individual, value creation (even segments with only one customer can be created). Different tailored offerings are provided to each different segment (2). The business model is therefore a result of interaction between the company and its customers. The company supports customer's, and its own, value-creating processes with its management structure, and with a network of partners and suppliers (3).

Concept development[23] is an essential part of the business model. It obtains a constant flow of information on the most dynamic interfaces, and links them to reinterpret existing business ideas. In effect, a central objective of the company is to enhance the quality of a continuous learning process for itself, and for others, to be able continuously to support changing customers' value-creating processes as effectively as possible.

When designing an IRP system, it is essential to look very thoroughly at, on the one hand, the future business model, and on the other, the already existing information systems. This is important because existing routines and systems form the starting point for defining the possible inputs for the new IRP system. In addition, 'sunk' costs in IT, which are often substantial, are many times the main alleged cause for *not* changing the business model, on the grounds that the investment needs to 'pay for itself'. To have the past colonize the future in this way is strategically very dangerous indeed!

In the development of an IRP system it is therefore necessary to involve both business and IT managers. The IRP process is actually a predesigned process to improve the interplay between business and IT.

The first step when entering an IRP initiative is to define a preliminary business rationale for the initiative, i.e. to establish why the initiative is defensible, why it is undertaken, and which problems need to be solved. For example, the established pricing logic might need to be readdressed. Or the firm may be facing a severe threat in a major customer segment, forcing it to manage that segment, or its whole customer portfolio, differently. Many times the ultimate implications of the implementation of an IRP system are that the firm has to fundamentally change its offering portfolio. This will be the consequence of an improved understanding of the value constellation of the firm and the value-creating potentials therein.

Because of what is at stake, commitment from top management is required for the launch of an IRP initiative. The launch usually takes the form of a kick-off meeting. At the kick-off meeting one of the main objectives is to ensure that participants get a clear view of the intention. Therefore, the kick-off meeting is preceded by proper preparation.

In the kick-off meeting the major ambition is to engage the participants in discussions around the design of the future system. The design, however, is at this stage not about what the system exactly should be, but about why it is needed and how it is practically possible to pursue the initiative, considering all other activities going on in the firm. The conditions for the new resource planning system have to be thoroughly investigated, emphasizing how implementation can take place. Early recognition that the initiative has to evolve 'iteratively' is helpful: the iterations will 'merge' planning and implementation, which then become two faces of the same coin. Constructive defying of the business model and realization of the new system take place hand in hand. Short- and medium-term goals are interactively set, based on realized activities and the pace that the initiative's expectations allow. The participants have to adapt their existing accountabilities and responsibilities in ways that allow them to understand how the envisaged future system would relate to their daily routines within the organization.

An IRP system development initiative will always aim at improving capability-leveraging efforts. It concerns dynamically matching value-creating potentials among existing customers with resources. An IRP system benefits from new technology, such as data warehousing and activity-based costing software, helping to obtain a better understanding of the profitability of both customers and offerings. An IRP system improves the effectiveness of customer portfolio management, offering strategies, pricing formulae, and resource allocation.

Implementing an IRP system in a large organization involves many efforts. It is in this respect similar to a traditional resource planning initiative. The major difference is however that the IRP initiative is implemented in an iterative way, and is best when considered as a learning initiative. Right from the beginning critical conversation will be allowed, and even encouraged, to get new perspectives. The conversations emerging around the IRP project will in themselves be role-modeling exercises, based on which the learning capabilities of the organization will improve.

Launching an IRP initiative is in many ways different from traditional systems development. In the traditional way there would be a first phase of intense system specification discussions, between managers requiring the system and the IT people in charge of design and implementation. The focus would be on matching the 'why' with the 'what'. And very rapidly the discussion would move into technical details in the 'what' area, such as the type of computer to have, database size, type of software, and authorized user interfaces, etc.

Instead, an IRP system focuses on developing an all-relevant integrated analytical information system based on whatever information systems are already used in the company. This means that an important question concerns what parts of what already exists can be made relevant. Indeed, a comprehensive, corporate analytical system cannot be built without using existing systems. It would be too expensive, and implementation would take too long.

Figure 6.11 exemplifies an IRP project, which aimed to improve how a large business-to-business firm did its pricing. This firm provided a broad array of offerings to a large customer base in many countries.

At the beginning, the CEO stated that he wanted a 'quick and dirty' support system to improve control pricing. This objective was presented in a management kick-off meeting in which it was agreed that activity-based costing was a required first step. It quickly became evident that existing production processes did not generate good quality cost/driver data. This caused the initiative to be totally redefined.

The new objective was stated as the design and implementation of an integrated IRP system which beyond acting as a support for pricing, would also become the glue holding together sales, production, marketing, and business development. The business model of the firm was redefined with the intensive use of data warehousing technology and decentralized activity-based costing systems. The product-based organization was transformed into a customer-based one. Resources would be allocated according to the strategy manifested in the business model, and not as a function of immediate, reactive, short-term, sales and capacity planning.

When developing an IRP initiative, it is important to keep IT and other related hardware and software ('what'-level) issues open.[24] The IRP's architecture has to be designed with the ('why'-level) business model (present and future) as its main referent. The 'why' of the business model has to be explicated, so that the IRP initiative can manifest it at the 'how' level. As one works, relating the 'how' and 'why' levels to each other, the characteristics of the 'what' which can be kept, and the parts which must be transformed, will gradually emerge, corresponding to the '*Pre-project phase*' and '*Phase 1*' in Figure 6.11.

In the IRP approach, activity-based costing plays a key role in the matching of the potential in the relations with customers with the resources and capabilities of the firm. If deployed correctly, activity-based costing in effect combines these perspectives from a supplier exchange value perspective.[25] Building on existing information systems, activity-based costing and data warehousing will shape the required IT-architecture. (*Phase 2* in Figure 6.11).

Extranets allow the IRP system to be shared with selected business partners, be they suppliers, or important customers. This further improves the 'lean management' effectiveness of both the prime mover firm and its constellation.

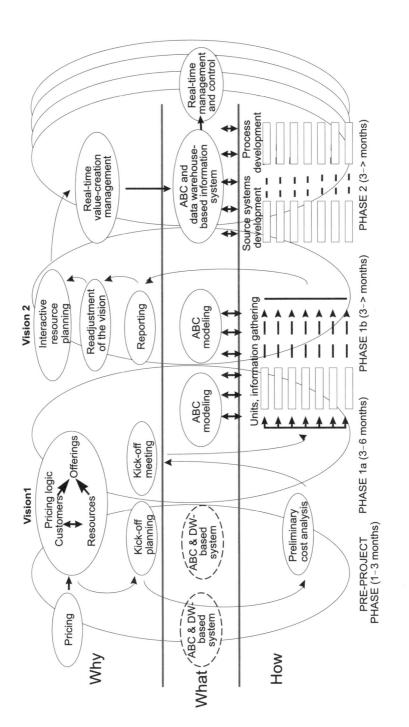

Figure 6.11 Implementing an interactive resource-planning system.

Actor-centered Market   7
Making: Leveraging *New*
Capabilities of the Firm to Create
New Offerings

This is the first of three chapters on 'Market Making', the business modeling priority built around both new capabilities and new customers. Specifically, this chapter:

- Explores the business environment of the firm, which consists of a *transactional* and a *contextual environment* (the business environment of the firm was first illustrated in Figure 4.4, at which point we referred the reader to this chapter for further explanation).
- Introduces the *AIC model* which shows how a firm's contextual environment is appreciated, its transactional environment is influenced, and the actual organization itself is controlled.
- Briefly introduces the *three types of market making*:
  - *Actor-centered market making*, in which a prime mover firm creates or expands a market in its transactional environment. The main beneficiary of such market-making is the prime mover firm, which very strongly influences (almost controls) key actors in its immediate environment.
  - *Co-operative market making*, in which a prime mover institution, created co-operatively by a group of actors, creates or expands a market for them. The key to the new market: the group's co-operation allows members of the group to not only appreciate, but also to influence factors in their contextual environment; while expanding the extent of their transactional environment. The beneficiaries of this form of market making are the members.

  – *Appreciative market making*, in which a prime mover develops a
    new market by influencing factors that others can only appreciate,
    and by controlling what others can only influence. The
    beneficiaries of this type of market making are both the prime
    mover and actors in its constellation.
- Explains in detail, through the case study of *Nokia*, the concept of the
  first type of market making: *actor-centered market making*.

BUSINESS ORGANIZATION AND ITS ENVIRONMENT

As early as 1965, two scholars, an Australian, Fred Emery, and a
Scotsman, Eric Trist, wrote the following:

> A main problem in the study of organizational change is that the
> environmental contexts in which organizations exist are themselves
> changing, at an increasing rate, and towards increasing complexity.[1]

Emery and Trist were among the first to analyze the implications of
considering organizations as living entities, laying the intellectual
grounds for much of our current understanding of both business and
management. They recognized that 'open' relationships with the
environment is what distinguishes living organisms from inanimate
objects, who are 'closed' to their surrounding environment.[2]

To survive, living entities must be, or become, resilient to changes in
their immediate environment. It follows that organizations considered as
living entities must be attentive to the nature of change in their
environments.

Emery and Trist analyzed the types of changes that environments present
for the organizations embedded in them. They introduced the term
'*turbulence*' for describing the environments which exhibit the most
fundamental, radical, and unpredictable changes. (Eric's wife has told us that
the term 'turbulence' came to Fred and Eric while, during a very turbulent
airplane flight, they discussed different types of conditions in which
organizations operate.) Emery and Trist presented these analyses in their
now famous paper 'The Causal Texture Of Organizational Environments'.[3]

In their paper, they distinguished between the wider contextual setting in which organizations and their immediate counterparts are placed from the closer transactional layer made up by these counterparts. Emery and Trist defined different levels of complexity which an organization faces in its environment by analyzing the causal connections between the two layers, and between the layers and the organization in them.

One of the things that Emery and Trist's research suggested was that *the environment is actor-dependent.* Thus, a third party may look at the environment of two actors who are close to each other, and conclude that they share a common environment. Although from the third party's point of view both close actors have an identical environment, however each individual actor will hold an extremely different, even incompatible, view of their respective environments. To illustrate this, we can borrow an example from Kurt Lewin, whose research on the 'topology' of social spaces much influenced Emery and Trist.

Lewin's research identified important differences between how a wife and husband place a woman colleague whom the husband has met at work. While the husband would map this colleague entirely and exclusively within his 'work' environment, the wife might consider that this person was present not only in the husband's 'work' environment, but also in her husband's 'marriage' environment.

In the same way, a helicopter pilot flying over landscape may thus consider that a factory and a hospital located next to each other share the same environment: the outskirts of a town, a highway crossing, a rail station. Yet, from the point of view of either one of the two individual actors, their own environments are very different from each other. Obviously, this is because the hospital is in the factory's environment and the factory in the hospital's, creating challenges and opportunities that do not concern the helicopter pilot. In other words, as your neighbor is in your environment, and you are in his, you cannot in your mind have the same environment as him – a fact not immediately obvious to a third party.

For us, these findings mean that *a strategy has to be defined from the individual actor's point of view.* This is because strategy has to do with what role one is to play in one's environment, in relation to the roles one expects others to play in this environment.

It follows from this that one cannot develop 'actor-independent' strategies, say for a given industry or market. Each actor will determine her or his environment, and thus the opportunities and challenges it poses, in their own, individual way. Each actor will thus interact with the environment to form its own, specific, individual value constellation(s). Strategies have to be developed in relation to the environment of each actor, and, as we saw in some of the cases we examined in Chapters 4 and 5, strategies have to be developed in relation to the environment of each customer.

Neuro-biologists Humberto Maturana and Francisco Varela[4] have even suggested that it is in this very interaction with one's environment that we obtain our identity. In effect, it is not by accident that the worst punishment human beings have invented is isolation. We need the other, 'our' environment, to be our living selves through interaction.

Thus, business organization exists in relation to, in relating with, its environment. This, of course, also applies to our customers!

TWO 'LEVELS' OF BUSINESS ENVIRONMENTS

Emery and Trist, and many of their students, studied how to deal with each of these 'levels of the environment', and the interactions among them. These studies suggested that from the point of view of the individual firm, the wider environment, the one that the firm cannot influence but only can *appreciate*, could be called the *contextual environment*. The transactional, or more immediate, environment is the one that can be *influenced* by the firm. Thus, fluctuations in exchange rates belong to the contextual environment for most firms, whereas George Soros, the fund manager who cornered the British pound, in certain cases has included this phenomenon into his transactional environment. Management practice holds that one can control what goes on inside one's organization.

Seen this way, contextual factors shape the way actors in our *transactional environment* act and interact. One of the most important sources of uncertainty managers have to deal with relates to how changes in factor behavior (such as recessions, foreign exchange rates, or demographics) are interpreted by actors, and enacted (as possible changes) in terms of their actions and interactions. One methodology developed to understand better the interface between the contextual and transactional environments is called scenario planning. By using scenarios managers prepare for futures they cannot predict and forecast.[5]

One of Trist's students, William E. Smith, further developed these distinctions. He concentrated his analyses on the relations between appreciation, influence, and control. Based on this he created a model which he consequently called the 'AIC' model.

The AIC model

Smith's AIC model related the three levels (appreciated contextual environment, influenced transactional environment, and controlled organization), to forms of power and purpose. The AIC model maps relationships between the whole and the parts.

Smith defines his model as follows:

> AIC is an organizing process that consists of
> * Identifying the *purpose* to be served;
> * Framing the *power-field* around that purpose, i.e. those who have control, influence and appreciation relative to the purpose;
> * Selecting those with the most influence relative to the purpose (stakeholders) and designing a process of *interaction* between them; and
> * Facilitating a *self-organizing* process which ensures that the stakeholders
>   1. Step back from the current problems to appreciate fully the realities and possibilities inherent in the whole situation;
>   2. Examine the logical and strategic options and the subjective feelings and values involved in selecting strategies; and
>   3. Allow free and informed choice of action by those responsible for implementing decisions.[6]

THE AIC MODEL AND 'MARKET MAKING'

We build upon Emery, Trist's, and Smith's work to determine how prime movers make markets.

The open systems model of the firm we introduced in Chapter 4 depicted the environment around the individual customer. We identified the value constellation surrounding the customer in terms of the customer's transactional and contextual environments.

Yet transactional and contextual environments apply, of course, to any firm, regardless of whether it sees its own role primarily as that of 'customer', 'producer', or 'supplier'. As we earlier noted, the notion of environment, and therefore of what each layer consists, has to be defined from the perspective of the individual actor.

This means that certain actors may consider environmental issues belonging to the transactional part, whereas the same issues for another actor are contextual ones. The importance that each actor will give to each feature will be different. *It is the exploitation of these differences that is at the core of the way prime movers make markets*, as we explore them in this chapter, and Chapters 8 and 9.

The possibility of exploiting different perspectives on what can be appreciated and what can be influenced to make markets can be illustrated with an example. Say that you are an entrepreneur operating a small agricultural farm producing 'bio-labeled' products. But your farm is located downwind from a coal-fired power station. From your perspective, the emissions from the power station would be in your *transactional* environment. But as a small actor, your influence on the power station would be close to nil. The acceptability of the levels of emissions, from your point of view, would belong to the *contextual* environment, as this acceptability relates to pollution legislation, government inspection, public policy, and public opinion. You can 'follow' the developments of these, and you *appreciate* how the way they develop could impact on reducing emissions. But one day you talk with your child, who tells you that in her primary school, the new science teacher has gotten her and her fellow students to closely monitor many measurable aspects of the power plant's emissions. You realize upon hearing this that if any one of the measurements your daughter is making registers levels exceeding the legally accepted bounds, the possibility for you and the school to *influence* the power station suddenly are considerable. You understand that the science teacher has transformed what you could only appreciate (polluting smoke), into something you can influence ('school detects unduly high levels of dioxide', says local paper headline). This is because the schoolteacher has in effect enhanced the 'granularity' of the contextual factor, transforming this factor from the vaguely identified ('pollution') to a specific, measurable substance (levels of dioxide).

'Colonizing' what for others remain contextual environments into one's own transactional environment is one of the ways in which prime movers engage in 'market making'. The more turbulent environments become, the more interest firms have to understand better how different environmental layers affect them, and the more interested they are in determining how they, perhaps together with others, can affect the definition of these environmental layers. This enables their becoming prime movers.

Market making is the notion we use to describe prime mover firms that proactively shape their environments, thereby setting the rules by which others play.

The three types of market making

Based on the AIC model, we distinguish between three different types of market making.

The first type of market making concerns a prime mover who sees an opportunity to shape the future by proactively supporting the building of both standards and constellations of actors working together, in its transactional environment. In building these standards and value constellations, others will benefit, but the point of doing this is to benefit the initiating prime mover most of all. We call this first type of market making *actor-centered market making.*

The most common way of achieving actor-centered market-making has been through proprietary resources or technologies, protected by patents, as was the case of Xerox's first configuration, surveyed in Chapter 2. Intel and Microsoft, or, much earlier, Standard Oil, are also examples.

Another, more recent and more daring way of making such markets is by introducing open architectures and stimulating others to support these architectures. Sun Microsystems is a good example of a prime mover firm which has determinedly promoted open architectures. It started to do so when evolving into a major player in workstations in the 1980s, and has lately continued doing so through its support for Java.[7]

The third way to obtain actor-centered market-making strategy involves combining proprietary technology and participation in the development of open standards. Nokia exemplifies this well, and is analyzed in detail in this chapter.

The second type of market making concerns a group of firms who decide to combine their resources and create a new infrastructure. The infrastructure is institutionally manifested as a prime mover organization, which from the point of view of the originating firms is located in their transactional environment. For example, Finnish pulp and paper manufacturers participated in exporting co-operatives and sales associations until the 1990s. Each member company held its share in this organization, but externally the sales association was the legal counterpart with whom big publishing houses dealt. The rapid consolidation of the European pulp and paper industry in the second half of the 1990s saw two of these companies, UPM-Kymmene and Stora Enso, become the leading European firms in the industry. The original sales associations provided these Finnish companies with contacts and knowledge that they later could use for their benefit in the consolidation phase that swept over the industry. In this reconfiguration phase the associations were dismantled, but they had proved to be very valuable, both during their existence, and in providing the platform for ongoing pre-eminence.

The prime mover institution which originating members thus create exists only for the purpose of bringing benefits to the original group of actors that decided jointly to pursue a prime mover, market-making strategy. Later joiners also benefit, though in many instances less so than the originators. Any 'union', 'confederation', 'partnership', 'federation', 'club', or 'professional association' entails this type of market making. But such market making can also be done for 'pure' business purposes. We use VISA, and its French representative, the Groupement Cartes Bancaires, to illustrate what we term *co-operative market making*, which we study in Chapter 8.

The third type of market making involves processes where the original ambition may have been one other than that of becoming a prime mover or market maker, but which involved rethinking and redesigning the factors which shape the behavior of actors who make up industries, or even parts of society.

Such market making often reflects the values of the original market-making prime mover organization, and typically these values have been enacted by the founder of the company. Such a market-making process will then be based on appreciating value-creating opportunities of systems which are broader than a given 'industry' is, in ways that are meant to improve its efficiency or effectiveness. We look at this third type, which we call *appreciative market making,* in Chapter 9, where we examine Tetra Pak.

NOKIA, COMBINING OPEN SYSTEMS AND PROPRIETARY TECHNOLOGY[8]

'Actor-centered market making' refers to the traditional way that a market is established by one prime mover company with a competitive advantage, often based on proprietary technologies or resources. Thus, Standard Oil's unbeatable access to petroleum allowed the company to establish the oil market. As noted above, however, proprietary technology or resources is just one way for an actor to make a market. Actor-centered market making can also result by developing standards that others follow (common in the computer industry) or by combining the two methods: proprietary technology and developing open standards. Nokia Group exemplifies this combination.

In 1998, Nokia overtook Motorola to become the world's leading mobile phone seller. And in June 1999 the *Financial Times* announced that

> Nokia, the innovative Finnish mobile company, has produced better returns for its shareholders than any other large European company over the past five years. (*Financial Times*, European Company Performance, 18 June 1999)

To explain the success of Nokia, it is necessary to overview the history of the context (of the environments) in which it developed.

The development of the Finnish telecommunications sector

1855 was the year in which the first telegraph line was built between St Petersburg and Helsinki, kicking off Finnish telecommunications as we have come to know it. The first telegraph message was sent from Helsinki to Vyborg in the same year. It was in 1865 that a Finnish engineer, Fredrik Idestam, founded a paper mill that later became the Nokia Corporation. This company quickly became one of Europe's largest soft-tissue manufacturers. The first telephone line was constructed in Helsinki in 1877, only a year after Alexander Graham Bell had invented the telephone. The first telephone company, Helsinki Telephone Company was established in 1882.

The Russian Czar ruled Finland at that time, and his government gave every town the right to have its own telegraph company. The number of local telephone companies grew as local telegraph companies adopted telephone technology. But the Russian telegraph bureaucracy was not considered by the Finns to be helpful, so they formed local co-operatives to become less dependent on the Russian authorities.

After 1917, the new Finnish Government inherited the imperial Russian role in telegraphy, and operated a long distance service. As independent local telephony was already in place in the cities, the number of telecommunications companies continued to increase until the 1930s, when there were over 800 firms!

Since then, driven by increasing investment needs, competition, and automation, smaller telephone companies have continuously merged into bigger units. In 1998 there were only about 40 local 'separate' telephone companies operating in Finland. These companies were tied up in a close co-operative agreement called the Finnet Group. One of its major functions has been to administer the joint ownership of the second largest mobile operator in Finland, Radiolinja. Radiolinja is in fierce competition with Sonera, (ex-Telecom Finland and ex-Posts and Telecommunications (P&T) of Finland), the national telecommunications and mail agency which, upon independence in 1917, had been founded by the Finnish Government.

The task of P&T had originally been to build long-distance lines and provide telecommunications services in scarcely populated areas, where local organizations did not exist. As the P&T in 1935 acquired the Interurban Telephone Company of Southern Finland, it established a monopoly position in long-distance services. As it continued to expand, it became the only provider of international service and telex.

The laws governing Finnish telecommunications had been set by the Czarist Telephone Manifest of 1886, the Telegraphy Law of 1919, and the Radio Law of 1927. While several efforts were made to update these laws, for decades there was no political consensus to accomplish more than minor changes. A new Telecommunications Act was passed and became effective only as late as 1987. It provided a legislative framework to promote the development of the telecommunications industry. With it, the Ministry of Transport and Communications became the regulatory authority, and P&T became a telecommunications operator, thus separating both roles – regulator and operator – for the first time. The Act has been amended several times since, promoting further steps towards liberalization in Finnish telecommunications. Today this market is arguably the freest in Europe (the world, maybe!), where operators no longer require licenses in order to open shop.

By 1999 the major players in the operator business were the partly privatized Sonera Group (the former telecommunications division of the P&T) and Finnet Group, the previously mentioned consortium formed by the local telecommunications companies. There was also the Swedish state-owned operator Telia and several small telecom and Internet service providers. In 1998, the total turnover of the Finnish telecommunications services was in excess of EU 2.5 billion, with Sonera and the Finnet group each having almost half of the market, and the rest of the actors less than 2 percent of the market.

The origin of Nokia's telecommunications business

Many observers attribute the initial success of cellular services in the Nordic region to the NMT services launched in 1982. However, the seed had already been sown earlier, in the 1950s when the telecommunications

operators in the Nordic countries began commercial radio telecommunications services.

Despite the fact that at the time the running costs of the radio
telecommunications service to users were high compared to today's
prices, and the quality of the service could not meet modern standards,
several business users adopted the offering. In 1980, just before the
introduction of NMT, radio networks in the region were estimated to
have around 100,000 subscribers. This first stage provided operators
and manufacturers with the possibility to develop their resources and
capabilities.[9] This development also, in many ways, shaped the events
leading to the formation of what the Nokia Corporation has become.

In 1963 the Finnish government had opened up a design competition
for a new military radio. Five competitors registered for participation:
Televa, the Finnish Cable Works, Salora (a local radio manufacturer),
Vaisala (a leading producer of weather measurement technology), and
Sonab (a Swedish manufacturer of radio telephones). Unfortunately for
the contenders, the Finnish government had to cut its budget the
following year, and the whole competition was canceled. Later, however,
many observers noticed that this event had a significant impact on the
development of the technical capabilities of the Finnish telecommunications cluster.

In 1967, Nokia merged with two companies, the Finnish Rubber
Works, a galosh and tire manufacturer, and the aforementioned Finnish
Cable Works, which primarily was a phone-cable maker, to form Nokia
Group. This new conglomerate consisted of four industrial groups: pulp
and paper, rubber, cables and electronics. Of these electronics was the
tiniest one, representing only 3 percent (FIM 15 million) of the total
turnover of the Nokia Group, which at that time was around FIM 400
million on a yearly basis.

The electronics group of Nokia thus, had its origin in the Finnish Cable
Works. The CEO of the Finnish Cable Works, Björn Westerlund, had
already in the 1950s recognized the growing importance of computers,
and in 1960 the electronics department was established. The first product
the department developed and sold was an analyzer for advanced
measurements in nuclear physics. The department also started to import

and distribute computers, and was by the mid-1960s a licensed distributor for Siemens, Elliot, and Bull computers.

Even if the government-sponsored competition for the new military radio was canceled in 1963, this initiative speeded up the development of radio telephones within the Finnish Cable Works, which started to develop its first radio telephone, the precursor of the cellular phone. Phones were produced for the army, public utilities, and emergency use. The first radio telephones were exported to the Soviet Union in 1966. These phones were used for communications during construction of gas pipelines and in oil fields.

In the mid-1960s the Finnish Cable Works also started to develop its own telephone switch, based on the experiences gained from its own product development in PCM (pulse code modulation), which represented new digital technology.

In 1971 the Finnish government opened a new mobile radio network called ARP (auto-radio-phone). And the following year the State Railroads announced a competition for a new train radio based on 24 channels. This new competition inspired the same actors that had been competing for the government order in 1963. Only Vaisala had withdrawn. The competition was won by Salora, which developed a new phone model based on new frequency synthesizing technology. This new technology was then transformed into products for the police force, navy and soon also for civil purposes.

In 1975 the Finnish government informed the mentioned four competitors about the joint Nordic decision to create a common mobile network for all Nordic countries, NMT (Nordisk Mobil Telefon). This challenge required considerable resources, and in November 1975 Nokia and Salora agreed to co-operate in the telecommunications field: Nokia would specialize in base stations and radio links and Salora would produce the mobile telephones. Later the Nokia/Salora combination became market leader for mobile telephones in the Nordic countries, with 60 percent of the Finnish market, and 30 percent in Sweden, Denmark, and Norway.

Nokia organized its own electronics department into three profit centers in the mid-1970s: telecommunications, industrial automation, and data processing. For the telecommunications part, Sakari Salminen was appointed manager. Salminen immediately recognized that for Nokia to become successful it had to enter into close co-operation with its own customers: the export customers in the Soviet Union, but also the Finnish P&T and the local operators in Finland. From this close co-operation, between the Finnish suppliers and customers within the tele-communications cluster, Nokia was able to gather a lot of experience. This helped the company continuously to maintain a position as a viable supplier to its customers in the northern part of Europe, even if the competitors (e.g. Siemens, ITT, LM Ericsson, etc.) at that time were manifoldly bigger than Nokia.

In 1977 Nokia and the state-owned electronics company, Televa, combined their units for telephone switches into a new company called Telefenno, of which Nokia and Televa both held 50 percent. During World War II, Televa had developed telephone switches. In the late 1960s a Televa engineering team started to develop a digital switch, the DX100. The project had almost been canceled several times, but finally in 1975 Televa got its first order for the DX100. The next version of this switch, the DX200, became very popular on the Finnish market, and by 1984 it had gained 50 percent market share of new telephone switches in Finland. The same year the first DX200 switches were delivered to the Soviet Union.

In 1979 Salora and Nokia agreed to combine their radio telephone businesses into a new company called Mobira on a 50/50 basis. Nokia was then offered the Salora company to buy, whose main business was television sets. But it was only four years later, in 1983, that Nokia bought Salora.

In 1987 Nokia bought the remaining 50 percent of Telefenno from the Finnish government. The foundation for Nokia Telecommunications was laid. The 1987 net sales of the Nokia Group reached FIM 14 billion. Fifty-one percent of the sales originated from traditional industries such as cables, rubber, and paper. Consumer electronics contributed 19 percent, data 13 percent, and telecommunications 17 percent.

The growth of the electronics part of Nokia had been quite remarkable over the 20 years since the new Nokia Corporation was formed in 1967.

From representing only 3 percent of Nokia's turnover (which at that stage was FIM 400 million), it represented 49 percent of the turnover in 1987. At this stage the telecommunications part generated sales of FIM 2.4 billion. This development had been possible thanks to the CEO of Nokia, Kari Kairamo, who had replaced Björn Westerlund when he retired in 1977.

Kari Kairamo was in the 1980s the most visionary leader in Finnish industry. He had started his career in the pulp and paper industry, and worked abroad in Poland, Brazil, and the United States for almost ten years. Kairamo wanted Nokia to become a leading European industrial company, and he recruited a team of young ambitious managers around him, including Jorma Ollila, who was recruited from Citibank and was placed in charge of corporate finance in 1985.

A European dream

In late 1987 and early 1988 Nokia announced two major acquisitions: the consumer electronics business of Standard Elektrik Lorenz and the Information Systems part of LM Ericsson. These two acquisitions made Nokia the third biggest producer of television sets in Europe and the biggest information technology company in the Nordic countries. Kairamo's dream of making Nokia a major European company had moved considerably forward. The strategic assumptions behind the acquisitions were the following:

- Nokia as a brand was unknown in Europe, therefore it was necessary to buy businesses with well-recognized brands; such a business was Standard Elektrik Lorenz.
- Building a distribution network was slow and difficult, therefore Nokia needed to buy companies with well-established distribution channels, which could also be used for distributing the Mobira phones.
- Nokia needed to buy acceptance in the protected central European countries; this was best done by acquiring companies with local manufacturing in the key markets.

The plan to buy Standard Elektronik Lorenz seemed to solve all three of these strategic problems. Nokia bought the most automated television plant in Europe in Bochum, a large tube manufacturing plant in Esslingen, and factories in Portugal and Spain. And in addition three brands were included in the deal: Graetz, Schaub-Lorenz, and ITT. Nokia thus became the third biggest television producer in Europe. But the plan proved to be wrong. Television production was an industry with excess capacity, and Nokia had to compete with Philips and Thomson. In addition considerable imports from Japan flooded into Europe. The consumer electronics business became unprofitable, and remained so for many years.

The acquired Ericsson Information Systems also brought trouble. Here the acquisition was a failure primarily because young managers coming from Finland to Sweden in a very short period spoiled the basis for co-operation through arrogant and unprofessional behavior. The dream of Kairamo became a nightmare. And in December 1988 Kairamo committed suicide.

Simo Vuorilehto, who for long had been the right hand of Kari Kairamo, was appointed CEO. He initiated the process of gradually consolidating the multi-business conglomerate. The tissue paper business was sold to James River Corporation. Nokia Chemicals was merged with Kymmene's chemical industry to form Finnish Chemicals Oy, in which both Nokia and Kymmene originally had 50 percent stakes, but from which Nokia later withdrew. In 1991 Nokia Data was sold to Fujitsu.

In the beginning of 1992 Simo Vuorilehto retired and was replaced by Jorma Ollila, who at that time was only 41 years old.

Providing the foundation for the transition

Jorma Ollila had already at a young age been an ambitious man with international aspirations. In 1967 he received a scholarship to study one year at Atlantic College in Wales. After graduating from college he studied applied mathematics and systems theory at the University of Technology, and economics in the University of Helsinki. He graduated from both places with masters degrees. His master's thesis in economics was called 'Uncertainty in the Theory of International Economics', and was honored as the best of the department when Ollila graduated.

During his years at university, Ollila was an active student politician, representing the central party. From the same party and of the same age was Esko Aho, who became Prime Minister in Finland in the early 1990s. After graduating in Finland, Ollila was accepted for studies in the London School of Economics, where he obtained a Master of Science degree in 1978. After graduating, he joined Citibank in London. Once Citibank opened its branch office in Helsinki in the beginning of the 1980s, Ollila joined the Finnish office, and became account manager for Citibank's two biggest Finnish clients, Rauma-Repola and Nokia.

In September 1984 the secretary of Kari Kairamo, Hanna Forsgren, called Ollila and informed him that Kairamo wanted to meet him. At that time Jorma Ollila was 34. He was appointed corporate vice-president of international business development as of 1 February, 1985. As the senior vice-president of corporate finance left Nokia the same spring, Ollila then became senior vice-president of corporate finance.

Ollila participated in the big acquisition round in the second half of 1980s as financial advisor, making sure that the financial aspects of the deals were sound. The business strategy behind the acquisitions was at that stage the responsibility of others.

Vuorilehto, who had succeeded Kairamo as CEO, held the opinion that to grow as a manager it was important also to have had line responsibility. In 1990 he asked Ollila to take responsibility for Nokia Mobile Phones.

When Ollila took over Nokia Mobile Phones, it was a fairly small unit with around 3,000 employees. In the late 1980s this unit had become very unprofitable. Ollila was the fourth person in charge within the last three years. For two years Jorma Ollila was responsible for the daily running of this part of Nokia, which in 1990 represented 10 percent of the turnover of Nokia Group with sales of FIM 2.3 billion.

When Jorma Ollila arrived at Nokia Mobile Phones, he encountered an organization which had almost completely lost its self-respect. Ollila in turn was convinced that the skills of the people were an asset that could be turned into a distinctive strength. But for some reason the formula on how to do it had not been found. Ollila adopted the managing-by-walking-around philosophy. Suddenly the workers recognized that they had a boss who was sincerely interested in how they felt, and what their ideas were. Gradually trust between the workers and management was rebuilt.

Besides building relationships with the workers, Jorma Ollila focused on developing the production management aspects of the plant. He considered production to be 80 percent psychology and 20 percent production technology. How to manage people was the more difficult part. By the end of 1990 the results of Nokia Mobile Phones started to improve. But then the beginning of 1991 was a period of increased global uncertainty. The Soviet Union collapsed and there was the Gulf War. The global finance system was very turbulent. And the demand for mobile phones did not develop according to expectations. Nokia Mobile Phones had to reduce its capacity. Three hundred people had to be made temporarily redundant. Ollila succeeded in doing this without initiating any strikes in the factories. As the situation improved most of the workers could later come back. Some of them became millionaires as the stock option scheme was introduced in the mid-1990s.

On 26 November 1991 Ollila was summoned by the chairman of the Nokia board, Casimir Ehrnrooth. Nokia was in real trouble. The board knew that the result for 1991 would be red, and Nokia Consumer Electronics, especially, was badly bleeding. Ehrnrooth wanted to hear Ollila's opinion: could Nokia be saved? Ollila had seen the potential that the telecommunications sector offered Nokia. He had also initiated the turnaround in Nokia Mobile Phones (in 1992 Nokia Mobile Phones produced 12 percent of net sales in profit). This, in his opinion, provided a platform for a possible recovery of Nokia. The board listened. And it decided to give Jorma Ollila the opportunity to prove his opinion. On 16 January 1992, it was announced that Ollila would become the new CEO of Nokia.

Ollila took the helm of Nokia at the worst possible time. The first six months were filled with ever worsening results, and no good news seemed to find its way among the bad ones. It wasn't until the summer of 1992 that the trend started to turn. New customers were solicited and sales in telecommunications improved. 1992 however, remained a year of losses before tax and minority interests. But the loss was halved from the year before. In 1993 operations already were profitable, but there was a one-time write-down of FIM 1.9 billion resulting from restructuring in the Picture Tubes and Home Electronics divisions of the Consumer Electronics business group. Because of this the net result for 1993 was negative as well.

The transformation

Kairamo had stressed the importance of corporate values in his leadership culture. This was even further emphasized by Ollila. Already when he was in charge of Nokia Mobile Phones he had started to communicate his values to the people on the shop floor and to his own business group management. Ollila had also received good support when Nokia bought Technophone in 1991.

Frank McGovern, who had been in charge of redesigning the production process in Technophone, was put in charge of production within Nokia Mobile Phones. His ambition was to re-establish the respect for production. And he strongly believed in the values presented by Ollila. He saw that if Nokia wanted to raise productivity and improve quality, management had to care about the people who worked at the factory. 'You'd better get into the loving and caring business.' And in relationships with the workers McGovern stressed the importance of always fulfilling all the promises that had been given to them.

The 1993 review by the President and CEO was headed 'Forward with Strong Values'. In this review, dated March 1994, Jorma Ollila laid forth his leadership philosophy:

> Outward success emanates from within a company. In 1992 we rediscovered the roots of our success anew. Nokia has always achieved its greatest success by applying new technology with spirit and boldness. In 1993 we began strengthening the Nokia way of operating, recognizing our shared values of *customer satisfaction, respect for the individual, achievement*, and *continuous learning*. This effort persists, and our

values function as a force that unites the whole of the Nokia Group. This is also reflected by our corporate slogan: *Nokia – Connecting People* (Nokia, Annual Report 1993).

In the same annual report, Ollila also stressed the need to define objectives clearly, and to set clear, quantifiable indicators for the common goals in everyday work. And on top of that mutual dependencies among Nokia's business groups and the development of common core technologies created a greater need for co-operation.

To put into place his own vision, Ollila also completely redesigned the management team at the top. He trusted his closest colleagues, representing young, internationally minded and competent telecommunications managers. The first three names of the Group Executive Board in March 1994 were Matti Alahuhta, Pekka Ala-Pietilä, and Sari Baldauf – all three younger than Ollila himself. These four individuals were most instrumental in the process of transforming Nokia into a global leader in telecommunications. Ollila characterized his team as consisting of people with different personalities and backgrounds (coming from different parts of Finland) but sharing the same values.

The years at Nokia Mobile Phones had taught Ollila the importance of outside partners. In no way could Nokia Mobile Phones have responded to the rapid increase in demand for mobile phones on its own. The network of suppliers was an important ingredient in the business model already in the early 1990s. Close co-operation with customers, something Salminen of the telecommunications business group had initiated in the early 1970s, was also a cornerstone of the Nokia Mobile Phones business model.

In May 1992 Ollila decided on the strategy Nokia was to take. It was built around four words: 'Focus', 'Global', 'Telecom-Oriented', 'High Value-Added'. To achieve this strategy, two elements were needed: to provide the financial prerequisites to carry through the strategy, and to change the business model of Nokia. In the first task he worked closely with his successor for corporate finance, Olli-Pekka Kallasvuo, to obtain the financial conditions supporting the telecommunications strategy. To change the business model, he had to get rid of what the strategy rendered non-core businesses, and at the same time shape the new way of working, enabling Nokia to challenge the big players in the rapidly growing field of telecommunications.

In the 1980s the whole of Europe gradually started to deregulate the telecommunications sector. In many countries mobile telephony was seen as the part which could first be deregulated. But it was from Turkey that Nokia got its first export order for a mobile network in 1986. The same year Nokia Cellular Systems became a separate business unit to focus resources and capabilities on building the infrastructure for mobile networks. This unit was headed by Sari Baldauf, and reporting to Matti Alahuhta. Alahuhta was at that time working on the strategy for the telecommunications business, and at the same time taking a doctorate in business administration. His thesis 'Global Growth Strategies for High Technology Challengers' provided a good foundation when, in 1992, he succeeded the man in charge of Nokia Telecommunications, Sakari Salminen, who retired after a long and successful career within Nokia.

One important conclusion Alahuhta made in his dissertation was that time had become a critical success factor. The faster Nokia could promise that the mobile network was up and running, the more customers were satisfied, and the better the profitability. To achieve this Nokia had developed flexible, modular product concepts for its network systems. Through modularity Nokia could combine existing knowledge into customized solutions. And fast.

The rapid development of the mobile telecommunications business created two separate markets: the market for network solutions, and the market for handsets. Nokia was a strong contender in both these markets. In the beginning, the networks had to be built. In 1992 the sales of Nokia Telecommunications and Nokia Mobile Phones were similar. But in 1993 the net sales of Nokia Mobile Phones grew by 73 percent and Nokia Telecommunications by 43 percent. This trend continued, and in 1999 Nokia Mobile Phones was double in size compared to Nokia Telecommunications. This remarkable development was also due to favorable contexts.

Growth through co-operation

Nokia had been fortunate to be situated geographically in the midst of the most progressive telecommunications area in the world. This area was characterized by simultaneous co-operation and competition. The Nordic telecommunications authorities had been very far-sighted when in the 1970s they agreed upon the NMT standard.

The NMT standard was developed based on the experiences from the early mobile radio networks. Because the Nordic countries were relatively small and scarcely populated, the early developers adopted an *open systems* approach and decided that the key specifications for NMT services should be delivered freely to all vendors. The same approach was also adopted later for the GSM standard.

Once the NMT standard had been agreed upon, the local authorities supported the domestic companies in building equipment for the new mobile telecommunications network. The Finnish P&T encouraged Nokia to build its own NMT base station, and later on to build a switch for NMT. The latter was achieved by doing some rather minor modifications to the successful DX200 digital switch.

Because of the open systems architecture, the NMT standard rapidly got wide support and the needed economies of scale. Consequently, the NMT services could be offered to customers some 75 percent cheaper than the earlier services. This, in turn, increased demand, and allowed the manufacturers and operators to enjoy even stronger economies of scale. By the end of December 1983, total subscribers to the region's five NMT 450 MHz networks ran to 73,000, up 360 percent over the year. By December 1986, there were almost 315,000 NMT users, with annual growth of over 50 percent, and in 1990, after the introduction of NMT 900 MHz networks, the total number of NMT subscribers was approximately one million.

The competition among Finnish telecommunications operators contributed to the high penetration rates of communications technology among consumers, thus making the 'cake' bigger for all operators. By the end of the 1990s, at least two alternative suppliers serviced all local telecommunications markets, and there were three alternative suppliers for long distance call services. Thus, despite the low population density, almost every household had at least one telephone subscription. By the end of 1998 Finland had the highest mobile phone density in the world (58 mobile phones/100 population), and twice as many Internet host computers/capita as the next country. In January 1997, the *New York Times* labeled Finland 'the most wired nation in the world'. This in turn, has created a relatively large, and very dynamic home market for the equipment providers as well.

In the late 1980s the opportunities presented by mobile telephony were also recognized as an important issue by politicians. The European Commission for Postal and Telecommunications Authorities (CEPT) established a special group to investigate mobile communications, Group Spécial Mobile (GSM). This group had the authority to define a common standard for European mobile telecommunications. As a first step it was agreed that digital technology should be applied. And the building of digital GSM networks should start in 1992 at the latest.

The challenge to develop a completely new technology for mobile telecommunications was of such magnitude that Nokia realized that it had to form alliances to be able to participate in this large endeavor. In 1987 Nokia, Alcatel, and AEG formed the European Cellular Radio 900 consortium. The objective was that this consortium should develop, produce, and market mobile networks according to the GSM standard. This happened in parallel with the forming of Nokia Cellular Systems, which should provide mobile networks. Mobira (and later Nokia Mobile Phones) would produce handsets. Each respective unit would operate independently, but when synergies were apparent co-operation would be recommended. By the end of the 1980s it became evident that the new GSM standard would radically increase the demand for mobile phones. In 1991 Nokia bought Technophone to expand its production base.

The 18 countries that had signed the original GSM agreement had defined the year 1991 as the year for the inauguration of the new network. By that year only Finland was able to open its GSM network, and the first GSM phone call in the world was made on 1 July 1991, in Finland. The network, owned by Radiolinja, had been delivered by Nokia Cellular

Systems. And the first handsets were produced by Nokia Mobile Phones. This first referenced case was only the beginning of the strong order flow generated through the new GSM standard.

As customers started to switch from NMT to the more developed GSM networks, Telecom Finland and its competitors had to cannibalize their own businesses and write off considerable investments quickly. This 'home' laboratory helped Nokia to understand better how the rest of the world's operators would need to develop from one standard to another, helping them to influence more how the industry would develop.

Building resources through co-operation was not only a strategy for network products, but also the strategy when developing the distribution of handsets. In 1984 Nokia had formed a joint venture with the Tandy Corporation with the objective of establishing a production plant for mobile handsets in South Korea. Tandy Corporation also owned the Radio Shack retail chain, which in total had 6,700 outlets throughout the USA. Gradually co-operation with Tandy developed so that Nokia took over the common mobile phone production facilities. The original joint ownership of the two production plants in Fort Worth, Texas, and in Masan, South Korea was transformed into full ownership by Nokia. When these plants were added to the two plants acquired through Technophone (one in the UK and the other in Hong Kong), Nokia had production facilities for mobile telephones in all important markets.

For Nokia the Tandy co-operation was more than just a distribution agreement. It was a way for Nokia systematically to follow the cost efficiency requirements from the world's toughest and most competitive consumer market. Through its close contact with Tandy, Nokia knew that if it could stay competitive and maintain or increase its market share in the USA, and maintain its profitability targets, then its cost efficiency would be world class; allowing it to meet the requirements of its business model's 'lean management' priority.

In Japan Nokia developed its distribution in co-operation with the oldest and biggest Japanese trading house, Mitsui. The reason why Nokia chose Mitsui was that Mitsui could provide a very good distribution network, and the Mitsui Group itself did not have competing production of mobile telephones. Mitsui was for Nokia an important partner also to provide a technology benchmark. In many areas the Japanese were ahead of the USA and Europe, and through its close co-operation with Mistui, Nokia could get a better understanding of the technological issues it had to master in order to stay competitive in Japan. Nokia took a very interactive approach towards the Japanese consumer: the product had to be competitive in its tiniest detail. By adhering to the voice of the customer Nokia was able to build a good reputation.

The battles for standards

Nokia had partly been fortunate in its first success in the field of mobile telecommunications. The NMT standard had provided the Nordic competitors Ericsson and Nokia with substantial advantages due to close co-operation with the tele-operators over the years. The GSM standard, developed in the 1980s and commercialized in the 1990s, was built to a large extent on experiences from the NMT standard. Thus the accumulated knowledge base was still a competitive advantage for Ericsson and Nokia. As this standard, which originally was designed as a European standard, spread also into Asia and partly into the USA, the position of Ericsson and Nokia grew even stronger.

Nokia was by 1997 in an enviable position. In February 1996 it had announced the divestment of its television business, and of its 1997 sales almost 90 percent originated from Nokia Telecommunications and Nokia Mobile Phones. And at the same time Nokia had reached a global market share of over 21 percent for mobile phones and was the leader of its industry.

But this position would only last temporarily. Just as the GSM standard had replaced the NMT standard, the GSM standard would not last forever either. Gradually every competitor had to start actively preparing for the next standard: third-generation (3G) mobile telecommunication services. This decision would become much more crucial, as the stakes now were higher than ever, and the outcome would have global consequences for the entire telecommunications sector for the next 10 to 15 years.

The first 3G discussions at the European level were initiated in the early 1990s within ETSI, the European Telecommunications Standards

Institute. These initial discussions were dominated by the incumbent telecommunications operators. Even if the manufacturers were represented, their voices were hardly heard in the discussions. Nokia was represented by Heikki Ahava, who initially mostly participated as a keen listener in the meetings. In pace with the success of the GSM, Nokia and other manufacturers gradually gained more weight within ETSI. The technical discussions took place in a sub-committee to ETSI, and Ahava was a member of this committee. Late 1993 Ahava noticed that things started to happen. The chairman of the sub-committee had to be changed in 1994, and Heikki Ahava felt that this would be the right opportunity for Nokia. But he knew himself to be too diplomatic to push strongly the interests of Nokia. Therefore he suggested his colleague, Juha Rapeli as chairman, and Rapeli was elected. Ahava knew that Rapeli was an action-driven person, and suddenly the atmosphere in the meetings was quite different. Juha Rapeli firmly guided the decision of the sub-committee into a direction that, from the manufacturers point of view, made sense.

Three possible technological alternatives for the 3G mobile standard had emerged: Time Division Multiple Access (TDMA), Code Division Multiple Access (CDMA), and a combination of the two, TD-CDMA. In 1995 Nokia still did not have a clear view of which standard to support.

By the end of 1996 Nokia had started to build its strategy for the battle for standards. It was evident that Nokia alone would not be able to force any decisions. There had to be a group of important actors that would be prepared to act jointly to pursue certain interests. Here Nokia was able to benefit from its existing co-operative relationships.

The standards discussion would be driven by the three major markets: the US, Japan, and Europe. Right from the beginning it was clear that the Americans would try to force their own technology on the other players. For the telephones this would not affect Nokia that much, but for the network development the situation was different. The networks built on the GSM standards would not be easily converted into the American standard. If this standard became the global standard, a lot of the path-dependent competitive advantage that Nokia had with its existing network customers would be lost.

Nokia therefore decided to target the Japanese market as the most important market in which to forge some form of co-operative bonds. Thanks to its good relationships with Mitsui, Nokia had established well-functioning relationships with NTT-Docomo, the mobile operating division of NTT, the biggest tele-operator in the world. In 1996 Nokia initiated a series of discussions with NTT-Docomo about the possibilities of jointly pursuing their 3G interests. The goal was to achieve a common standard for both Europe and Asia. This would further strengthen Nokia's position in Asia, where tough competition was expected also from the American solution providers. And at the same time NTT-Docomo would find it much easier to enter the European market as a global service provider. In early 1997 it became evident that NTT-Docomo had chosen which standard to support: CDMA. Just a couple of weeks earlier Nokia and the other European manufacturers had jointly stated that they supported a combination of CDMA and TDMA called FMA, Frames Multiple Access.

The decision on how to treat the new situation had to be made by Yrjö Neuvo, senior vice-president in charge of product creation in Nokia Mobile Phones. Neuvo had a brilliant background as a scientist, but had, since he joined Nokia in 1993, very rapidly learned the commercial realities of the world Nokia lived in. Neuvo could easily see that for Nokia the most important goal was to be able to create a unified standard for Europe and Asia. And as it became evident that not only NTT-Docomo, but also other Asian operators favored CDMA he decided to suggest to the board that Nokia go for CDMA as well.

The decision was not automatically supported. Nokia Tele-communications had been successful based on GSM. TDMA was the technology which most naturally followed GSM. Jumping on the CDMA train meant considerable higher risks for Nokia. But during internal discussions a compromise was found: Nokia should aim at accepting CDMA as the communications standard between the handsets and the base stations, but the third generation GSM-derived technology would be the communications standard for NTT-Docomo between the base stations and the switch. This same strategy had also been adopted by Ericsson. The two Nordic telecom manufacturers were thereby united in their goals.

During spring 1997 Nokia and Ericsson very closely negotiated their joint 3G standard strategy. The main objective was to find a compromise that could satisfy NTT-Docomo. In June 1997 four American manufacturers stated their ambition to develop their own technology for the next generation mobile phones. Nokia and Ericsson decided jointly to announce publicly their support for CDMA at the Asian telecom exhibition in Singapore. The co-operation between Nokia and Ericsson thus became public. This was not appreciated by Siemens, which thus far had not been involved in the negotiations. Nokia and Ericsson tried in July jointly to convince Siemens to join them, but without results.

In September Siemens, Alcatel, and Nortel announced in a symposium for GSM-operators in Cyprus that they had developed their own proposal for a European standard for the third generation of mobile communications. Siemens had during spring 1997 understood that Nokia and Ericsson had a good opportunity to reach an agreement with NTT-Docomo. Siemens had never been fully competitive with GSM, and felt the need to try to develop a completely new technology platform, upon which the path dependent advantages of Nokia and Ericsson could be reduced. Siemens therefore aimed at creating a group of European and American actors, who would be able to establish a joint European and American standard, which the Japanese would have to follow as well. During autumn 1997 this group around Siemens grew – for example, Motorola gave Siemens its support. This was not something the European authorities had expected, nor wanted. In the end of October 1997 Jacques Santer, chairman of the EU Commission, called a meeting to discuss the situation regarding the coming European decision on a standard for third-generation mobile telecommunications. From Nokia the participating delegation consisted of: Jorma Ollila, CEO; Veli Sundbäck, executive vice-president, corporate relations and trade policy; and Heikki Ahava, vice-president, new system technologies. The meeting did not lead to any results. On the contrary, the fight grew even more intense. Nokia however still had one card to play. The Finnish President, Martti Ahtisaari was paying a visit to the UK in November 1997. Nokia informed him about the ongoing dispute over the telecommunications standard, and asked him to take their message to Tony Blair, the Prime

Minister. Two weeks after Ahtisaari's visit, the British tele-communications authorities announced publicly that they supported the technology suggested by Nokia and Ericsson. This support was important, as the big tele-operators in the UK were important and influential participants in ETSI, the body in which the final decision would have to be made.

The decisive ETSI meeting was on 28 January 1998. Neither party could gain the necessary 71 percent, but the suggestion by Nokia and Ericsson got 61 percent. Based on this result there had been a preprepared compromise solution, which was based on the Nokia and Ericsson suggestion, but included some adaptations from the Siemens proposal. By late in the evening this compromise was accepted by everybody, and Europe got its decision on the future mobile telecommunications standard. At that moment it was felt that the standard for Europe and Japan would provide a good foundation for developing the new technology. The Americans were expected to keep their standard, but this would not affect the decision made in Europe. And the European GSM standard had also been different from the American standard.

But certain forces in the USA driven by Qualcomm did not just accept that Europe would go its own way. They announced that they wanted a global standard for the third generation of mobile telecommunications. And they wanted ITU (the International Telecommunications Union) to decide which standard to follow. According to Qualcomm there were two alternatives: the European CDMA standard, or its own CDMA2000. The reason that Qualcomm was fighting was that they had certain patents relating to the CDMA standard, and Qualcomm wanted to gain the highest possible benefits from its own Intellectual Property Rights (IPR).

In spite of the divergent opinions regarding the standard for the third generation standard, Nokia, Ericsson, and Motorola agreed in spring 1998 to form a joint venture called Symbian. This company was established to develop a tailor-made operating system for the new media phone, the handset for the third generation network. Microsoft was not invited to this joint venture, and later formed an alliance with Qualcomm.

During autumn 1998 the conflict regarding the standard escalated. Motorola talked about a 'holy war', and Qualcomm announced that

Europe was applying grave protectionism in its efforts to pursue its standard without having waited for the possibility for a global standard to emerge. But the Americans were not united: Lucent and Motorola had different opinions in this matter. And Ericsson had ongoing fights with Qualcomm regarding IPRs. Qualcomm announced that it would prohibit the whole use of CDMA technology for European manufacturers. And Qualcomm continued its lobbying, which in December 1998 resulted in a letter to the EU Commission signed by Madeleine Albright, Secretary of State; Chalene Barshefsky, Chief Trade Negotiator; William Daley, Minister of Trade; and William Kennard, chairman of FCC (the Federal Communications Commission). This letter meant that the US was considering a trade war with Europe, if the decision on the standard was not reconsidered.

On 18 January 1999 Martin Bangemann, the commissioner in charge of telecommunications affairs in the EU, replied to Ms Albright and denied the accusations. During spring 1999 the conflict was gradually solved. In a TABD (Trans-Atlantic Business Dialogue) meeting on 17 February 1999 in Washington, a formal agreement between Europe and the US was reached, and this agreement was further ratified in the ITU meeting in Brazil in March 1999. In this agreement it was accepted that the third-generation mobile telecommunication services would be based on CDMA technology, but that the individual operator could choose from the different available CDMA alternatives. Basically this was what the European manufacturers had suggested at the beginning. The reason why this decision was not resisted by Qualcomm became evident on 25 March 1999 when Ericsson announced that it had acquired the network business and product development of Qualcomm. Thereby the IPR conflict between Qualcomm and the European manufacturers also came to an end.

At the end of April 1999 NTT-Docomo announced that it had ordered the next generation mobile phones and base stations from Ericsson and mobile phones from Nokia. The competition had now moved from competition for standards between groups of actors towards competition for commercial orders between individual actors. Ericsson got the first order for a third generation network. By spring 1999 Nokia had not produced a second generation CDMA network. And Ericsson had acquired Qualcomm. The close co-operation around the standards was a different issue from the fierce competition to provide value-adding offerings to customers.

REVISITING NOKIA AS A MARKET-MAKING PRIME MOVER

When the Finns formed local co-operatives to become less dependent on the Russian authorities, they began the market making which has made Nokia so successful. The co-operatives were manifested as companies which helped their members, involving the second, *co-operative* type of market making we introduced in this chapter, and which we explore in detail in the next.

For Finnish operating companies, the 1987 Telecommunications Act increased the industry's granularity, for it separated roles between regulator and operator in ways that had not been evident before.

For suppliers such as Nokia, however, the Act did not change much. The development of resources and capabilities to which it would gain access had started well before, going back to at least the 1963 military radio design competition which prompted Salora to begin to put a together bid.

The 1967 merger between Nokia and the Finnish Cable Works (FCW) added one more step to the capability-generating path Nokia was to undertake. Recall that electronics – which FCW had brought to Nokia – then represented only 3 percent (FIM 15 million) of the total turnover of the Nokia Group. This unit first manifested what would become mobile phone offerings later in the form of the much earlier radio telephone offering. As it was too expensive for individuals, the first customers the Nokia found were public institutions: the army, utilities, and emergency intervention crews as well as isolated energy infrastructure construction crews in the Soviet Union.

It is worth noting that electronic capabilities were developed in two ways. One involved developing capabilities without clear ideas of the offerings that would manifest them; that is, without having a clear idea of how the capability under development would help given customers to create value. The PCM (pulse code modulation)-based digital switching capability development of the 1960s is a good example.

The other was in response to precise requirements by identified customers. The 1972 State Railroads 24-channel train radio competition is a case in point. To win it, Salora developed an offering in the form of a phone manifesting new frequency synthesizing technology. The capability was then further manifested in offerings for the police force, navy, and civil purposes.

Soon after, developing innovative capabilities and winning competitions for single offerings gave way to a more demanding game. This involved positioning oneself as part of the prime-mover set in constellations which involved standards. 'Standards' can be interpreted in the terms of this book as a 'code' for value creation which will make it possible for suppliers and customers to relate through offerings which can be related to other offerings fitting the standard. The standard is the 'guarantor'[10] of the interconnectivity of the offerings. The standardized interactions, manifested as offerings, make it possible for those who enter the constellation determined by the standard to be connected to each other.

The first standards challenge which Nokia entered was the 1975 NMT (Nordisk Mobil Telefon) one. To be present, as we saw above, economies of scale in R&D were required, leading actors to work together. But the co-operation brought with it enhanced granularity. Recall that in its linking with Salora, Nokia agreed to specialize in base stations and radio links, leaving Salora to concentrate on the mobile telephones. It is the need for greater granularity which led to distinguishing internal capabilities that same year into three distinct units: telecommunications, industrial automation, and data processing.

As we saw above, Sakari Salminen recognized the importance of thinking of the business as a relationship-based learning one and not a transactions-centered one. His establishment of close and long lasting co-operation with his customers manifests this. As Nokia's Finnish customers were already in a competitive environment, while the rest of the world still saw its operators as monopoly suppliers, Nokia's customers were the most sophisticated customers one could learn from in the world.

This 'sophistication differential' gave Salminen's Nokia unequaled co-productive R&D advantages.

Nokia's ill-fated attempts to become a leading player in household electronics, and in particular television sets, remind us of Xerox's finding itself lambasted by Japanese makers of cheap, high quality photocopiers. While Nokia's history is more complex than that of Xerox, it is similar in that nothing in its past, not even its pulp and paper background, had prepared it to be a successful world-class leader of a commoditized offering.

One of the patterns that becomes visible in Nokia's phone success is its successful collaboration with partners, followed eventually by buy-outs; which in turn forms a platform for successfully influencing other actors. This was the case with Televa, with which it formed the joint-venture Telefenno, which Nokia bought out 12 years after its being formed. In the same way, the coming together of Salora and Nokia's radio telephone businesses into Mobira existed for four years, until Nokia absorbed first Mobira and Salora another four years later.

The environmental context providing the 20-year growth of the electronics part from 3 percent of turnover in 1967 to 49 percent in 1987 contributed to seeking out parties external to the corporation in order to access required capabilities. Because the overall telecommunications industry was nationally protected, the partners which Nokia sought were first Finnish ones, and when required, Nordic ones.

The 'closed' environment of worldwide communications para-doxically moved the Finnish actors to be 'open' with each other. By the time that the world's telecommunications started to become deregulated and privatized, the Nordic players (notably Nokia and Ericsson) had acquired 'prime mover' skills that others were at pains to comprehend.

Kairamo's recruitment of young, competent managers with international experience in the 1980s capitalized on the structural opportunity which openness had obtained to develop world-class capabilities.

As we saw, Vuorilehto and Ollila honed the capabilities which allowed Nokia to be a prime mover, and sold those in which it could not to other parties that aspired to such a role in their respective value constellations.

Ollila's line management experience at Nokia Mobile Phones strengthened his belief in Nokia employees' experience and skills as assets to be developed. Ollila hired and promoted people like McGovern, who also stressed the importance of always fulfilling all the promises that had been given to the workers.

One can argue that such values prospered particularly well because of the size of Finland. With 5 million inhabitants, people who work in similar professions often know each other quite well. In such small circles, people are bound to be more closely related by family, and other social bonds than in many other countries. The central place of mutual dependencies in Nokia's business values also reflect the historical roots of Finland as a country geographically located in a strategic position between east and west. This experience, combined with a harsh winter climate, has formed a society known for its ability to perform under considerable constraints (e.g. the post World War II reparations to the Soviet Union), having become very adaptable to changing conditions.

Ollila sought to enhance the internal variety of his management team as much as possible so as to face the increasing complexities which becoming a world-class prime mover supposed. Nokia's main historical client, Sonera (previously Telecom Finland) also pursued the same strategy in composing its own top management team.

Alahuhta's modular product architecture allowed Nokia to fit capabilities and customer-specific offering requirements more effectively than many of its competitors. This modularity in effect brought the 'standards' logic internally into Nokia's own value-creating organization.

NMT's open systems architecture matched the modularity developed by Alahuhta. Developing the new GSM standard in ways relating to this logic was of great interest to Nokia, who was organized to do well in it. Note that this logic would have appeared to be 'turbulent' to a player organized to fit an alternative one.

Nokia's formation of the European Cellular Radio 900 alliance with Alcatel and AEG followed the logic it had earlier used with Finnish actors, but this time at a Europe-wide level. The fact that Finland was the only one of 18 countries able to deliver a working GSM network in time attests to how well the interactive logic (internally with workers, externally with partners, and in particular, commercially with customers) worked.

Its joint venture with the Tandy Corporation and its Radio Shack chain of 6,700 outlets simply extended the interactive logic to the USA. As it had done in the past in Finland, Nokia bought out part of its partner's operations. Its agreement with Mitsui in Japan is yet another extension of the interactive logic.

Notice that entering agreements with foreign actors (European, American, Japanese) allowing it to reach customers went hand in hand with its developing capabilities. This is why Nokia is situated in Chapter 7 ('market making') of this book, and not in Chapter 5 ('customer focus') or 6 ('capability leveraging'). It became a prime mover by developing *both* customer orientation *and* capability leveraging as business model priorities at the same time. It fed the one to the other and vice versa, opening up markets before others.

CONCLUSION: WHAT'S NEXT FOR NOKIA

The global market share of over 21 percent for mobile phones in the NMT and GSM standard world which Nokia's exemplary market making obtained will be challenged in the new millennium by the coming of the new G3 standard. This time, the game is not Finnish/Nordic as it had been with NMT; nor European, as with GSM; but global. The complexity of the business environment is much, much tougher as a consequence.

Nokia's prime mover strategy has however not changed, not fundamentally. It still goes full-blast for the market-making business modeling at which it has come to excel.

We saw how both Ahava and Rapelli influenced decision making at the ETSI technical sub-committee. Nokia then ably navigated the constellations that respectively backed the TDMA, CDMA, and TD-CDMA formats. Its compromise with NTT-Docomo to obtain what in effect became an Asian-European *modular* standard that would isolate the Americans, while fitting the interests of both Nokia and Ericsson, is a perfect example of how sophisticated appreciation of factors, influence of actors, and (joint) control of technologies makes actor-centered market-making prime movership possible.

It is worth noting that the Siemens-Alcatel-Nortel initative attempted to counter Nokia's efforts with a European/American standard. But none of the players, excepting perhaps Nortel, had the same interactive and modular capabilities which Nokia had developed. And Nortel was Canadian, not American. Motorola's support was thus not a surprise. Motorola's falling behind in its mobile phone capabilities compared to Ericsson and Nokia, as well as its ill-fated Iridium satellite-based global phone alternative, in effect made the stakes of G3 literally vital *for its survival.*

Securing a British leg to its Northern Europe–Asian constellation strengthened Nokia's and Ericsson's position against the prime suppliers of continental Europe operators, enhancing the credibility of the 'European' part of its Euro-Asiatic proposition. After the January 1998 ETSI meeting, the real battle would be played out in terms of how each party would 'colonize' North America. And the stakes were big, as the US 'trade war' letter showed.

The TABD meeting on 17 February 1999 in effect saw the old Nokia market-making pattern win again. The result was a high resolution, enhanced granularity 'modular standard', helped by the fact that Ericsson, which had teamed up with Nokia, had bought out important parts of Qualcomm.

The April 1999 order from NTT-Docomo for joint offerings from Ericsson and Nokia signaled that the market making would move back from standards (competition 'for' the market) to offerings (competition 'in' the market). Based on the available information, one can draw different possible scenarios of how the contextual environment may evolve. Two broad ways of linking capabilities deployed to transform the transactional environment come to mind with our value-creation model.

In the first view, different possible futures are determined by not-yet-existing, or currently underdeveloped, capabilities. In such possible futures, these future capabilities would allow mobile phone suppliers to make offerings which existing customers in the future, and desired future customers, would require. Nokia showed in the G3 standard battle that it could influence what in the GSM standard decision it only could appreciate. A big player, like Nokia is today, therefore appears to have a 'larger' transactional environment than smaller players. Considering Hamel and Prahalad's[11] notion of 'strategic intent', one can therefore see that one of the most important features of the 'strategic intent' is to shape *and enlarge* the transactional environment. As the G3 standard is now set, the following challenge is double: what the actual offerings provided within this standard will be; and how to prepare for the next standard.

In the second view, possible futures are related to not-yet-existing, or not-yet invented, customers, with whom firms would benefit from existing, or 'pipeline' (expected) capability developments. This view is particularly interesting when the capabilities have the potential of becoming competences, i.e. form a basis for sustained competitive advantage. The customer in this view is not a 'given', independent variable around which the capability dependent variable would be developed. On the contrary, it is the customer who must be developed, and/or invented, from the foundation of dynamic capability development. In this second view, once the new 3G standard is in place, Nokia has to start to consider how capabilities fitting the G3 standard can be combined in commercially attractive offerings. Important questions are: How to design and technically produce a media phone which attracts customer interest, and which has an acceptable cost? How to develop user-friendly, interesting multi-media features of the media phone? How can moving pictures be properly displayed in the media phone? How will 9-year-old girls relate to the phone? And 50-year-old fishermen? And crews fueling aircraft at airports? And ... any other relevant customer profile? And how do we go about exploring these possibilities with all these different types of potential customers? And ultimately ... how many consumers will in the end buy a media phone-based offering? Nokia's agreement with Sabre to enhance flight information effectiveness for passengers signals developments in this direction.

The redefinition of how prime movers further develop market making in the telecommunications sector has by no means come to its end.

Co-operative Market Making: Prime Movers Acting for Others, Not Themselves

8

In this chapter we explore the second type of market making: co-operative market making. More specifially, this chapter:

- Analyzes how companies can design value constellations by *influencing* how their constellation's key members relate to each other.
- Uses an in-depth case study of *VISA*, the prototypical co-operative market-making organization, as the framework on which to base this analysis.

A PRIME MOVER ACTING FOR OTHERS

As opposed to the previous chapter, in which actors design the value constellation to suit *themselves* in the first place, this chapter looks at another, entirely different type of prime mover. Here the prime mover acts *for others* in the first place, rather than *for itself*. These 'others' it typically refers to as 'members'.

If one tells a classroom full of MBA students that VISA is a not-for-profit organization, working for its *members,* one will get lots of sarcastic laughs, smirks, and dubiousness. Yet VISA's claim to this effect is, strictly speaking, true. And VISA uses this fact to compete – successfully – against American Express.

VISA can credibly tell retailers, for instance, that just like they (the retailers) do, VISA works for its customers, except not in order to make a profit. It can thus afford to depict AMEX as greedily pocketing what it makes on the retailers' back ... While the caricature does not fully stand up to careful scrutiny, VISA has a point.

To explore this second ('influence') type of value constellation making, we overview how two quite similar institutions, VISA and the Groupement Cartes Bancaires in France, built their value constellations and carry out business.

The link between VISA and the Groupement Cartes Bancaires is as follows. All financial institutions issuing cards that access VISA and/or MasterCard brand rights in France belong to the Groupement Cartes Bancaires. Those that access the VISA brand also belong to the Groupement Carte Bleue, which licenses the VISA brand; those that access the MasterCard brand belong to the Groupement EuroPay/MasterCard. Several institutions are members of all three Groupements, but many of only two of them.

We close the chapter by investigating some of the principles upon which both VISA and the Groupement Cartes Bancaires have become successful prime movers.

VISA: AN OVERVIEW

In 1999 VISA had over 21,000 member banks, which together provided more than 1 billion cards for their members' customers around the world. These are accepted in over 14 million locations.

This makes VISA the world's largest credit and payment supplier, and contributes to render it one of the most widely recognized brands.

In 1998 VISA held a 54.7 percent market share in credit cards, followed by MasterCard with 37.5 percent. AMEX held only 3.5 percent, as did Japanese-based JCB.

VISA states that its mission is to enhance its members' pre-eminence, profitability, and competitiveness. To do so, it helps members with:

- Licensing.
- Promotion and protection of the trademark.
- Providing a global electronic system to authorize transactions.
- Process clearing.

- Process settlement data.
- Provision of rules and by-laws.
- Development and/or enhancement of products.
- Establishment of global standards.
- Development of strategic alliances.

VISA does not itself issue cards, sign up merchants, or retain profits (as compared notably with American Express, who does all of the above on its own account). Instead, VISA helps its *member* banks do so.

VISA has no information on member banks' customers. The only information VISA has concerns the number of cards each issues, the number of transactions each card is used for, and the number of retailers which the banks have signed up to accept payment with VISA cards.

VISA was formally founded in 1977, though its roots lie with experiments conducted by Bank of America, which issued its first card (BankAmericard) in 1958. BankAmerica Service Corporation was established in 1966, giving way to NABANCO in 1970, which became VISA USA in 1977, the same year that VISA International was established.

VISA is headquartered in San Francisco, and is owned by financial institutions. But *members control it* through the International and Regional Boards, by acting as advisors and in working groups, and by participating in regional sub-meetings. Because of US banking law, there are many small and medium-sized banks in the USA, which means that until recently at least half of the VISA member banks were American banks. As we see below, this fact has created some controversies for VISA's international expansion.

Like the Groupement Cartes Bancaires, VISA is a good example of an organization which is itself situated in the 'influence' level of Smith's AIC model.[1] VISA has self-consciously situated itself in the 'influence' part of Smith's model *from the point of view of its members*. VISA is located there precisely to 'shape' the transactional environment of its member's businesses. It does this by influencing others in ways that no single member can. From the point of view of its members, then, VISA is thus an 'agent of influence'. It succeeds if it gets the behavior of actors in its members' individual and collective transactional environments to fit better their present and future desired value creation.

Thus, *from VISA's point of view*, the 'control' part of Smith's AIC model is entirely carried out by its members.

In effect, the way in which both VISA and the Groupement Cartes Bancaires exercise their prime mover role works as follows. They both convert what for members would otherwise remain 'appreciated' contextual environment factors into parts of their transactional business environment. This is because they can, for example, determine the type of technology which banking payment systems will use by setting standards which suit its members' business interests. In this way, VISA and the Groupement Cartes Bancaires convert what would otherwise remain a 'technological factor' which an independent (non-member) bank could only appreciate into something which they transform into an influenced aspect of members' transactional environments. It is thus very difficult – very costly – for a bank to decide not to become a VISA member, or a member of an equivalent, typically competing institution such as MasterCard.

HOW VISA DEVELOPED ITS VALUE CONSTELLATION

VISA has developed differently in different countries and regions of the world. Yet, overall, it seems to have undertaken the following activities, although not necessarily in the order we present them.

1   Rethink the role of the 'customer' into a plurality of roles for each counterpart.
2   Rethink roles VISA ('we') hold in relation to (1).
3   Rethink roles 'others' hold in relation to (1).
4   Redesign roles 'customer', VISA, and 'others' play in relation to each other.
5   Manifest (4) in actual offerings.
6   Enable VISA's ('our') people, the 'customer', and 'others' to engage with VISA's ('us') in (1–5).

We examine each in turn.

Rethink the role of the 'customer' into a plurality of roles

VISA's most immediate customers are its members. These pay VISA for technical and marketing services, including use of the brand. But VISA also gets them to work for it in many other roles – for example, as providers of advice, information, and even of governance.

For VISA, the notion of 'customers' extends beyond its members (the banks), to also include members' (banks') customers (households, companies, retailers). VISA also has found that many 'stakeholders' (that is, any actor which has a stake in its value constellation, or is affected by it) in its constellation hold – among others – the role of 'customer'. They pay both VISA's customers, and these customers' customers, for the right to participate in VISA's constellation. Such stakeholders include hardware and software suppliers, regulators, automated-teller machine enablers such as cash transport companies, and phone companies. All such actors play multiple roles in the VISA-designed payments constellation, in ways defined, enabled, and organized by VISA in its prime mover role.

As is the case with Xerox's 'documenting' offerings surveyed in Chapter 2, VISA's business is to redesign activities that would otherwise remain cumbersome. VISA acts to render them smoother and/or more cost effective. Typically it does this on behalf of its members, often also for its members' customers.

Thus, for instance, VISA's Corporate Purchasing Card program reduces invoice-processing costs for corporations that subscribe to it by an average of 73 percent. A study carried out by Deloitte & Touche on VISA's behalf showed costs related to invoice reconciliation, expense reports, and purchase orders fall from an average of $83 per transaction to $23. Alternative systems to the ones depending on this offering appear to be particularly costly when the purchase amounts are small, which represents a substantial proportion of the purchases which units in companies – e.g. secretaries – typically make.

Rethink roles which VISA holds

On behalf of its members, VISA holds many different roles:

- Product developer.
- Brand value guarantor.
- Trademark protector and licensor.
- Technical standards setter, lobbyist.
- Marketer, buyer.
- Systems architect and provider.
- Rule maker and enforcer.
- Negotiator of strategic alliances.

Each of these roles influences other parties in its members' constellations.

For example, being the guarantor of the brand – which in 1999 is the fourteenth most important brand in the world, well ahead of AMEX, which is twentieth – supposes co-ordinating advertising actors in all regions in which VISA is present. Its current (1999) organization includes six regional organizations (USA, Canada, Latin America, Asia/Pacific, European Union, and Central Europe/Middle East/ Africa). In all of these regions, VISA must interact with legal authorities to ensure that its trademark and licensing correspond to the standards it has set in order for the brand's value to be protected and enhanced.

In the same way, as a buyer and systems architect, VISA has created the VISA Technology Fund, a venture capital partnership open to member financial institutions. The fund invests in:

(a) 'strategically core' companies whose offerings VISA buys on behalf of its members, or which its members buy to meet their membership requirements;
(b) companies which support VISA's strategy, but which do not necessarily have VISA or its members as customers, and
(c) companies which VISA reckons will fit either the (a) or (b) categories in the future.

Rethink roles 'others' hold in relation to the 'customers'

VISA has been better than the competitors (MasterCard, AMEX, JCB, Diners') in mobilizing 'others' to help it develop its constellation. It has been a pioneer in co-branding cards,[2] which means sharing its brand with other actors such as large retailers, airlines, telecom operators, or gasoline retailers, to extend the reach of its brand. It is now actively engaged in promoting new generation smart cards (inspired by those of the Groupement Cartes Bancaires), and in enhancing the security of e-commerce on the Internet.

At the time of this writing (mid-1999), VISA is involved in an interesting 'prime mover' battle with one of its premier members, Citigroup (previously CitiBank). Citigroup wants the highly recognized VISA brand, which is now displayed in the front part of the card together with the logo of each member bank issuing it, to go on the back of its cards. Citigroup wants its own brand in the front, alone. Predictably, VISA refused, as this would challenge not only its role in its constellation, but its very *raison d'être*. In our view, VISA saw Citigroup's request as a challenge to its being positioned in the transactional environment of every one of its over 21,000 other members. Citigroup, which is attempting to build a global financial services brand of its own, resigned its VISA board seat, and approached VISA's rival, MasterCard. On 25 June 1999, MasterCard agreed to move its own brand to the back of its cards, allowing Citigroup to put its brand on the front, alone.

A few scenarios can be envisaged. One is that large banks with international aspirations, whose capability-focused business model requires strong brand recognition, will attempt to emulate Citigroup' initiative and seek a similar deal to the one it sought with MasterCard. If this worked, MasterCard would have created a 'glocal' (global *and* local) value constellation alternative with which it could challenge the 'global' logic of VISA's value constellation. In announcing the deal with Citigroup, MasterCard

> said its market research showed that consumers would view the movement of the logo as simply another card design, with no impact on their perception of the brand.[3]

A second scenario is that VISA would make the exit expensive, and that in the worst of cases (from VISA's point of view) only a handful of very large, very rich banks would afford this option. Thus, most members would remain with the VISA offering. Banks that exited would in effect have transformed their business models so that they would have a more limited 'capability-focus' (refer to Figure 4.5 on page 106).

But as we see further below, both scenarios are subject to more fundamental changes which electronic commerce is bringing to the payments business.

Redesign roles 'customer', VISA, and 'others' play in relation to each other

Customers' customers are activated in many different ways by VISA, by its member banks, and by the retailers. This can involve typing a 'PIN' number on a keyboard to obtain cash at an automated cash machine or to pay retailers, or signing one's name on a copy of the receipt, as in department stores and restaurants, or examining one's monthly statement.

Obviously, many member banks are actively involved by VISA in defending the 'prime mover' role they collectively hold through VISA. In doing so, they influence members of their own value constellations. Thus, retailers significantly change their behavior when they have their customers pay with VISA. To assess the change, try to pay for a leather bag in an Italian shop, as one of the authors did. If after agreeing on the price you offer to pay by cash, you immediately get – at least – a 10 percent reduction. This is not the case in Finland or France, where the authors now reside: the high-speed telephone infrastructures which local actors such as the Groupement Cartes Bancaires have obtained are extremely reliable, and do not require the repeat dialing which is commonplace in Italy. At the same time the commission to be paid by the retailers for VISA transactions have remained comparatively low, further supporting retailers also to encourage the use of the card.

Below, in examining the Groupement Cartes Bancaires system in France, we show how the redialing difficulties which in Italy make it rational to avoid paying with VISA both manifest, and contribute to, the failure which payment cards have met with in Italy.

Manifest the redesigned roles alluded to above in actual offerings

There are many different kinds of payment and credit cards. The distinctions are not so much technical or legal, but often – as is the case in France – they are commercial distinctions. The different categories of cards we depict below in effect manifest the commercial offering that a bank has chosen to make available to its customers, be they individuals or business firms.

Among the most important types of cards, which can also be offered in the form of combined offerings, are:

- *Debit cards* – purchases are immediately deducted from cardholder's bank account.
- *Deferred debit cards* – purchases are accumulated during a certain period and then deducted from cardholder's bank account. Eventual refinancing should be negotiated with the bank.
- *Credit cards* – purchases are accumulated during a certain period and monthly balances can be automatically refinanced.
- *Co-branded affinity cards* – these are debit *and* credit cards that also display specific brands (usually non-financial brands) aiming at specific market segments.
- *Stored value cards* – cards issued with a certain nominal value. Purchases are deducted from this original value. These cards can be rechargeable or non-rechargeable.
- *Smart cards* – multifunction cards that incorporate payment card and other card functions (ID, door key, car key, driver's license, etc. ....).

In addition, cards can have different services attached to them (e.g. travel insurance, frequent flyer mile loyalty program awards, tracking sales expenses, etc.). This variety is bound to explode soon.

For example, early experiments with smaller, mobile phone-based smart cards for payment are under way in Finland. There, the leading mobile phone operator, Sonera, has equipped some Coke machines with mobile phone equipment. This allows a mobile phone user to type a certain code, and get a Coke. The price of the Coke then appears in the user's monthly bill. A similar experiment has been developed with car wash machines. The possibilities are endless, and will soon become evident in other realms of everyday life, be they transportation, health care, entertainment, or whatever.

Enable 'VISA people', the 'customers', and 'others' to engage simultaneously in the continuous process of improving value creation

VISA invests a considerable amount of money in training both its own employees and those of its members. With IT innovation enabling many new offerings to come on stream, VISA requires that people employed by different stakeholders review their roles many times during their careers.

For example, a company adopting the Corporate Purchasing offering referred to above, must have people
- obtain a Corporate Purchasing software package from their bank;
- check that its hardware and software can sustain it;
- get the company to become referenced;
- inform all the company's suppliers that the system has been installed, and allocate them a Supplier Number;
- inform all staff authorized to make purchases that the system has been installed, train them to use it, and allocate them a Purchasing Number;
- ensure that the company's bank is equipped, and that its staff are trained to authorize and to authenticate the buyer, to verify the purchase limit and the merchant category code;
- set purchase limits individually, and determine criteria changing these;
- organize the relationship between authorization, authentification, and delivery; and
- redesign internal and external auditing and reporting processes to accommodate dematerialized invoicing.

All of these activities require coordinated mobilization of individuals on the part of, at least, VISA, the company setting up this system, its bank, its suppliers, its auditors, its 'systems' (hardware and software) suppliers, and government inspectors.

THE CARTES BANCAIRES EXAMPLE IN FRANCE[4]

France is the third largest market for VISA in the world, behind the United States and the UK. It accounts for 9 percent of world VISA cardholder sales volume, with its residents holding 2 percent of VISA cards. Within Europe, French cardholders hold 12 percent of European VISA cards and they account for 29 percent of VISA's European sales volume.

This means that French cardholders have a higher than average use rate for their cards. In effect, French cardholders use their cards six times more often than Americans, and nearly three times more than their British counterparts. From VISA's point of view, the French market is a big success, and a testing ground for new ideas.

The Cartes Bancaires (hereinafter referred to as CB) system is by far the most important payment card system in France, boasting 29,000 ATMs and being accepted by nearly 700,000 merchants. Like VISA, it is administered by a co-operative consortium of French banks.[5]

The Groupement Cartes Bancaires[6] today includes more than 200 banks, bank groups or financial institutions. Like VISA, the CB system is in part an interbanking system enabling card-based payment and cash withdrawal. Only banks can participate in this part of the system.

What got the Cartes Bancaires system going, paradoxically, was the May 1968 uprising in France. The negotiations that followed May 1968 resulted in the banks getting a customer base for free. This is because the agreements reached included a measure to the effect that all salaries would have to be paid to a bank account. The unemployment rate was very low at the time – meaning that all French households not uniquely dependent on pension income immediately became individual bank customers; and all dual or multiple income households would have at least the same number of accounts as income earners. But the agreement stipulated that, in return, the banks would have to offer checking for free.

As processing checks is expensive, the banks negotiated for, and obtained, the possibility of not paying interest on the monies deposited in such accounts.

As could be expected, this gave rise to two initiatives: the development of measures to reduce the cost of processing checks, and – later, when inflation was successfully vanquished – the opportunity to develop financial products (such as unit trusts) that better remunerate the money that was deposited.

The development of the CB system obeyed the first, more urgent requirement. Developing a cards-based payment system was originally conceived of as a way of reducing the high cost of processing a check-centered payment system. This demand for cost efficiency accelerated earlier explorations for card-based products. Between 1985 and 1995, the proportion of non-cash payments which were made by check decreased from 73 percent to 51 percent, thanks to the use of cards going from 5 percent to 25 percent in that period.

To this day (mid-1999), the French card system features a rather unique profile in the world. This is because there is very little card-based credit business in comparison to the penetration of cards in its payment system. The card-based credit business came relatively late to France, compared to many other countries; with many of these credit cards being offered by companies other than the banks, although some were at least partly owned by banks. It is only since the 1990s that banks have developed specific 'revolving credit', card-based lending offerings. But the law has stipulated that these offerings must have a distinctive card manifestation. Consumer groups have complained that the 'distinction' is not clear enough, and that many households inadvertently use credit cards with very high lending rates while thinking that the bank has simply renewed their old payment card.

But let us get back to the story of how the system came to be. Some time before May 1968, a group of French banks[7] had jointly decided to launch the first electronic payment system in France. In 1967 they created a limited interbanking card system called Carte Bleue (blue card). In 1971 two other French banks, the Crédit Agricole and the Crédit Mutuel, profiting from their traditional strengths in rural areas, created an alternative card system focusing on cash withdrawal. They installed a large network of automated teller machines, or ATMs, in small cities but had relatively low penetration among merchants.

These two systems were known as 'the blue ones' (Carte Bleue) and 'the green ones' (Crédit Agricole and the Crédit Mutuel) because of the color of the cards they issued. According to a CB Director:

> At the beginning the Crédit Agricole and the Crédit Mutuel had a lot of ATMs in the countryside and the Carte Bleue banks had ATMs mainly in the large cities. The Crédit Agricole's and the Crédit Mutuel's ATMs had a huge demand peak in the holidays period (especially in August). The Carte Bleue banks were strong in the big cities like Paris, Lyon or Marseilles and among the merchants but they were weak in the small cities.[8]

In 1977 Crédit Agricole launched an independent payment card in association with Eurocard/MasterCard. In 1983 the Crédit Mutuel bought 50 percent of Eurocard France, a firm created by the Crédit Agricole, which represented Eurocard/MasterCard in France. This company developed a second interbanking network parallel to Carte Bleue system.

The CB interbanking system as we know it today was created in 1984 through the merger of Carte Bleue and this second network formed by the Crédit Agricole and the Crédit Mutuel.

On 31 July 1984 the member banks of the Groupement Cartes Bancaires – Carte Bleue[9] (together with VISA) along with Crédit Agricole and Crédit Mutuel (together with Eurocard France) signed an agreement laying the groundwork for the CB interbanking system. The CB system was to make these systems (that of Carte Bleue, Crédit Agricole and Crédit Mutuel) compatible, overcoming the differences in their technical architectures, procedures, and equipment network.

By creating a single payment card system at the national level, French banks created one large network that in effect bypassed VISA and MasterCard at the national level:

The Cartes Bancaires (CB) system was made by a group of French banks issuing and managing payment cards. It is a domestic system, not an international one. In the beginning of the 1980s some clients had to change banks because of the cards (VISA or MasterCard). Some of them had to have accounts in two banks in order to operate the two-card systems (VISA and MasterCard). This was not economically efficient. At that time there was a kind of cold war among the banks, a terror equilibrium. Each bank was well established in one segment. At a certain point they decided to stop this competition that benefited the international networks. Then the banks decided that competition would henceforth concern attached services but would not concern access to the network by the customers.[10]

The interbanking agreement signed in 1984 was based on three main axes:

- Technically standardized cards, leaving the possibility of customizing the service offerings attached to the cards of each bank.
- Procedure standardization: the banks would sign a standard contract, the ATMs and terminals would follow standard specifications to allow compatibility.
- 'Free' access to all terminals and ATMs in France to all cardholders.

The central entity established to co-ordinate the CB system was the Groupement d'Intérêt Economique Cartes Bancaires, which was the institutionalization of the consortium created in 1984. Its mission, inspired by VISA's, is to implement, co-ordinate, and promote the interbanking concept in the payment cards market in France.

According to one of its directors:

The GIE-CB is a club, a non-profit association composed of French banks and other institutions that have banking activities. The GIE-CB exploits a French system of electronic payment. It is, in a way, a competitor of VISA and MasterCard[11] at the domestic level.[12]

Members of the GIE CB included by 1999:

- Over 200 banks that are members of the AFB (Association Française des Banques[13]).

- Three decentralized structures (networks of regional and local banks):
  Crédit Agricole (65 regional banks),
  Crédit Mutuel (17 regional federations), and
  Banques Populaires (30 regional banks).
- The national center of Caisses d'Epargne (34 institutions).
- Some credit institutions.
- Some other institutions like the Post Office (La Poste), the Public Treasury and the Banque de France.[14]

The interbanking system permitted the early adoption of advanced technologies, such as cards with built-in microprocessors ('smart' cards), which in France were launched much earlier than in the rest of the world, as of 1992. State-of-the art 'smart' cards have embedded micro-processors that can store about 32 kilobytes of information, about 100 times more than magnetic strips. They have very low levels of fraud compared to the magnetic ones.[15] Part of the reason that the French were the first to adopt smart cards has to do with the fact that it is a French invention. Gemplus, created by the inventor, is the world's leading producer of smart cards.

The system which the 1984 agreement created helped co-ordinate the actions of a variety of economic agents including banks, credit card administrators, electronic equipment manufacturers, telecommunication companies, major retailers, and the French government.

According to a CB director, the CB system was originally presented to politicians by some of its promoters as an instrument of national economic autonomy. Recall that at the time, significant parts of the banking system, and all of the telecommunications sector in France were nationalized. Those promoting CB knew how sensitive national monetary independence was in some political circles, and they cast VISA and MasterCard (MC) as something of a 'Trojan horse' used by American banks wanting to enter foreign markets:

> [seen in that way] the CB system [could be presented] as a question of national autonomy. [Thus] behind the international schemes [VISA/ MC] one would find the American economy, American standards, and American practices . . . .[16]

The argument which was used was as follows:

> For example if two Brazilian banks have two VISA credits, the compensation of such credits will not be a domestic transaction, [instead] the credits will be compensated by VISA in the USA and both banks will pay fees to VISA. In France, because of the CB system, all French[17] banks together [would in effect] pay VISA and MC the same amount that each one of the foreign banks pay to them individually. This [was thus presented as] a question of political autonomy.
>
> The worst case [which promoters used in their presentations] happens when a bank has to have access to both networks – VISA and MC. In this case the bank will pay double fees. All those problems have been avoided with the CB system.[18]

Over time, VISA actually collaborated a lot with CB members in product development, for instance in the design of electronic purses based on smart-card technologies.

At the time of this writing, most CB cards are debit cards, whereby purchases are directly deducted from the cardholder's bank account. There are basically two kinds of CB cards:

1　The regular CB cards, valid only within the French territory. In this case the cost of purchases are *immediately* deducted from customer's checking account (more often there is 2–3 day delay between purchase and payment to allow for processing and settling).

2　The international CB cards, valid internationally and issued by the French CB consortium jointly with a major credit card company (VISA and Eurocard/Mastercard). In this second case purchases are, depending on what the client prefers, either immediately deducted at every purchase or accumulated during a whole month and automatically deducted from the cardholder's bank account in full at the end of each month. Cash retrieved at ATMs is deducted immediately. Bills are not automatically refinanced, as they are in the regular credit card formula. In case of non-payment clients have to negotiate terms with the banks which hold their accounts.

The regular CBs are directly administered by the issuing banks through the Groupement d'Intérêt Economique (GIE)-CB. International CBs are processed as a regular CB card when inside France, but they are processed as VISA/MC cards for international operations. Thus, the CB system treats all the domestic transactions, which account for 96 percent of all transactions made by French banks' clients. VISA and MC are used just for the *processing* of the remaining 4 percent of transactions, those which take place internationally. Cost differences are very important. For a typical French bank the 96 percent of domestic CB transactions cost as much as the 4 percent of international VISA/MC transactions.

HOW THE CARTES BANCAIRES CONSTELLATION WAS DEVELOPED

As in many businesses that depend on volume, the main challenge when implementing a new card system is to attain 'critical mass'.

In order to remain a viable, resilient, robust value-creating system, a new payments card system has to break the vicious circle shown in Figure 8.1. If a payment card system is trapped inside this vicious circle, it will require skillful management to avoid collapse. Often low-volume payment card systems adopt the strategy of being niche players, dominating specific sectors of the market where they can offer clients some attractive advantages to compensate the lack of general acceptance. Local retailer's payment cards often follow this route. One can also argue that VISA in Italy has been confronted with this situation.

But, if and when the value-creating system reaches a given level of 'critical mass', the vicious circle becomes a virtuous one. This virtuous circle implies a positive feedback where more clients → mean more retailers → which mean more clients and so on. Such a virtuous circle is shown in Figure 8.2. After a certain point the system is 'locked in' and it is very difficult for competitors to break its reinforcing logic.[19] This is an example of increasing returns economics.

A competitor confronted with an actor such as VISA, which is enjoying this 'virtuous' lock-in loop, loses its advantage, which

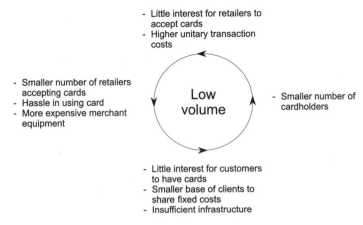

Figure 8.1 A low-volume vicious circle.

subsequently will mean losing further advantage (and so on). Virtuous and vicious circles thus feed on each other.

This virtuous ↔ vicious circle relationship applies both to established players left behind because they did not reach the critical mass, as well as to new players. The virtuous circle thus not only feeds itself, but also 'causes' vicious circles for other players to remain stuck. As we saw in the comparison between Netscape and Microsoft in Chapter 3, it is only when

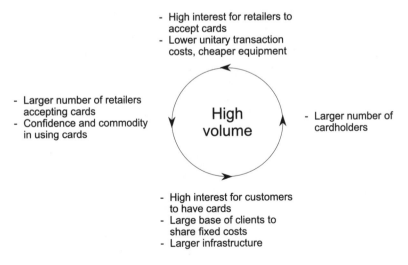

Figure 8.2 A high-volume virtuous circle.

other offerings are brought into the fray, that the dynamics of this logic can be broken.

These reinforcing dynamics make life very difficult for challengers to CB like American Express and Diners Club who did not succeed to create the needed 'critical mass' and are now marginal players in the French market, although their own business model allows them to remain profitable in such conditions.

Once the CB system worked so as to grow beyond its critical mass threshold, it behaved as an 'attractor'. By this we mean that its 'gravity force' pulled other economic actors inside the system. This rendered the value constellation robust, resilient, and reinforced its chances of survival.

A key question in designing value constellations of this type, then, is how to build this critical mass, how to get enough volume to lock in the market?

The French banks made it by assembling through the GIE-CB a group of banks that grew to over 200 members, simultaneously 'pulling' their clients to adhere to the 'Carte Bleue' system. The construction of a virtuous circle was also enabled by the complementarity of Carte Bleue strengths in big cities with the Crédit Agricole/Crédit Mutuel strengths in the countryside. The GIE-CB also relied on privileged alliances with large retailers who could help to build critical mass for the system. Financial service subsidiaries of large hyper-market and super-market retailers such as Leclerc, Auchan, and Carrefour were accepted as members of the GIE-CB.[20]

The CB system also had to create the infrastructure needed rapidly to make the cards operational at a large number of sales points. The high initial volume generated by the association of hundreds of banks enabled the GIE-CB to negotiate with other companies such as the electronic equipment manufacturers Schlumberger, Gemplus, Bull, and the telecommunications company France Télécom.

To the banks, the CB system offered the possibility virtually to monopolize the payment cards market, which proved to be profitable. CB also helped banks to increase the use of attached services and the brand loyalty of their clients, as the cards are branded by each bank.

To the merchants, the CB system opened up the possibility of selling to a large number of customers holding CB cards. It also simplified payment operations, adding safety and avoiding the hassle of dealing with cash and checks.

The CB system was made possible because the French banks gave up part of their individual independence, relying on an interbanking organization to obtain collective independence. However, the co-operation became the ground for intense competition among the banks. It is a bit like formula one racing, or soccer, or many other sports: teams collaborate to build up the interest of the sport, and then compete fiercely within the rules they have agreed to play by. Both the VISA and CB systems rendered collaboration and competition compatible and complementary.

According to CB Administrator Max Auriol:

> Without competition there is no stimulation to improve the services offered to clients. The services that banks offer to their clients are subject to commercial competition. But without interbanking agreements the payment card system is impossible. That's why the interbanking services within the CB system are not subject to competition. They are the heart of the interbanking concept and are not subject to competition because this would destroy the system.[21]

THE CARTES BANCAIRES CONSTELLATION IN TERMS OF CONCEPTS INTRODUCED IN EARLIER CHAPTERS

One way in which readers can grasp the existing CB model is to present the business in terms of concepts introduced in earlier chapters of the book. Figure 8.3 presents the CB constellation in terms of the co-productive, offering-centered, value-creation framework we introduced in Chapter 3, and which was presented in Figure 3.1.

Figure 8.4 presents CB's offering's dimensions, which was a framework which we also introduced in Chapter 3, and which was illustrated in Figure 3.2. The initial CB offering replaced the peopleware intensive check offering. It did so by changing the architecture of the offering, designing instead much more hardware- and software-intensive offerings.

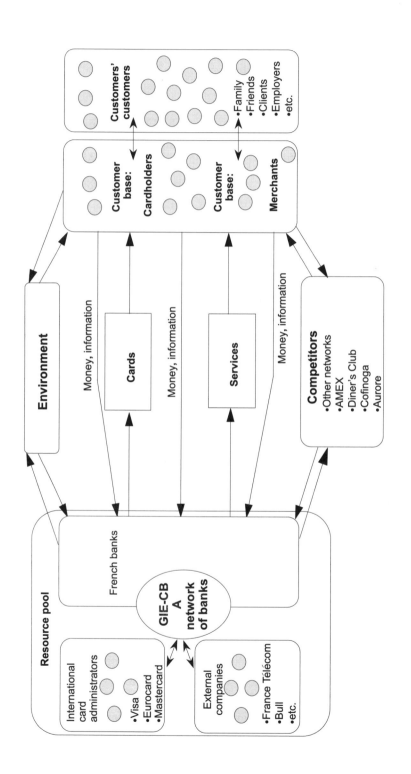

Figure 8.3 The CB value-creation system.

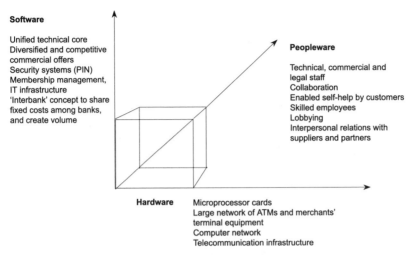

Software

Unified technical core
Diversified and competitive
commercial offers
Security systems (PIN)
Membership management,
IT infrastructure
'Interbank' concept to share
fixed costs among banks,
and create volume

Peopleware

Technical, commercial and
legal staff
Collaboration
Enabled self-help by customers
Skilled employees
Lobbying
Interpersonal relations with
suppliers and partners

Hardware   Microprocessor cards
Large network of ATMs and merchants'
terminal equipment
Computer network
Telecommunication infrastructure

Figure 8.4 The three dimensions of the CB offering.

The costly peopleware made up by bank employees who provided cash for people in their branches was transferred to the customer, who was glad to enter a self-service logic because of the convenience that a very extensive set of automated machines offered. In effect, the constellation which CB created made it attractive for banks to establish ATMs, whose use obtains about 30 percent of all gross revenues into the system. The 'back office' intensive use of peopleware was thus eliminated. The CB offering replaced it by a combination of hardware and software with far fewer people employed.

In addition to succeeding in its cost-reduction objectives, the new offering had the advantage of giving member banks access to information which checks made difficult, if not impossible, to obtain.

The information which the CB system enabled banks to collect increased the granularity, or resolution (see Chapter 3) with which they could relate to customers. This allowed them to segment customers more 'finely', better matching offerings to customers' value creation.

Finally, the system provided a level of security unheard of in other markets. In France, the fraud rate is 0.03 percent for lost, stolen or falsified cards. Including abusive use by the owner, the fraud rate is 0.05 percent. Compare this with the USA, where the risk for lost, stolen or falsified cards is between 0.10 percent and 0.15 percent. Including abusive use by the owner the American fraud rate is 0.30 percent. Including the credit risk (non-reimbursed credits) the total risk in the US is close to 2 or 3 percent. The high interest rates for credit cards in the US (up to 18 percent per year) are partially explained by this higher risk.

As explained before, the CB system is mainly based on debit cards. The lateness with which French retail banks expanded their card-based relationship with households into lending/credit offerings is explained by a CB director as follows:

> Credit cards and banks are two different activities. Risk management is also different. In France we have a Catholic and Mediterranean cultural profile. Consumer credit is not well developed. Banks are not very interested in these sectors because French customers are hostile to debts. Consumer credit is mainly made by specialized institutions like Cetelem, Sofinco, and Cofinoga.[22]

In the next section we overview how this winning combination is now challenged with the arrival of new, e-commerce technologies.

REDESIGNING THE CARTES BANCAIRES AND VISA OFFERINGS

The constellation established through Cartes Bancaires, and the related offerings, are being challenged by the advent of electronic commerce.

E-commerce will for example affect the software aspects of risk management. CB is well ahead of VISA in this respect, thanks to its early adoption of smart cards. The fraud rate for Carte Bleue cards now stands at 0.02 percent of sales volume, having decreased from 0.27 percent in 1987. This is because the equipment required to make 'false' smart cards is much more expensive than what magnetic strip cards require, and because software to trace use is much more effective.

But new Internet standards will replace the existing ones, at least in part. Monitoring and combating fraud within the new standards is being pursued by VISA in an initiative called SET (for 'secure electronic transaction'), which converges with joint ventures launched by VISA's

Technology Fund, a venture capital partnership it has opened to member financial institutions.

Through its Technology Fund, VISA outsources part of its R&D, just like Xerox (see Chapter 2) has done. It has invested in a speech-recognition technology with Nuance, in an e-commerce certification and infrastructure venture with Veriphone, and with Trintech in the SET protocol. To 'escape' the French smart card leadership, VISA has strategically invested in Proton, a Gemplus competitor.

The Groupement Carte Bleue launched Secured Electronic Commerce on the Internet with the first international card transactions in October 1997. These transactions were performed within the framework of a pilot program led by Carte Bleue in France, which itself was part of the VISA SET initiative in Europe. Eighty member banks of VISA, representing 16 countries, took part in this operation. In France, the banks participating in this program are part of the 'Club SET', whose main objective is to promote the implementation of the international SET norm. The norm makes it possible to secure exchanges on the Internet, and to authenticate merchants and cardholders via their respective banks. For VISA, which has encountered problems (for example in the USA) of converting magnetic card systems into smart card ones, SET has the advantage of being compatible with both magnetic stripes as well as smart cards. This interoperability makes SET the universally recognized standard applicable to electronic commerce.

Such technical advances lead to changes in laws that allow offerings' architecture to be transformed. Thus, on 15 December 1998, the Carte Bleue VISA Purchasing Service obtained approval from the French tax authorities for the dematerialization of its invoices. This is the first time that an agreement of this type has been concluded in France in the financial sector. This agreement allowed Purchasing Service customers to legally rid themselves of paper-based invoices, officially recognizing the legal value of electronic invoices, which serve as the basis of any audits by tax inspectors. To take advantage of this dematerialization, users simply replace hardware for software, in the form of a software package which is provided by their bank.

As we saw above, this software is made up of very flexible, yet standardized functions allowing processing systems of 'buyer' and 'supplier' firms to be fully integrated.

As other aspects of life become digitalized, VISA and CB can broaden their offering to wider aspects of customers' value creation. Insurance and medical assistance are examples. Some banks are extending their services to include items such as medical assistance coverage, or a 'Snow and Mountain' insurance package. Studies conducted by Carte Bleue on healthcare card payments, which in France includes 1.2 million professionals, have shown that there is a major opportunity for French payment systems to 'invade' this world. Carte Bleue is working to increase co-operation between its members and the computerization of French healthcare reimbursement.

In 1996 Carte Bleue and VISA signed a new agreement aimed at boosting the development of the two brands. Marketing and advertising actions are jointly financed and organized, e.g. advertising and communication for the Olympic Games.

Yet the technology revolution that e-commerce poses is bound to fundamentally transform the relationship which has existed to date.

> For instance, the EMV norm, which was developed jointly by EuroCard-MasterCard and VISA, was chosen as the standard for the next generation of chips by CB. Chips on the Carte Bleue will have migrated to EMV by the year 2000. While this norm reinforces security, it also further facilitates interoperability with non-French chip card programs, meaning that the 'technical advantage' isolation of the French system will be further breached.
>
> But EMV chips also make it possible to broaden the payment offering, enabling future cards to contain multi-application functions. Java is the programming language chosen by VISA to develop EMV multi-application smart cards. The Java Card makes it easier to broaden the offering to include other value-creation activities by bank customers such as transportation, health, loyalty.

To secure the opportunities which new technologies afford in terms of innovative offerings, GIE-CB is also testing a PME, 'Porte Monnaie

Electronique' (Electronic Purse), a payment card specially designed to pay for small amounts. This card has been initially used for paying for parking spaces, phone calls, and public transportation (bus, metro). It can later be expanded to other uses – it is attractive from a cash flow point of view. Basically the PME is a rechargeable stored value card, that can be 'charged' with a certain amount of money in a bank ATM, allowing one to then use this stored value (the 'charge') to pay for small purchases. The use of the PME does not require the client's signature or the typing of confidential codes. Just the insertion of the PME in a specially designed slot is enough to validate the transaction. So in effect, the design of the PME card implies the creation of yet another alternative monetary circuit, which again offers members the transformation of what would otherwise be a contextual environment factor into a part of their (collective) transactional environment.

The GIE-CB is also discussing electronic commerce norms with other potential partners.[23] The present system is based on software encoding of the credit card numbers. This system is entirely based on software following a VISA/MC encoding norm.

According to a CB Director:

> Internet is an excellent opportunity but it is also dangerous, very dangerous. If the payment system through the Internet is not well conceived it can destroy the payment cards industry. The possibilities for fraud are enormous. The software encoding of card numbers is not enough because all codes can be broken.[24]

The GIE-CB is proposing a different system, based on its microprocessor-equipped cards. It has the advantage of already having the cards. According to GIE-CB's proposition, Internet money transfers would be authorized only if the customers insert their individual payment card in specially designed card readers linked to their personal computer. The advantage is that the card numbers do not enter the Internet. Following these procedures, the security level would be much higher. The problem with this proposition is that each computer connected to the system would need to be equipped with a special card reader.

Regarding the Euro, as the bulk of payment operations are done at the domestic level, the arrival of the currency is not considered as presenting an immediate, enormous danger. CB cards have technical resources (codes) that enable the payment with Euros using the same CB cards now used. While the same authorization procedure can be used, sales terminals require adaptation. The transition period (from FF to Euro) is scheduled between 1999 and 2002. From 2002, customers will be able to use all CB cards to make payments in Euros.

Yet the arrival of the Euro in Europe, which renders the monetary unit of analysis common among the EU countries, may make the 'national' aspect which CB used as a support to reach its 'virtuous circle' more difficult to refer to. Perhaps the virtuous circle no longer requires this 'nationalistic' support which helped to get it going in the first place. But like Netscape/Microsoft, the test for its ongoing viability will be challenged by actors offering things other than payment facilities to the customers of CB's customers.

REVISITING THE LESSONS OF VISA AND CB

Just as Nokia does (see Chapter 7), VISA and CB extend their activities to include what for members would otherwise remain 'contextual' infringements on their transactional environments. They influence these widened environments in ways that make business sense for these members.

Thus, for example, despite changing technologies, VISA and CB can get involved in, and shape technical standards and their evolution, setting a pace of innovation that their members can afford.

> We made huge productivity efforts. Our commissions are low and the fraud rates are among the lowest worldwide. The CB system is a success. French banks may not be excellent in other activities but with the cards we are among the best ... Client satisfaction rates are very high. The average age of merchants' terminals is 7.5 years. We made efforts to anticipate standards. A merchant who buys a CB terminal can be sure it will be usable for at least seven years. Banks and merchants have the same interest in keeping the same standards.[25]

Because of their role as influencers of their members' transactional environments, both VISA and the CB system exhibit a duality between co-operation and competition which regulators accustomed to policing only actor-centered organizations find hard to deal with. On the one hand, there is competition among the banks to get the clients. On the other hand, members joined forces to be able to enhance their effectiveness.

According to some European Community officers, some of the practices which VISA and CB have engaged in should be changed to enhance free competition among the card systems. Yet, according to two CB directors: 'The best evidence of the existence of a cartel is the stability of market shares. In our case market shares are not stable.'[26]

In recent years the CB system has been in conflict with some European Community (EC) organizations that try to change the contracts the CB system imposes to the affiliated merchants. EC officers say that the CB system attacks merchants' freedom by insisting (via the standard CB contract) that they charge the same prices, whether the payment is with CB or with money or checks. These EC officers say merchants should be able to charge clients more if payments are done with cards.

The GIE-CB opposes this position, saying that the essence of the system is to offer the best service to customers. They argue that the commission they charge the merchants covers insurance, and a built-in accounting system which should not be paid for by the merchants' customers.

But the problem, in our view, is that the EC position does not take into account the specific, influence-based market-making position which VISA and CB occupy. They are not in the same actor-centered market-making business that their members are in. The influence that they offer is inherently interactive. Thus, according to a CB executive, the very existence of a payment system implies the constitution of an agreement among several partners:

> What we sell is an agreement. We sell a pack of agreements: between merchants and customers, between merchants and banks, between customers and banks, and among banks (to accept payments). The agreement is the essence of the business. We sell an agreement. But an agreement is illegal according to the Rome Treaty (articles 95.1 and 95.3). We spend a lot of our time explaining to EC officers why our

practices are not blocking free competition. . . . It is illegal to try to control prices. So the CB system does not have detailed data on costs which could be interpreted by regulatory organisms as signs of a tentative to control prices. . . . Some banks doubled their market shares of CB transactions in 10 years. This only can happen because there is competition.[27]

It is precisely because of their influence-centered positions that both the VISA and CB systems can be regarded as not offending free competition principles. The prime mover position which this role affords means that the argument it entails would apply even if there was only one payment network: no one to our knowledge has argued that 'money' prevents competition! This is because the payment networks that both VISA and CB offer are interaction-facilitating ones. The offerings of both VISA and CB render it possible for their members to make many more different offerings available to retailers and households, to companies and their employees, because their offerings increase the available level of granularity (see Chapter 3). The VISA and CB offerings do so by better linking 'information' and 'money' for households, retailers, and banks than any alternative systems have allowed to date.

Both the VISA and CB systems can be seen as (single) network(s) having many access doors. The competition among the access doors (the banks) is to get the resources (the clients – consumers and merchants). The network makes strong competition among a large number of differentiated offerings possible.

The CB system was made possible because the member banks gave up part of their individual independence, relying on an inter-banking organization to influence other actors in ways that would enhance their obtaining collective independence; or even better and more accurately, collective interdependence. However, the co-operation is ground for intense competition among the banks. In this interactive sense, collaboration and competition are not incompatible, but complementary.

We can expect that as Internet-based e-commerce takes hold, many more prime movers making markets by influencing others will emerge, and that thus, the VISA and CB form of market making will be seen as forerunners of what will become a common breed.

Appreciative Market   9
Making: When Becoming a
Prime Mover Is Not the Driving
Goal

In this chapter, we explore the third type of market making which prime movers engage in: appreciative market making. This type of market making results from an original ambition that may be different from that of becoming a prime mover or market maker, but which involved rethinking and redesigning the factors which shape the behavior of actors who make up industries, or even parts of society. In some cases, the result may benefit society as a whole. This rethinking is the driving force of the firm's activities, which results in the prime mover firm making a market for itself and members of its constellation.

Built around a case study of Tetra Pak, the Swedish packaging giant, this chapter

- Describes how a global corporation got its start in a small country where one man had *an idea:* package milk into easy-to-use cartons.
- Shows how developing and acquiring the *capabilities* needed to make the idea a reality took decades of trials and errors; and how Tetra Pak continued to expand its market with new *innovations* that, again, required years of capability building.
- Offers a overall review at the end of the chapter of the succession of *different business models* that allowed Tetra Pak to first appreciate and then act on the opportunities to offer and improve packaging for milk and juice products.

THE ORIGINS OF A COMPANY BASED ON AN IDEA

In 1895 a man called Ruben Rausing was born close to Helsingborg in the southwest of Sweden. He graduated from the Stockholm School of Economics in 1918. He then won a scholarship and traveled to the USA for further studies at Columbia University in New York, which resulted in a Master of Science degree in 1920.

During his stay in the United States, Rausing studied American industry. Touring the East coast in an Overland car, he learned how recently devised economic systems theories were applied in practice. He was so impressed by the United States that he even considered moving there permanently.

Rausing was especially interested in the packaging field, as he had worked for a company in the packaging industry before he left for the US. In spite of his predilection for 'God's own country, the United States' he decided to go back to Sweden. He continued to work for the packaging company until he decided to leave in 1929 due to differences of opinions with the board.

What Rausing had recognized during his stay in the US was the opportunity radically to improve the packaging industry with the help of new technology. From his position within the Swedish company to which he had returned, he had wanted to pursue his ambitions and put these ideas into practice. But the board considered his suggestions too revolutionary.

So instead Ruben Rausing became part-owner of a smaller packaging company, the name of which was changed into Åkerlund & Rausing. The other major owner, Erik Åkerlund was primarily a financier, and Ruben Rausing was responsible for the operations of the company. The business was not very successful in the beginning, so in 1933 Rausing bought the shares from his partner and became the sole owner of the company. Gradually the company became more and more successful and grew to become a major packaging supplier to the Swedish food industry.

Åkerlund & Rausing made traditional packages at the time. Yet Rausing had a grand idea: to redesign the way milk was packaged. During his stay in the United States, he had seen carton milk packages, and he thought such packaging held interesting opportunities which could be further developed. As early as 1932, he asked a colleague, Holger Crafoord, to visit the USA and investigate how the methods for packaging milk in cartons had progressed in the United States.

Rausing had a vision about 'creating something new, but also something useful'. He believed that the role of organizations in society was to create a need for something hitherto unknown and then fulfill that need. In the 1930s, he made the following mission statement for Åkerlund & Rausing:

> The idea of the company, and the principles for its operations, form the foundation on which the company is built. Based on this idea the company gets its direction, will, spirit and life, it becomes a living creature instead of a dead mass. Its physical shape, buildings, machines and working procedures are built upon the guidelines from the idea. People who work in the company get their direction from the idea... If the company can create a need in the long term then the idea, on which it is based, has been right. The company has then fulfilled a function in society. The idea of our company is very simple: to rationalize the distribution of goods through purposeful consumption packages and proper transport packages.[1]

Ruben Rausing was convinced that dominant companies were built on ideas. He was also convinced that good ideas were the only thing which allowed a company, based in a small country like Sweden, to become internationally successful. While he measured the quality of an idea based on how well the idea contributed to enhance society's effectiveness, Rausing at the same time knew that an innovative company could survive only if it had earnings high enough to finance the implementation of its idea.

We consider the history of Rausing's success to correspond to the previously presented (see Chapter 7) AIC model's 'appreciative' category because the Rausing's convictions correspond with Smith's descriptions to a remarkable degree. Smith tells us:

> The human figure in the center of the [AIC] model is always we – the individual me, or the collective us. Our current purpose determines the

relevant power field. ... Our power is directly correlated with our purpose enacted within the space/time constraints that we choose. We are always the individual[s] in the center that is [are] in control. We make our choices [i.e., exercise control] based on the whole of our appreciation and influence, no matter where it comes from or no matter how conscious or unconscious. ... No matter what happens in our influenced or appreciated environments, information is passed through us as whole individuals or whole social units, families, organizations, communities. What goes through each individual passes through a unique set of filters. We cannot control the output. The uniqueness of each individual and each social unit has to be appreciated. By developing systems and processes that recognize that it is only the individual part of the system which has control, we automatically recognize the uniqueness of each individual. After appreciating the whole situation and sorting priorities and relationships with the other interested parts, the individual part makes its choices based on its own unique sense of the situation and its interests both conscious and unconscious. When we design systems and processes that value equally the appreciative, influence and control relationships, we make much more power [capacity to achieve purpose] available to that system.[2]

Ruben Rausing's big idea to change the way one could package milk, was something he worked on all the time. But its realization had to wait until 1944, when a new assistant in the research laboratory, Erik Wallenberg, was able to completely re-think the way the milk package should be designed. Wallenberg's insight was that if the package was based on the form of a tetrahedron, many of the technical problems which, until then, had been impossible to solve could be addressed and solved. This 'tetrahedron' idea was revolutionary. Erik Wallenberg first presented his insights to his own superior, Stig Sunner. They did not dare present the idea to Ruben Rausing until they jointly improved the prototype. It would be an exaggeration to say that the reception was highly enthusiastic, but Rausing was prepared to support some further investigations. As he later dryly commented: 'This is what can happen when one employs somebody who doesn't know anything about how a package shall be made and how it shall look'.

In spite of his skepticism, Rausing, a couple of weeks later, made the first patent application for the new package, in March 1944. The idea of using the tetrahedron as the basis for the package became gradually more and more promising, in step with the continued efforts to make this package adaptable to an industrial process.

Once the preliminary testing showed that the package could be used for packaging milk, some critical questions started to emerge. How should the package be formed, filled, and shut? Which form of paper should be used? How to make the material waterproof? And how should the filling machine look? The technical engineering that was required to solve all the problems related to the packaging machine called for the co-operation of many individuals, both within the technical department of Åkerlund & Rausing, and with outsiders.

The finding of the proper material was attacked in the same manner. Everybody involved worked continuously, with a strong conviction that the problems would be solved even if in the beginning nobody could clearly recognize how. At the end of 1950, the activities around the new package for milk were separated into a new company, Tetra Pak. Ruben Rausing's sons, Hans and Gad, were in 1954 appointed managing director and deputy managing director respectively. At this stage Tetra Pak had six employees.

The Rausing family cultivated a very 'low key' style, as was expected by Swedish culture, which at that time tended to frown upon deviation from established norms. Its members' ambition was to be, but not be seen. Both Gad (born 1922) and Hans (born 1926) had joined Åkerlund & Rausing in the late 1940s. Gad Rausing had studied chemical engineering, and Hans had studied languages, with Russian as his primary subject. Both brothers were fully committed to carrying forward their father's heritage. The management style they applied has been characterized as 'management by conviction'. When in 1993 Hans Rausing left his position as Chairman of the Tetra Pak board he commented: 'Things have not proceeded too badly in this small southern Swedish family company.'

The first explicit efforts to move forward on the idea of packaging milk in cartons took place in 1932, and sixty years later the Rausing brothers were among the ten richest people in Europe.

ADDRESSING CAPABILITIES

Several incidents contributed to rendering the idea of using the tetrahedron as the physical design for the package a commercial success.

A key person in this chain of developments was Harry Järud. He was a civil engineer who had been appointed by Ruben Rausing to take charge of time studies in Åkerlund & Rausing in 1942. Järud was the person who was convinced that the filling of the tetrahedron packages should take place continuously. This involved a process where the carton first was formed in a cylindrical shape, then the cylinder was filled with milk, and finally the cylinder was shut at both ends, forming the tetrahedron. He presented his idea for the first time in the beginning of 1945. But other development engineers were working on a different construction. When the head designer suddenly became ill, Järud was offered the position as head designer. In May 1946 Rausing gave him four months to produce a prototype. Järud was able to develop a prototype thanks to the participation of a number of smaller regional workshops, which contributed different parts of the prototype. During the years many of these workshops have maintained this subcontractor relationship with Tetra Pak, and have themselves grown along with the company.

Beyond Järud's innovation, a key missing link was still the carton. The whole second part of the 1940s involved a process of trial and error to deal with this issue. Numerous alternatives were investigated, but none worked properly. Yet Rausing was convinced that some day the material problem would be solved. And his son, Gad, was in the latter part of the 1940s given the responsibility of overseeing this part of the development. In the summer of 1946, people from Åkerlund & Rausing visited ICI in the UK to find out about a new plastics material, polyethylene. The following year, a group from Åkerlund & Rausing led by Gad Rausing visited the United States for four months. They visited some 90 companies to examine alternative material solutions. Many new ideas were found for Åkerlund & Rausing, but for the Tetra milk packaging problem, the only possibility identified was a new plastics material, a polystyrene, coded S-50.

Many visits to the USA followed. In 1951, a Chicago-based company called H.P. Smith was visited. This company had developed a method to laminate paper with polyethylene. This method was called extrusion. The Swedes asked whether this method could be used for the S-50 material as well. And the answer was yes!

Laboratory trials by Tetra Pak showed that the S-50 material was well suited for the required purposes. But as Tetra Pak started to negotiate the purchase of the S-50 material from the United States, it became evident that the producers of this material had been allocated for the Korean War's strategic production, and were not allowed to produce it for civilian purposes.

However, at the same time, in 1953, news reached Tetra Pak that new results with PE-coated paper might be a substitute. This proved to be the case. And Tetra Pak was involved in close co-operation with both ICI and DuPont in developing the material and the extruder. Thanks to its own developmental contribution, Tetra Pak got its own license for the extruder-laminator, and was not forced to pay any royalties to DuPont, who had developed the original extruder.

The same type of detailed product development was conducted also for the base paper, the carton. This development took place in close co-operation between, on the one hand, Åkerlund & Rausing (later Tetra Pak) and on the other hand, the Swedish pulp and paper industry. In addition, when the different parties discussed printing on the paper, substantial technological developments also took place. In this case most of the work was done within the company, but was based on closely following which technologies were available on the market. When Ruben Rausing commented on these developments, he once said: 'When you do something that nobody has ever done before, then it is actually quite difficult.'

The idea of packaging milk in carton board was something that Ruben Rausing had pursued for about 30 years before it became a commercial success. All the knowledge to make this idea a reality had been gathered into one single company, Tetra Pak. As they are here described, the elements were the technical concept, the design of the package, the material for the package, and the filling machine. They were all developed in parallel over these years. Rausing was convinced that one day all the pieces would be in place. And when that happened, Tetra Pak found itself holding a capability base which was completely unique in the whole world.

One could say that within the milk industry, Tetra Pak had become the equivalent of a 'world-class' Internet 'portal'. Tetra Pak had a knowledge hub that nobody else could challenge, and this knowledge would be manifested in a way of packaging and delivering content (milk!) that would prove to be much more effective than anything else available. In addition, the underlying demand was very much stronger than the one surrounding many of the 'virtual', digital portals that have been desperately fighting each other in the late 1990s. Tetra Pak built the foundation of its portal over a period of 50 years.

CREATING A MARKET

The patents and activities relating to the development of the concept of packaging milk in carton board started to create interest outside Åkerlund & Rausing at the end of the 1940s. As Tetra Pak was formed, it became necessary to make some official declaration about the future of the company. On 18 May 1951 Tetra Pak's first press conference was arranged. The press conference was a big success. One newspaper wrote:

> After almost 20 years of research and confidential trials, the iron curtain was raised, and the machine the whole dairy industry had waited for was presented. Those who had expected a sensation were not disappointed. It is more than a good package, it is a genius process.

The truth was that the presentation to the press was planned to the highest detail, and the impression given was of a machine that was much further developed than it actually was at that time. The major problem Tetra Pak still had to address was leaking packages. This proved to be such a challenge that as late as the 1970s, Ruben Rausing made a speech which he titled 'My leaking life'. During the press conference the participants were told that the packages, during the process, went through a 'secret part of the machine' behind a curtain. What actually happened behind the curtain was that a person manually changed the package into another one, which was secured not to leak!

In December 1952 the official commercial introduction of Tetra Pak was made. A small local dairy had used the Tetra Pak process on a trial basis since September, and in time for Christmas, this dairy started to offer 100 ml of cream in the tetrahedron package. The second customer was Mjölkcentralen (now Arla) the biggest Swedish dairy. They launched the same 100 ml cream package in November 1953. Expansion in Sweden was rapid, and the first 1 liter package was introduced in a dairy in Linköping in March 1957. The new package however, met with resistance from a considerable proportion of consumers. The glass bottle was preferred by many, and strong resistance was found especially in Gothenburg, which was the location of the glass works where most of the Swedish glass milk bottles were made. However, by the end of the 1950s the majority of Swedish milk was packaged in Tetra Pak packages.

For the Rausings Sweden was the platform from which a global conquest should take place. Already in a board meeting in January 1951 it had been decided that the trade mark 'Tetra Pak' should be registered in 57 countries. As the commercialization emerged, a key question was how to bundle the offering. It was heavily debated internally whether to sell or lease the machines. The final decision was to offer the machine on a lease basis.

Tetra Pak also considered what type of sales organization it should build. The solution was that in each country there could either be an agent who represented Tetra Pak, or they would establish a local subsidiary. As the market penetration grew, it also became necessary to establish local production of the laminated carton board, 'the Tetra paper'. Tetra Pak had in the beginning no financial resources to establish its own paper manufacturers locally, so production was arranged by licensing the rights to local producers Such agreements were. rapidly made in England, Finland, France, Holland, Norway, Germany and Austria. In 1960 the first production plant for packaging material outside Sweden was started up in Mexico.

As sales efforts increased, it became evident that the contractual leasing agreement, with strict commitments from both sides, was a difficult challenge for agents to meet. The agreement implied that the agent had to supply customers with continuous support, effective paper delivery logistics, technical maintenance, spare parts, technical services, etc. For many local agents, it was difficult to provide all these offering elements well. And so, in many cases, the start up with a local agent was followed by a gradually increased presence of Tetra Pak personnel in the country – first, through the establishment of a local sales office, and later, through the establishment of a local plant to produce packaging material.

CONQUERING THE WORLD

The first Tetra Pak machine to be exported went to Alster Milchwerk in Hamburg, Germany, in 1954. The next year Hans Rausing made his first trip to the Soviet Union. As he had studied Russian at University, he was well equipped to take responsibility for this market.

It took Hans Rausing four years before the first Russian order was received, in the autumn 1959. It was for eight tetrahedron machines. To get this business, Tetra Pak had to compromise on its lease agreement, as in Moscow only purchasing was possible. This was something which created great concerns within Tetra Pak management, but the board decided to approve the Russian requirements because it was felt that the first deal would open up opportunities for continuous business in the future. During the 1960s, this business was more or less restricted to the orders for carton. No additional filling machine orders were obtained, to the disappointment of Tetra Pak. But then, in 1969, Tetra Pak got a new order for some 20 aseptic tetrahedron filling machines. This solution was very attractive for the Soviet Union, due to its relatively undeveloped distribution system. And soon after, Tetra Pak got an additional order for material for six packaging plants, to deliver material for the tetrahedron machines. This order was in total about SEK45 million, one of the biggest Tetra Pak had ever had. They discovered, however, that the Russians had copied the Tetra Pak machines and installed their own copies in a number of dairies. As one

Tetra Pak salesman joked: 'We delivered 28 tetrahedron machines, of which now 1,350 are installed.'

But the locally copied machines did not work properly and the Tetra Pak system soon got a bad reputation. This was not Tetra Pak's fault, as Tetra Pak had nothing to do with the machines that the Russians themselves had produced. Neither had Tetra Pak any responsibility for the material production for these machines, as this also was done entirely by the Russians.

Yet, with the introduction of Tetra Brik, the situation changed for two reasons. First, the Soviet Union now had become a member of the International Patent Union. As they wanted protection for their own patents on the world market, they also had to respect the patents belonging to Tetra Pak. Second, the technology around Tetra Brik was so complicated that this process was much more difficult to copy. The first Tetra Brik order for the Soviet Union took place in 1973, and since then Tetra Pak has had a continuous, and successful, business with Russia. Tetra Pak had been prepared to take risks in the Soviet Union because it had seen that the development of food processing and distribution in the long term would be one of the major areas for investment. The central promoter of the relationships with the Russians had always been Hans Rausing. He became, over the years, a highly recognized and respected person within Russia, and was, for example, elected in 1995 as a member of the Russian Council for Trade and Industry, which has only 25 members.

Hans Rausing's approach to the development of the Russian part of Tetra Pak was evident in the early 1990s. He responded to a question asking when he thought the conversion of currencies would enable Tetra Pak to bring profits home from Russia:

> This question is not actually something I am very much bothered about. All profits are needed locally, to continue further to edify the food industry in the country. Countries like Russia, Ukraine, etc. have a crying need of our help, and of our products. It is our responsibility to assist.

Like his father Hans Rausing expressed the conviction that the idea about genuinely doing something important to help society become effective was priority number one. Later on profits would come. These laudable humanitarian values luckily coincided with what turned out to be extremely good business, enabling the Rausings to avoid facing a situation where they would have to chose between business and ethics.

Tetra Pak started its penetration of the important European markets in the first half of the 1950s. The first French order, in September 1954, for 14 tetrahedron filling machines for a 500 ml package, was made by one of the biggest dairy companies in France, Les Fermiers Réunis. When the tetrahedron packages, *les berlingots*, entered the retail shops in France, the glass bottle manufacturers did all they could to maintain their position. The 500 ml size did not attract the French either, as they were used to the 1 liter bottle. Once the 1 liter package was introduced, the 1960s saw the market share for Tetra Pak products gradually increase. An important element in this development was that Tetra Pak France rapidly recognized the interest of actively educating retailers about the distribution advantages which the Tetra Pak packaging system afforded. The catch-phrase they came up with was: '*Don't take the bottle* – buy the Tetra Pak'.

Italy was the focus of the dairy industry in 1956, when the tri-annual International Dairy Federation Conference was held in Rome in September. This conference also hosted an exhibition of dairy machinery. Tetra Pak was present at the exhibition. As the Italian market expanded, Tetra Pak in 1963 decided to place its first European packaging material plant outside Sweden in Rubiera, Italy. Production commenced at the new plant in 1965. For over two decades, Italy would be the number one market for Tetra Pak by volume.

Tetra Pak also entered the American market and Japan in the 1950s. China would not come into the picture until 1972, when Tetra Pak participated in an industrial exhibition arranged by the Swedish Export Council. And it would wait another seven years before the first order from China was received. This was a filling machine for production of juice. The problem Tetra Pak faced in China was access to packaging material. The volumes were too small to support local paper production, but without this in place, it seemed impossible to create a genuine interest in the Tetra Pak system.

Gad Rausing had the responsibility for developing Tetra Pak's Chinese strategy. Helped by his history and archeology interests, he quickly managed to become a respected counterpart for the high level Chinese authorities. In discussions with them, he decided that Tetra Pak was well advised to make a licensing agreement with a local paper manufacturer. But the negotiations were difficult, and it was not easy to find a solution that could satisfy both parties.

In July 1984, the Chinese prime minister, Zhao Ziyang, officially visited Sweden. As Tetra Pak was one of the major Swedish exporters to China, Rausing was invited as an honored guest at a dinner arranged for the prime minister by the Swedish minister for foreign affairs. After the dinner, late into the evening, Rausing and Zhao Ziyang discussed the license negotiations. A couple of weeks later Rausing was able to close a deal with Beijing Pulp and Paper Mill regarding licensing the paper production. Production of local Chinese paper started in 1987, and in the 1990s the Chinese market rapidly developed. In the discussions regarding the continual development of Tetra Pak's Chinese business Gad Rausing became a close business partner also to Zhu Rongji, at that time still Mayor of Shanghai.

As all these examples have shown, the perseverance with which Tetra Pak developed its markets, one by one, has been helped by the fact that the company has remained family owned. This has enabled Tetra Pak to take a genuinely long view. When Tetra Pak has had to take on the most important challenges, family members themselves, with the authority this brings, have been the ones in charge.

TRANSFORMING THE BUSINESS MODEL THROUGH EXTERNAL CAPABILITIES

Since the 1950s, Tetra Pak's management had recognized that further developing its capabilities would allow milk not only to be pasteurized and packaged into carton, but also aseptically treated. This would render milk completely free of bacteria, which would open enormous possibilities for Tetra Pak and for the actors in its value constellations. It would become possible to store milk for considerably longer, no longer requiring cold storage. Savings, as well as enhanced convenience for household customers, would be significant.

Again the Rausings proved to be open and flexible in pursuing this goal. In 1954 they learned that a Swiss industrial development group, called Ursina, had achieved important scientific advancements regarding milk processing. In November 1954 the first contacts with Ursina were made. The discussions with Ursina, and their development company, Alpura, immediately revealed a common interest.

The process equipment developed by Ursina, called the Uperisator, was based on steam treatment providing a fast and gentle sterilization of milk. This process had only minor impacts on the taste and nutritional value of the milk. Ursina had brought its own process capabilities into industrial production offerings by producing milk-based desserts this way. The package used by them was a metal can. For regular milk, however, this package was too expensive. So Ursina was interested in finding a new package in which milk could be filled, using their sterilization method.

Some first joint trials took place in 1955, but they were not very successful. Ursina however wanted to proceed. Tetra Pak was reluctant as it felt that confidential elements of the Tetra Pak technology might be used by Ursina, constituting a form of industrial espionage. Two years later, in 1957, a legal solution was worked out allowing the joint experiments to continue. The research and the experiments proved to be a much more demanding task than either party had expected.

But the efforts were worthwhile. At a press conference in Bern, Switzerland, in September 1961 the management of both Tetra Pak and Alpura presented the revolutionary new aseptic method of filling milk into carton packages. The process consisted of the following steps:

1   The plastic-coated carton material goes through a mixture of peroxide of hydrogen to sterilize the material.
2   The material is formed into a tube, which is vertically sealed.
3   Radiated heat from an electrical element within the tube develops an

ascending stream of sterile hot air, and at the same time all peroxide of hydrogen becomes steam.

4   In the lower part of the carton tube is a filling pipe, through which the sterilized milk is continuously flowing. The filling pipe is below the surface of milk within the carton tube, avoiding the building of foam.

5   The sealing of the carton tube, to form the tetrahedron, takes place below the liquid level, through the filled package. The entire process is continuous, and takes place in a single machine which both forms and fills the packages.

The method was simple enough to be industrialized and enabled Tetra Pak to build a filling machine that could fill the package aseptically using the process developed by Ursina/Alpura. The commercial name for the milk produced this way was aseptic milk. And the process was called UHT, Ultra High Temperature. This referred to the fast heating of the milk to considerably higher temperatures than those which pasteurizing involved.

The UHT process was revolutionary. Milk could now be bought and stored for relatively long periods. But the risks were also considerable. If some part of the process was not sterile, then the package would contain contaminated milk. And as milk was nutrition for both children and the very old, contamination risks had to be treated very seriously. Because of this, Tetra Pak proceeded carefully and quite slowly with this new offering.

The first markets entered with UHT milk, after Switzerland, were France, Italy, and Germany. The method still had its problems, and had to await the mid-1960s, when the carton was laminated with aluminum, to become sufficiently reliable to make more aggressive penetration possible. Aluminum also provided better protection against the impact of light and air.

Thanks to the 'capability focus' initiative it had entered in its business modeling (see Figure 4.5 on page 106), Tetra Pak again had developed an offering which was unique in the whole world. To offer long-life milk was something nobody had been able to do previously. The interest around the Tetra Pak concept grew rapidly. This allowed Tetra Pak to stipulate very demanding conditions in its contracts with producers on the first part of the production process, the sterilizing equipment. The bacteriological requirements were defined in greatest detail to secure the quality of the aseptic process. Dairy customers had to be educated to respect the requirements of super hygienic procedures in the plant. Tetra Pak required the personnel of the dairy to go through its educational program to make sure that the operators were sufficiently trained, allowing them to handle the process in line with the hygienic requirements that rendered it effective.

The new offering, consisting of UHT-sterilized milk and aseptic packaging, was more expensive than pasteurized milk. But Tetra Pak sales people did all they could to convince the dairies, and their customers (the wholesalers and retailers) that the higher cost per liter would be offset by cost savings in distribution and logistics. Retrospectively, some of the calculations supporting the arguments may have been partly inaccurate... Yet, the final decision was made by the consumer. During the second half of the 1960s, aseptically produced milk gained market share all over the world. The UHT method was also applied to juice.

In the first installations of the aseptic process technological problems still emerged, and many customers complained. To face these, Tetra Pak management launched a saying reflecting their 'think positively' attitude:

Remember that every complaint is the entering gate to a new order!

The success of Tetra Pak was sealed by yet another revolutionary innovation: the 'Tetra Brik' package.

We saw above that the 1-liter tetrahedron had been a technically challenging product. But it was also a cumbersome package from the consumer's point of view. It was difficult to carry in the shopping bag, and on the table it was hard to handle without spilling milk. In spite of this by 1959 there were filling machines for the tetrahedron in 30 countries. But most of them were for smaller packages, such as the 100 ml cream package. Tetra Pak calculated that about 1 billion packages were produced by Tetra Pak equipment per year at that time.

In the spring of 1959, Tetra Pak management participated in an exhibition called Wiener Frühjahremesse. In this exhibition, they discovered that a German company was presenting a new milk package called Zupack. This package could be described as a paper package, with thin walls, in rectangular form. Tetra Pak took this very seriously, as it recognized that a less cumbersome form of the package would be an attractive, more practical option for both the dairies and the consumers. The person who was appointed in charge of the development of a rectangular package was Åke Gustafsson, director of research and development at Tetra Pak.

The competition was also moving. In 1962 Elopak, a Norwegian firm, acquired the European license for the American Pure Pak package, which was a rectangular, gable-top package. Elopak aggressively promoted its own solution, and there were campaigns in the press against the clumsy 1 liter tetrahedron package. In March 1963, the first Tetra Brik-packaged milk (the name Tetra Brik came from the word brick, as the form of the package was more or less similar to a brick) was offered to the market in the Stockholm region. The product was far from finalized, and Tetra Pak had to offer the dairies considerable support during the first year of production. As one dairy manager expressed it: 'It required blood, sweat and milk, but never tears!'. The amount of milk that spilled during interruptions in the production process was considerable.

The difficulties Tetra Pak had this time offered a good set of opportunities for Elopak, which was able to gain considerable market share in Sweden and in the rest of the Nordic countries. The Nordic dairy market has since then been divided between these two companies. Afterwards, Tetra Pak expressed its thanks to its very good sales force, which was able to maintain customer relationships during a period when its offering's technical quality could by no means be classified as excellent...

The major advantage of the Tetra Brik package offering was the way it revolutionized the logistics around milk. The Tetra Brik package was designed so that it was compatible with the new distribution logic based on bulk handling and standardized pallets. The new standard was manifested in the so-called EUR-pallet, a transport pallet measuring 80 x 120 centimeters. Over the years, Tetra Pak developed a whole logistical concept relating this standard to its own offering:

- the 1 liter Tetra Brik package,
- the Tetra Wraparound solution, a corrugated carton box for 6--24 liters,
- the Tetra Tray, a corrugated carton tray for 12--18 liters,
- the Tetra Multi Shrink, a film-covered transport package,
- the Tetra Crate, a returnable plastic box for the small retailer,
- the Tetra Mini Pallet, and
- the Tetra Roll Container.

Tetra Pak first tested its distribution and logistics solutions mostly on the Swedish market. Based on these experiences, the solutions were later exported to other markets. And in doing so, Tetra Pak was instrumental in changing the whole milk industry in many countries all over the world. One such example is Spain.

RECONFIGURING THE SPANISH MILK INDUSTRY

Spain has a population of about 40 million people. The annual milk consumption in the mid-1990s was about 106 liters per capita. Of the total milk consumption, Tetra Pak estimated that 83 percent of the total volume was UHT milk, one of the highest percentages in the world. And this milk was almost solely packaged into Tetra Pak packages.

In about 20 years the whole structure of the milk-producing industry had changed, thanks to the revolutionary offering developed by Tetra Pak.

In 1969, a dairy company called Leche Pascual, SA was founded. Its initial production capacity was 30,000 liters per annum. In 1973 this company bought its first Tetra Pak equipment, a production line for Tetra Brik UHT milk.

Gradually more and more production lines were introduced. Twenty years later, Leche Pascual had three production plants. The original factory at Aranda de Duero had reached a production capacity of 400 million liters of milk per annum. The Lugo milk plant, produced 180 million litres of milk per annum, and a milk factory in Montauban, France, had a production capacity of 100 million litres per annum. The equipment used by Leche Pascual was, in all these outlets, provided by Tetra Pak.

By 1997 Leche Pascual did business under four different trademarks, and its offering range included, besides UHT-milk, juice, mineral water, yoghurt, puddings, butter, and infant milk. A specialty produced by Leche Pascual with the help of Tetra Pak was liquid eggs.[3]

By 1997 Leche Pascual, was the second biggest producer of liquid milk in Spain, and by quality it was regarded as number one. It had an ISO 9000 certification as well as a 14 000 environment certification. Its turnover exceeded US$500 million.

As part of the quality concept, Leche Pascual proudly described the production process in the following way in a company brochure:

> During the production process, milk is submitted to a direct vapor injection at 148°C for 2.4 seconds (uperization process) which conveys its long life, whilst maintaining its vitamins, proteins and minerals, as well as its natural taste and color. Milk is packaged in Tetra Briks, which avoids any alteration of the product and facilitates its storage. Samples are taken at the beginning, during, and at the end of each production batch, to control the quality of the product, and its packaging. Testing includes the most advanced analytical methods, such as the bioluminescence technique for the analysis of milk microbiology.

For Leche Pascual, the Tetra Pak process offering represents the standard and benchmark for good quality. And it is not only Leche Pascual who holds this view. In its Spanish customer newsletter *Tetra News*, one can read the advertising campaigns of Tetra Pak's Spanish customers includind Asturiana, Ato, Lauki, Puleva, García Carrión, Juver, Ram, Nestlé etc. – in other words all the major dairies in Spain.

When representatives of Leche Pascual were asked by one of the authors to evaluate their co-production with Tetra Pak, they enthusiastically praised the close co-operation and trusting relationship. They said that the most important thing in the history of Leche Pascual had been the pioneering work done on UHT and Tetra Packaging in 1969--73. The technology that was adopted then was considered by them to be the basis for the whole success story of Leche Pascual.

For Leche Pascual, Tetra Pak is a genuine partner who supports the company well beyond solving technical matters relating to filling machines and packaging problems. Tetra Pak makes its own international network available as a source of knowledge, helping Leche Pascual develop its business. The responsiveness of Tetra Pak staff was also mentioned as an important element in the joint value-creation process between Tetra Pak and Leche Pascual.

Tetra Pak Spain has developed into one of the biggest Tetra Pak subsidairies outside Sweden. The activities handled by the local office can be divided into two parts: ongoing handling of day-to-day activities and development projects. Both these activities are supported by Tetra Pak's technical service organization, which has regional service offices around the country. Technical service is extremely important to keep the customers' plants running. Technical service provides preventive and corrective maintenance, spare parts, exchange parts, problem solving and trouble shooting, modifications of equipment and machines, and training.

From the point of view of Tetra Pak, not all customers are like Leche Pascual, whose business model is to be a high quality, premium price supplier in its own market. Tetra Pak has also customers whose business model is one of cost leadership. For such customers, it is important that Tetra Pak can provide very cost efficient, not fancy, offerings. Tetra Pak's large market share in Spain has proved that the company has been able to understand thoroughly how-value creation processes vary between different customers, finding a role in different business model orientations.

CONCLUSIONS

In 1965 the Rausing family became convinced that the milk industry was the value constellation on which they should focus as prime movers. They sold the original company where Ruben Rausing had started his entrepreneurial career, Åkerlund & Rausing. All capital gained from that sale was used to finance the expansion of Tetra Pak.

During the period 1970--85, 17 factories for production of packaging material were built all over the world. By the mid-1990s, Tetra Pak produced more than 75 billion packages a year, to distribute 45 billion liters of liquid food. To support this, Tetra Pak employed more than 20,000 people and had 50 plants producing packaging material and 10 plants for machine assembly. A total of 127 countries had customers directly supported by Tetra Pak. In 1996 the sales of Tetra Pak reached 9.2 billion Swiss francs.

The company monograph of Tetra Pak was written in 1995 by Lars Leander, a retired Tetra Pak senior vice-president. Leander, makes the reflection that Sweden should be recognized as an important spring board for Tetra Pak's success. Sweden had established capabilities, leading resources, and a long tradition not only to provide but to develop the inputs Tetra Pak utilized. These included, first, the steel for the filling machines, and the carton for the packaging. Second, together with dairies in Denmark, Finland, and Holland, Swedish dairies were among the most sophisticated in the world. Milk consumption has always been exceptionally high in these countries. Third, the geography of Sweden called for world-class distribution effectiveness, and Ruben Rausing could, first at Åkerlund & Rausing and then in Tetra Pak, follow the development of Sweden's distribution sector. And fourth, the retail sector developed earlier in Sweden than in most other countries due to the comparatively high standard of living in the 1960s and 1970s. Tetra Pak not only built upon these pre-conditions, but actively contributed in the shaping of what was to become the 'Swedish model'.

The co-production between Tetra Pak and the biggest Swedish dairy, Arla, was an important reference for Tetra Pak's commercial expansion. Numerous visiting delegations from abroad were brought to Sweden to see how the total redesign of the milk handling process, from the farm to the consumer, had taken place. These developments had been made possible by offerings developed by Tetra Pak and Alfa Laval, the other Swedish systems developer for milk processing which Tetra Pak acquired in 1991.

When describing the reasons behind the success of Tetra Pak, Leander attributes a major role to Tetra Pak's corporate culture. Its decision-making style has been flexible and fast, but when necessary, serious and in depth considerations were allowed. 'The best decisions come about by themselves' became a favorite saying in Tetra Pak.

The need to think before acting was widely accepted and promoted. The fact that the original idea took more than 20 years to become a commercial reality rendered this approach credible. Another aspect of the culture which Leander underlines is responsiveness and availability. Both brothers, Hans and Gad, made sure that they were always available to the organization. During trade exhibitions, the two brothers themselves made sure they were there, all day, at the fair. These occasions were seen as extremely important information-gathering opportunities as well as settings in which new business possibilities were found or exploited.

The Rausings were also very cost-conscious. In the beginning this was a necessity, as there was a long period when the investments were larger than cash flow. But as times improved, the same conservative approach to spending continued. One statement that Ruben Rausing always used with his colleagues was that 'a package has to save more than it costs'.

Perhaps the most important ingredient in the picture laid forth by Leander has to do with *intuition*. In difficult decision-making situations, the management of Tetra Pak relied on their personal perceptions, often not yet explicable in formal rational reasoning. This *appreciation-based* decision-making process was also used in groups.

The management team's longevity has facilitated individuals challenging, but also trusting, each other. To one young manager Hans Rausing once sent an article with the title: 'Good managers play it by ear – they just muddle through' ... This took place just before the manager entered a six-week course in marketing. The message was clear: don't lose your own judgment irrespective of new improved techniques. Another popular quote from the management philosophy was "Long-term views – yes, but long-term forecasts – no!'. In the 1990s these insights have been highly appreciated outside Tetra Pak as well!

But Leander does not forget the most important part of the success: the lease agreement – reminiscent of Xerox's as reviewed in Chapter 2. This contract stipulated that the filling machine had to be operated with carton produced by Tetra Pak. The production of this carton was something where Tetra Pak in practice created a monopoly situation towards its customers. The most important aspects of Tetra Pak's income flow, and of its profits, were generated through selling carton, not through the sale of machines. And carton was the most critical piece in the reliability of the production process.

REFLECTIVE ANALYSIS

Tetra Pak was a market-making idea which was first cultivated in the environment of a more traditional company, Åkerlund & Rausing, for more than 20 years.

The idea, first presented by Ruben Rausing, and subsequently energetically followed up by his sons Gad and Hans, was not primarily focused on the business side, in the sense of quarterly earnings, profits, cash flow, shareholder value, or market share. It had more to do with the conviction, the intuition, that something big and important had to be done, and could be done.

In the beginning the idea reflected 'needs' which from Rausing's point of view were in the contextual environment: food production, processing, and distribution. Through his actions and, more importantly, though interactions, the idea became manifested institutionally as Tetra Pak. As a prime mover, the organization Tetra Pak transactionally shaped a market. This market reflects phenomena which originally could only be appreciated. As Tetra Pak expanded and redefined the boundary between control and influence, and – more importantly – between influence and context, it converted parts of the contextual environment into something belonging to its own value constellation. So the whole milk distribution system in Sweden changed thanks to Tetra Pak's role as prime mover. For other firms in the dairy industry, like the producers of milk bottles, this development had to be regarded as a change in the contextual environment. But for Tetra Pak, the market-making prime mover, this change was a result of its own decisive efforts to develop its own offerings, and at the same time strongly influence the environment. For Tetra Pak the transactional part of the environment, which could be influenced, encompassed a much bigger portion than for the bottle manufacturer, for which most of the environment had to be treated as a contextual one.

The evolution of Tetra Pak is reflected in the evolution of its business model. Its offerings enhanced efficiency and effectiveness for a whole industry (milk processing), and then other industries (juice), constituting an unprecedented value constellation that did not correspond to the established 'industry'-defined boundaries. As the example of Leche Pascual illustrates, those who co-produced the value constellation with Tetra Pak as prime mover participated in a new, unprecedented value constellation, sharing and jointly shaping the value creation.

All through these developments, the Rausings were very cost-conscious, as they knew that the milk industry could not increase the cost of milk for the final consumer. This meant that within Tetra Pak's business model, *lean management* was a central issue. Initially, *customer orientation* played an important role. Introducing semi-finished offerings to some of the more sophisticated, high-potential dairy customers meant that handling customer relationships became a very important capability within Tetra Pak. As technical problems were mastered, the common history of sharing the pain in many cases created even stronger bonds between the customer and Tetra Pak. Such struggles cemented a co-productive trust which competitors would find impossible to break into.

Tetra Pak in the 1950s could be characterized as exhibiting a business model that simultaneously contained *market making* and *customer orientation*, and some elements of *lean management*. But this business model changed in the 1960s. As the technologies became more reliable, Tetra Pak very swiftly and firmly shifted its business model into *capability focus*. As the offering's technical capabilities became robust, Tetra Pak's main challenge was to make its offerings available to new customers all over the world, and as quickly as possible. But as market after market became saturated, Tetra Pak has had to change its business model to become more *customer orientated* again – for different reasons than those which sparked its 1950s customer orientation. At that time, customer orientation concerned gathering information from customers, and addressing problems relating to the hardware part of the offering. In the 1990s, the reason for adopting a customer-orientation business model related to diminishing growth potentials. Tetra Pak had reached the most interesting customers worldwide, with its basic mix of offerings related to carton packages for liquid food. And so, in acquiring Alfa Laval in 1991, Tetra Pak clearly signaled that it wanted to build additional capabilities to serve its existing customers better. Subsequent to the acquisition, the role of the newly merged Tetra Laval was described as follows:

> Tetra Pak's integration with Alfa-Laval Liquid Food means that the company now has the equipment and expertise to prepare and process liquid foodstuffs. Resources now allow for the development, processing, marketing, installation, and servicing of equipment, production lines, and complete factories.

In 1989, the International Food Institute nominated the Tetra Pak aseptic offering for long-life milk 'the most significant invention in the food industry in the last fifty years'. Significance is an important element in open systems thinking.[4] Significance is the ultimate reason for one actor to become more influential than another one. The ultimate test of significance is if an actor is able to change the world. Tetra Pak has passed this test for significance.

PROSPECTIVE ANALYSIS: POSSIBLE FUTURE FOR APPRECIATIVE MARKET MAKING

For the twenty-first century Tetra Laval foresees a trend whereby dairies will be consolidated into even bigger units. For example, in the Nordic area, the late 1990s have seen on-going discussions about combining the biggest dairies in Sweden, Denmark, and Finland into one single dairy. Rational large-scale production of high-demand products would be the guiding concept for such a business.

In our view, Tetra Laval will need to revisit its market-making history to continue its success. It will need to understand better how the appreciative skills – which rendered it successful in the past – can be articulated within the context of a large, successful corporation. Tetra Laval's current large size, recognized market-making authority, and control of the many capabilities and resources it has successfully developed, may hinder this reflection on the past.

As Smith put it:

> I had thought that knowledge, authority, or control of resources were
> the sources of power. . . . [But] appreciative power . . . depends more on
> being in tune with the whole – the whole person, group or community –
> [and] is not very dependent on [the] control of resources. . . .
>
> To understand the appreciative-centered organization, we have to
> stretch our imagination a little . . . An appreciative-centered organ-
> ization . . . is an even higher order of organization than an influence
> centered-organization.
>
> The most formidable . . . development we can produce in ourselves or
> others is to help enlarge our appreciated world (which) opens up greater
> possibilities for influence and for more control . . . The future of the new
> Systems Generation will be, I believe, to take the lead in developing new
> appreciative-centered models.[5]

For 60 years Tetra Pak could prosper by continuously rethinking its
business model, building on the original appreciative idea of Ruben
Rausing. The business origins were appreciative. Specifically, Rausing
appreciated that milk could be packaged in a more convenient package. Its
development combined innovative customer orientation and capability
leveraging which insightfully reinterpreted and integrated technological
innovations. The combination of the three (appreciation, customer
orientation, and capability leveraging), together with a vigilant eye on lean
management, contributed to making Tetra Pak the market-making prime
mover which shaped the milk industry over many decades. Throughout its
development, Tetra Pak enlarged not only its transactional environment,
but also its appreciated contextual environment. For example, Tetra Pak
not only appreciated the potential for better milk packaging, but also for
the packaging of all liquid foodstuffs. It also achieved this for and with its
closest customers, like Leche Pascual. In enhancing its appreciation, Tetra
Pak created possibilities for influence and control which were once difficult
to imagine, obtaining untold advantages for itself and other members of the
value constellations it so created.

But, as Dorothy Leonard-Barton[6] has shown, there is a risk that what
once were core capabilities should become core rigidities. For Tetra Pak

this may mean that the offering has to be further expanded, or rethought. In a business context in which outsourcing and co-producing become common, many dairies might prefer to have the Tetra Lavals of this world take over the whole of their production cycle. The dairy would then concentrate on its farmer relations, and on its product development and marketing efforts. There are a number of players who see this 'facility management' as a business opportunity.

Tetra Pak has so far shown remarkable insight in shaping and exploiting new opportunities, appreciating the potential for possibilities better than any other actor in the constellations it has been involved in. Its experience, reputation, relationships, and consolidated knowledge base makes it a formidable competitor.

The future will show if Tetra Pak will disprove the saying 'Nothing can save a successful company'.

Value Creation as Prime   10
Movers See It

Finally, we revisit the ideas presented in this book and their implications. Specifically, this chapter:

- Reviews *basic characteristics* of prime mover companies and their business models. A sample of these characteristics: no business model can be pursued forever; prime movers actively create their opportunities; and ideas, not financial calculations, are the driving forces behind market-making firms.
- Shows how managers of successful prime mover firms focus on the *interactions or relationships* between (a) a company's purpose (its values and goals); (b) its business model; and (c) the value-creating processes of its counterparts. This chapter explores how the interactions among them are changing each of these three elements of the firm, causing a re-evaluation of the meaning of purpose, transforming business models, and changing the nature of value.
- Explains the *organizational implications* that follow from the changes in the three elements explored in the previous section. We overview some of the challenges facing managers who start to organize based on the co-production logic which prime movers utilize.

CHARACTERISTICS OF PRIME MOVERSHIP

In the previous chapters we have seen how companies like Xerox, Finnsugar Bioproducts, ABB Fläkt, Caterpillar, Port-Express, Nokia,

VISA, Groupement Cartes Bancaires, and Tetra Pak invented or transformed one, or in some cases several, business models. We overviewed how these prime movers enacted successful value constellations.

The message from the experiences of these prime mover companies is clear: *There is no single business model which can be pursued by one company forever.*

The development of the models, and the enacting of the value constellations which convert them into realities that meet with economic success, has sometimes involved very long time spans.

> Tetra Pak and Xerox both struggled for decades to convert good ideas into commercial successes.

And upon meeting with considerable success, both fundamentally redesigned their business model.

> Xerox went from 'photocopying' to 'documenting' and must now recast this in terms of 'knowledge management'. Tetra Pak decided to redesign its business model by acquiring Alfa Laval and forming the new Tetra Laval Group.

> Even Caterpillar, whose prime mover role had been established for so long, and who has demonstrated a continued ability to keep itself dictating the state of the art of earth-moving equipment, experienced severe difficulties in the beginning of the 1990s. And to remain as prime mover, it reacted by adapting its business model, strengthening the model's customer orientation.

The above-mentioned companies have all been faced *with the same fundamental dilemma:*

> Whether
> **they** *will be the prime mover* that configures or reconfigures their constellation,
> or
> *allow some other company* to come and do the configuring or reconfiguring, for or against them.

The configure-or-be-configured dilemma can take place in a narrow domestic setting, as ABB Fläkt illustrates. Or it can involve a global quest for dominance in a standard-based business, as Nokia's efforts to shape the 3G mobile telecommunications standards or VISA's efforts to remain a key payments system player both illustrate.

In all settings, big or small, *a prime mover role* in configuring or reconfiguring one's value constellations involves *one unavoidable requirement: understanding the value-creation logic of the firm's counterparts*, if at all possible individually, but, in any case, with a much higher resolution (or granularity) than that which was used in industrial-era value creation.

Let's look at how *Business Week* compared Nokia's and Motorola's approaches to the same challenges in the mid-1990s.[1]

Business Week analyzed how, from being one of the most admired companies in the world, Motorola got into deep trouble as, in *Business Week's* view, it failed to realize the impact of new technologies, rapidly changing markets and shifts in customers' needs. Shareholder return in Motorola averaged 54 percent a year between 1993 and 1995. Between 1995 and 1997 the average was less than 1 percent annually.

Big customers started to ask Motorola for digital phones which could enable services such as Caller ID, paging and short messaging. However, *Business Week* tells us, Motorola believed that most customers would want better, smaller, and more stylish analog phones. As a result, Motorola customers launched digital services, but without Motorola phones. On top of this, Motorola initially meant its new analog phone StarTAC to be distributed only to carriers who bought most of their phones from Motorola, and who agreed to promote the phones in stand-alone displays. Carriers reacted sharply, and sales dropped.

When Motorola finally decided to develop digital phones, it initially intended to buy semiconductors from a competitor, to enter the business faster. But Motorola considered the competitor's prices too high. So Motorola decided to develop the technology in-house. It turned out to be a costly project, which took two years and lost Motorola much needed, valuable, time.

Business Week's analysis of Nokia offers a stark contrast. *Business Week* overviews how Nokia managed to take the lead position in the fast changing cell-phone market, and the new market of pocket-sized Net devices. Its success is ascribed to its unconventional risk seeking, yet collegial management style; as well as to its ability to build strategic alliances with suppliers and complementary high-tech companies. But above all, *Business Week* considers that Nokia focused on the requirements of key customers.

Before developing its successful 6100 series, Nokia went to big service providers, who buy thousands of cellular phones and resell them in subscription packages. These customers required that their own customers should be able to communicate across frequency bands used by different formats – analog and digital. Furthermore, they wanted the cellulars to be switched on as long as possible, to maximize the number of calls received. Nokia managed to fullfill the expectations of the big service providers, and gained considerable market share, in particular in the US.

On top of this, *Business Week* emphasizes how Nokia has set off on a journey of customizing its phones for every major market, in order to outrun its rivals. It uses the high-paced Japanese consumer culture as its testing ground as it breaks one product into dozens of niche offerings. Nokia's share price doubled over the first months of 1998 and second-quarter net income soared 66 percent.

We have in this book concentrated on examining how prime movers understand and shape the value creation of customers, as well as suppliers and partners. But *this requirement for 'high resolution understanding' of value creation* can be extended to other counterparts, such as employees and their unions, lobbies, interest groups, regulators, and any other relevant stakeholder in the constellation.

The prime movers we have studied show that the requirement for greater, individualized understanding of the value-creation logics of counterparts applies both

- to the present situation, statically and dynamically; and
- to the possible future states in which such value creation can plausibly take place.

We have seen the many ways in which prime movers are different. For one, they do not only wait for opportunities to present themselves to them. Instead, *prime movers actively work on manufacturing or creating opportunities.*

Prime movers have great respect for possible changes in the way value creation can take place. *Prime movers listen actively* for early signs of such changes. These early signs can first appear in terms of customers's value creation, but can also first become manifested in how employees, shareholders, suppliers, and other stakeholders with an interest in the firm create value. They may concern technological breakthroughs which reshuffle the cards of what is possible.

Another important finding from the companies we have studied is that *prime movers seem to favor the stakeholder approach to business*, over the pure shareholder maximization axiom. This does not mean that making money for shareholders is not important for prime movers. On the contrary, making money is the only way prime mover firms survive in the long run. But market making cannot always be precalculated, and too much attention – particularly at the early stages of the game – on quarterly earnings would often disallow prime movers from succeeding.

As most of our cases show, *'financial' calculations are rarely the basis upon which the major decisions for prime movership are based.* Calculations and financial results are of course often at the core of the signals that managers get about the need to reconfigure (as Xerox illustrates so well). But if such calculations define the problem, they rarely contribute to defining the solution. If anything, they are used later, to test and verify the reconfiguration business model prototype once it has been defined.

Thus, in the early 1930s Ruben Rausing did not have a clear business plan, or a return on investment calculation, as the foundation of his idea to package milk in carton. Neither could Ollila of Nokia in detail foresee the development of Nokia when he wrote his four words: 'Focus', 'Global', 'Telecom-Oriented', 'High Value-Added'. And no one foresaw, for nearly a decade, that customers would get Xerox to grow at the rate it did.

What the examples we have studied show is that *prime mover companies are built on ideas*. Prime mover ideas motivate people within and around these companies, and help them to co-produce value with customers, suppliers, and other possible stakeholders.

Because of this resonance with people in and out of their formal organization, *prime mover companies tend to be explicitly vigilant about values, not just value*.

> Donald Fites at Caterpillar goes out of his way to render explicitly the values which dealers and Caterpillar share, and which make this combination trustworthy for their customers. Jorma Ollila's personal values, reflected in his management style, greatly contributed to having Nokia employees adhere to the vision he built with them and outsiders on the future of the businesses they were in.

As we see below, we expect this connection between values and value to become a much more evident feature in the managing of such companies in the coming years.

At the same time these *prime mover companies appear to be able to move in a fluid way*, weathering very unstructured and open-ended phases.

> Examples of such phases include: Tetra Pak looking for solutions to its material problem in the beginning of the 1950s; ABB Fläkt digesting the emerging Finnish recession in 1991; and Xerox's struggles to figure out what 'focusing on the document' actually meant.

And then, when their ideas become clear, and they assemble the constellation of interactions which enables them to enact their idea, *prime movers surprise us with their ability to quickly, decisively, and effectively co-develop their new business model into an actual value constellation*.

Think of Tetra Pak rapidly rolling out its revolutionary tetrahedron package all over Europe in the late 1950s. Or ABB Fläkt immediately moving into implementing its export and 'Eastern Europe' efforts, once it was clear that the volume of business with domestic customers had been declining, and would continue to do so.

This type of 'decisive' management has been characterized by Nokia's CEO as 'combining winning foresight and excellent execution in a balanced way'.[2] He considers three attributes to characterize such management:

- ability to read the market through wide and open market interfaces,
- ability to translate intuitions into right actions at the right time, and
- ability to execute a global strategy fast.[3]

THE NEED FOR MORE HOLISTIC THINKING POSED BY PRIME MOVERSHIP

Using these attributes, defined by Nokia, we can go back to the model of the firm as an open system, which we introduced in Chapter 4.

This model of the firm contained three crucial elements:

1 the purpose (the values and goals),
2 the priorities (or the business model), and
3 the actual value-creating processes.

These three elements relate to Herbert Simon's now 40-year-old description[4] of the organization as a three-layered cake:

- In the bottom layer of Simon's cake one finds the basic work processes – corresponding to our model's 'actual value-creating processes'.
- The middle layer of the cake houses programmed decision-making processes which govern the day-to-day operation of the system – corresponding to our 'business model priorities' or 'recipes'.

- The cake's top layer consists of the un-programmed decision-making required to design and redesign the entire system, to provide it with its basic goals and objectives – corresponding to our model's 'purpose'.

The three layers and three elements have been typically structured as three different, hierarchical, layers within a company's actual functioning. Even today, many companies still exhibit organizational designs which conceptually are 40 years old. Thus, issues related to the relationship between the transactional and contextual environment of the firm are handled at the purpose level of the board of management, supported by strategy-staff personnel. Immediate issues relating to specific value-creating activities occupy most of the time of individuals in the lower echelons of the organization. Middle management is concerned with the middle layer.

But as the companies we have studied show, today these three main elements of the firm as an open system (purpose, recipes, and actual value creation) are much more interdependent than they were when Simon wrote about the three layers. The three elements, both individually and in combinations, also hold multiple interactions with the actors in the transactional environment, whose own behavior changes in unpredictable ways as the relationship between transactional and contextual environment evolves.

As a result, we see a growing number of senior executives in prime mover firms (Barnevik in ABB, the Rausings in Tetra Pak, etc.) explicitly allocating a substantial amount of their time to actual value creation for and with customers. The issues forcing their rethinking of the business model arrive and are resolved on a schedule that is dictated by the pace of events in their customers' and suppliers' and partners' value creation – not according to the annual 'business planning cycle' calendar. Preparing responses to such challenges now often involves work groups, multi-unit taskforces, and special project groups, which involve more and more members of 'lower' layers of the hierarchy. As we see below, the most challenged layer of the cake is the middle one, as is attested by the widespread practice of 'de-layering' corporations.

As the three major elements (purpose, recipes, and actual value creation) *interact more densely,* considering the interactions among them takes on an unprecedented level of importance. People at all levels in such companies now hold more, and more different, interactions per hour and per day. They have more, and more different, interactions per location and per conference room; more, and more different, interactions per actor interface and per mobile phone call and e-mail than they ever did in the past.

The reason for the now high priority of understanding these interactions is obvious. If the multiple and different interactions and relationships are not mastered, the enhanced density of relations among the three layers of the cake will not allow companies to fuse the three elements into prime mover effectiveness, but, instead, will only bring in confusion. Such confusion will be called 'turbulence' for managers who do not understand the relationships. The confusion or 'turbulence' will relegate companies, whose managers experience the three elements in this manner, to the category of 'out-configured' players. Only companies that understand the interactions and relationships well can pretend to become configurers of winning value constellations. Prime movers cannot afford not to understand these relationships.

We proceed by examining how these enhanced relationships are changing the very notions of 'purpose', 'business model', and 'actual value creation'. In so doing, we explore the interactions and relationships among them. These analyses provide the foundation for how the relationships among the elements can be used by firms to become prime movers.

PURPOSE (VALUES AND VALUE-CREATING GOALS)[5]

Since the ancient Greeks, and perhaps even before, the notion of 'value' has a long and complex history. This complexity arises from two fundamental definitions of 'value':

1   a moral or ethical definition, such as a person's values; and
2   an economic definition, such as the monetary value of an object.

Value, both moral and economic, was studied by moral philosophers until the eighteenth century. At that time, economics became a field of study in its own right, which sparked an ongoing debate, which continues to this day, between the economic and the ethical aspects of value.

The debate takes many different forms. It includes differences of opinion regarding the responsibilities corporations have with respect to the physical and social environments around them. It also concerns the controversies of doing business in countries with terrible human rights records. It increasingly involves the ethical issues around cloning and other genetic-related activities developed by 'life science' firms. In Europe it all too often gets manifested in terms of the priorities managerial decisions give to individual stakeholders (in particular, employees and shareholders).

Since at least the eleventh century, the meaning of the term 'value' held two definitions simultaneously. Value denoted both (a) what people have done and become, and the actions they can perform and (b) how goods were traded. This duality in the origins has created both much confusion and has accounted for enriching debates since then.

By the middle of the sixteenth century, value began to be viewed as being a measurable unit itself, a unit which acquired at the end of the seventeenth century a specific new term: the 'price'. At the beginning of the eighteenth century, '*une valeur*' was the generic name given to negotiable securities. By the beginning of the twentieth century, '*valorisation*' and '*devaluer*' respectively denoted the enhancement or the decrease of merchant (exchange) value.

Both the utility of an object, and the exchange value based on that utility, were in effect considered to be objective until the eighteenth century. It was then that value began to be taken as a 'subjective' assessment. The role of 'personal judgment' in this assessment became widely recognized in the nineteenth century.

Many 'values' thus were taken as no longer being determined by society, but rather by the individuals in that society. What are the reasons for what anthropologists describe as the 'delegation' of certain values from society to the individual? The rise of the market economy has been presented as a key driver of this change. Markets break the stability or uniformity of values embedded in a society by offering choices to individuals.

These individuals were taken to 'have to' make choices which had, up to then, been chosen for them by society, and the way in which they made such choices was supposedly guided by their own, individual, values. Judgments of what is true, beautiful, and/or good, and the values these supposedly express, led to notions like 'scale of values' and 'value systems' that differentiate one culture from another.

But today we believe that this idea, originating in the nineteenth century, whereby one's personal values 'determine' once actual decision making is no longer self-evident. The problem with this view is precisely that so-called 'personal values' are expressed only in personal judgments. Today we know that such judgments are context-dependent, not 'driven' by eternal, unchanging values. In effect, recent research shows that 'value-based modes are difficult to apply to complex, real-world decisions'.[6]

Thus, for example, someone who expresses non-violent values when interviewed by a Gallup pollster at home may hit a pickpocket he discovers attacking an old lady in the subway the next day.

Furthermore, empirical research shows that people don't know how to choose, or even how to determine objectives upon facing unprecedented situations.

For instance, polls made in Israel at the height of the Kosovo bombings in 1999 found that some Israelis identified themselves with the Serbs, while others identified themselves with the exiled Kosovars in the Kosovo war.

The dynamics of global connectivity bring forth ever-more situations for which previous experience is not a guide. In such conditions, it is difficult causally to connect the judgments made and the values which supposedly guide these.

Today 'values' therefore appear to be much more *contingent* than 'subjective'. Values are also more *actual* than 'objective'. Individuals do not have 'totally' absolute values that remain untouched by what happens to them or to dear ones, or which are independent of the actions they take.

> Thus, if I am an American citizen, I may have been 'pro-gun' until the killings in a Colorado high school just like the one my son attends push me to support the outlawing of – at least – automatic weapons.

In the same way, an object does not have a single, given, value embedded in it. Its value depends on the interactions to which it is subjected.

> For a rising film star, diamonds will be of bigger (show-off) value in a 'glitterati' social event such as the Cannes film festival than they would be if stored away in a safe.

At the end of the twentieth century, thus, we have to admit that values are neither subjective nor objective. Instead values as we know them today are enacted and contingent. They are defined according to how individuals make choices in a context in which they hold dense relations to each other.

In such a setting, companies aspiring to have a say in how they do business, who are prime movers, or who at least are part of a prime mover group, have to take into account issues which go beyond creating value for shareholders. Arie de Geus, formerly the head planner at Shell International, suggested in his book *The Living Company*[7] that managers be held accountable for investments in value creating which people other than shareholders (employees, customers, other stakeholders) make – *as well as* ensuring return on money invested by shareholders. He suggested that the company itself is primarily a community whose purposes are longevity, and the development of the potential of this community. Profitability is a means to this end.

Companies as de Geus sees them have traits which the companies we have studied in this book also exhibit. Such companies define membership, establish common values, recruit people, develop their capabilities, assess their potential, live up to a human contract that is not only monetary, manage relationships with outsiders and contractors, and establish policies allowing members to exit the company gracefully.

We see a growing number of young individuals also interested in achieving something more than just creating value for shareholders.

Look for example at Michael Saylor, founder and CEO of MicroStrategy, a leading company in decision-support software. Mr Saylor likes to compare his company with a beaver. A beaver engineering a dam, creating a habitat for not just 1,000 people but also for the 5,000 that depend upon them, and a few thousand customers. He wants his company to build a better world.[8] He has been able to attract a number of very brilliant young professionals to join his company, and make it successful. One of the reasons the company is attractive as an employer is the values it represents.

BUSINESS MODELING FOR PRIME MOVERSHIP

Business modeling for prime movership has been the focus of this book. We have looked at how companies have done this, in the past, successfully. We have garnished some lessons from examining their experiences.

We have found that the *'low-resolution' concepts are now giving way to 'higher resolution' ones*. 'Products' and 'markets', the low-resolution terms with which business modeling was carried out in the past are replaced with *'capabilities'* and the *'specific value-creation logics'* of individual customers.

As a result, what competes in the marketplace changes. The 'high resolution' unit of competitive analysis is *offerings*, not the 'low resolution' one of companies. The competition between companies takes place on the resource market, to make sure that physical and financial resources and competent individuals are available to provide competitive offerings.

We developed our understanding of business modeling with this notion of offerings at the center. We proceeded to explain that value is perceived in actor-specific ways. And we proposed formulae which make it possible to compare how an actor who, in a given offering, plays the primary role of 'supplier' values this offering compared to the actor who in that same offering plays the primary role of 'customer'.

Our view of business modeling thus involves a shift from position into potential, from a static perspective into a dynamic one. This is because the referent which calibrates the whole model is the interaction, not the actor, nor the activity. The interaction is dynamic, and it is of primary interest because of its future potential, not because of its present position. In other words, the interactions, articulated through the offerings, define the business model of a firm. Offerings thus complement the 'activity' unit of analysis which characterized actors in 'low-resolution', industrial-era business modeling. That is, actors should no longer be only defined or analyzed by their activities, but also – and first – by the interactions (and resultant offerings) in which they engage. The activities are important from an efficiency point of view. But the interactions are even more important, as they provide the future potential in the dynamically changing context of the firm. *For prime movers, interactions frame activities.*

We moved on to propose a three-dimensional topology with which to analyze offerings. Software that allows us to manipulate easily three-dimensional representations on two-dimensional media such as paper, overhead transparencies, projection screens, and computer monitors has existed at least since painters invented perspective.[9] But computers and object-oriented programming today facilitates this much more. A three-dimensional conceptual framework is thus not the impediment it was only a few years ago.

We suggested that companies are developing business by strengthening the 'software', or 'services' dimension of the offering. This enables some of what had been expensive peopleware to be transferred as self-service to customers. It also renders the competitiveness of the offering less dependent on hardware, and enhances the relationship logic of offerings.

We suggested that more and more *offerings are now becoming competitive by establishing a relationship logic*, rather than having their commercial logic depend on one-off transactions. In effect, we can consider that offerings have intellectually gone through three generations of thinking.

- The first stage resulted from the observation by Richard Normann and Rafael Ramírez[10] that 'service logics' permeated all activities, regardless of industrial sector. The co-productivity of services was thus extended to the whole of economic activity.
- Building on this work, in his analyses of customer-oriented businesses, Johan Wallin[11] developed the three-dimensional view of offerings we have described in this book.
- The current book takes this work further, emphasizing that for prime movers, offerings now form the platforms for relationships in which 'timeware' is important.

It is important for prime movers to understand that the understanding of offerings we have developed has to be placed in an open-systems framework. *This involves taking an approach which is contrary to the one which has been taken in the 'low-resolution' business modeling,* whereby actors are taken and broken down into activities. Instead, we find how our unit of analysis, the offering, is a media for interaction with others in this open context. Russell Ackoff[12] has found these two approaches not to be contrary to each other, but complementary to each other. We believe that the open approach should frame (or configure) the 'breaking down' one.

In this book we *explored this open-systems perspective and rendered it operational for prime movers to engage in actual business modeling.* This was depicted in a simplified view that we presented in Figure 4.4, which we here reproduce as Figure 10.1.

We suggested *that 'prime movers' are those companies that define how others will act.* Prime movers are the architects of the value constellations that

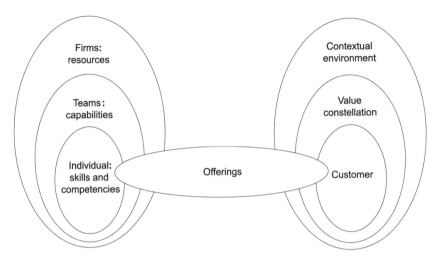

Figure 10.1 The operational business-modeling framework for prime movership.

they define. We provided a multitude of examples of firms that historically have proved to be prime movers.

Prime movership is by nature a high-risk venture. To some extent, you have to drop the company's historically and presently successful tools and set off on a journey into unknown territories. However, if prime movership is a high-risk venture, neglecting it means an even higher risk. If you do not define the prosperous game of tomorrow, you can be sure that someone else will. As we saw, both Xerox and Caterpillar have experienced periods in which they desperately sought a way out of the downturn that was caused by their previous success.

The prime mover companies we studied and which we have here described all follow the basic principles of creativity, with a clear opening up of the processes and an end with a distinct converging stage.

The first phase includes a thorough re-evaluation of historical drivers and distinctive competences to clarify what business you are in today. Thus, Ruben Rausing carried out many investigations into the possibilities of packaging milk into cartons. And Finnsugar Bioproducts evaluated what the combination of itself and the distributor actually meant for the ultimate user of betaine.

With the present business model as a basis, the next step is to conceptualize the present situation in a broader context, in which either customer value creation (Chapter 5), capabilities (Chapter 6) or both (Chapters 7–9 inclusive) became focal. ABB Fläkt identified the inconsistency between signals from their customers and the official future presented in the form of long-term plans and budgets. Nokia identified the telecommunications sector as one that would provide more than enough business opportunity, and decided to move away from being a conglomerate and concentrate all its resources into this field. Xerox regarded photocopies as but an element of broader documenting cycles.

Rethinking the business involves rethinking the context it will be in. Some aspects of what is often implicitly the 'official future' have to be surfaced and reconsidered. Xerox had to study what the futures of paper could look like. This phase can in many cases be a very time-consuming, confusing and/or frustrating part of the process of aiming for a prime mover position. For instance, Tetra Pak was occupied with this question for almost 20 years. Not until certain technical breakthroughs were achieved was it possible for Tetra Pak to generate more concrete options about how to actually move from idea to concrete implementation.

Such efforts allow the business model and offering alternatives to be explicated. ABB Fläkt looked at different co-operation partners and different geographical areas to target, once it was clear that the domestic demand was not sufficient to meet the sales targets. VISA looked at how e-commerce will affect payments. Nokia made detailed forecasts and plans for their assault on the telecommunications market, but they also worked with scenarios. And as the 3G standard battle showed, they were prepared rapidly to change previous decisions to be able to form a European–Japanese alliance.

We have borrowed the word 'windtunneling' from the car industry. The same notion has already been used by Kees van der Heijden in his scenario methodology.[13] The 'windtunneling' exercise is aiming at testing and verifying the robustness of the different business models and offering alternatives generated in the previous phase. The 'windtunneling' can also be done through small experiments and trials. Tetra Pak and Xerox show how concepts are gradually tested in the market. The Tetra Pak incident of showing the first prototype to the press, and faking the quality of the process was an example of 'windtunneling' the new concept. The very positive response of the press conference strengthened the belief that the concept was genuinely path breaking. Xerox's decision to advertise 'documenting' outside and inside the company simultaneously offers another way of doing this.

The 'windtunneling' results in a commitment to choices upon which concrete action plans can be made. Even if the stages here are presented as taking place in sequence, they are often overlapping. The transformation from 'photocopying' to 'documenting' can be characterized as a phase in which conceptualizing, generating forward-looking options, and windtunneling were going on at the same time from 1985 onwards for a period of 10 years. But in the mid-1990s Xerox had enough insight into the implications of the new business model and the corresponding offerings. This permitted the firm to commit itself heavily to the new model. Based on this commitment the action plans became much more focused and detailed.

In many cases the business model continuously adapts itself to changing environmental conditions and increased learning within the organization. Nokia clearly shows how the business model has been updated and fine tuned in pace with the changes taking place outside the company.

Incumbent prime movers have very explicitly to question their business model, as new and potential entrants – often from other industries – actively challenge their model in an attempt to dethrone them. These new entrants do so by exploring how asset liquidity can be exploited to create a challenging value constellation. They – and the incumbents – have a great interest in understanding how value creation actually takes place. We overview this in the following section.

ACTUAL VALUE CREATION

As the history of Xerox, which we presented in Chapter 2, and that of Tetra Pak in Chapter 9 both illustrate so well, technological breakthroughs offer new opportunities, which, often with difficulty, are seized by innovators. These innovators configure entirely new businesses ('Xeroxing', 'UHT milk'), or substantially reconfigure existing ones (from 'photocopying' to 'documenting'; from 'tetra' to 'brik'), thereby becoming prime movers.

Technological breakthroughs remove constraints. The electric motor removed the constraint of locating factories near waterway-based power sources. Mobile telephones remove time and location constraints for calling or being reached.

Technological breakthroughs also allow what was joined to become separable, in time and space, and among actors. A lot of the service elements enacting the software dimension in Caterpillar's offerings are based on extensive investments in information technology. To see the possibilities created by information through databases all over the world, enabling experts to arrive at a customer's site at very short notice, consider the following:[14]

Boeing's maintenance of their 777 airplane is centered on a 'Digital Data for Airplane Maintenance (DDAM)' program. DDAM allows maintenance workers employed by Boeing's suppliers, customers, customers' sub-contractors, and/or Boeing itself, to access the required information of any 777 airplane which is flying into any airport, and whose on-board computer signals to the pilot that repairs are required. Before the 777 has landed, DDAM enables the workers to obtain information on (a) that plane's particular configuration; (b) its up-to-date maintenance records; (c) required spare part availability; (d) the needed competencies to carry out the repairs; (e) the plane's expected, and because of the incident, redefined future maintenance requirements; (f) possible courses of action to follow here and now to bring competence, spare parts, and the airplane together as quickly, or cost effectively, as possible; and (g) training instructions to prepare staff to carry out the repair themselves, even before the plane has landed.

All graphic and other instructions are available through a modem-equipped personal computer. All operations done on the plane are automatically built into the DDAM data base. DDAM's interactive, decentralized, highly liquid architecture replaces illiquid paper-based repair manuals, micro-films, and magnetic tape recordings. DDAM organizes the value-creating activities of (a) the airline's pilots, (b) the airline's and (c) its sub-contractors' ground staff, (d) logistics operators stocking and flying in competencies and/or parts, (e) the airline's maintenance department, (f) the airline's 'alternative to programmed flights' contingency planning systems, (g) insurance and/or self-insurance providers for lost flying time, (h) and Boeing's and (i) outside supplier spare part operations.

DDAM is now becoming available for all of Boeing's aircraft in operation. In the process, Boeing, with the consent of customers, sub-contractors, suppliers, and other actors, is configuring a more effective offering than the unbundled set of offerings which used to tie together the constellation of at least nine economic actors (a) to (i) above). The company is making the overall value-creation system more effective through reconfiguring roles, risks, and activity sets. Most significantly, DDAM makes Boeing's clients more effective – while simultaneously increasing the costs of their switching to other aircraft suppliers.

The work practices which technological breakthroughs such as those which DDAM exploited offer bold alternatives for organizing value creation. Value creation can be rendered more interactive, involving more actions and more actors working together.

Thus, all kinds of new designs for actual value creation ('hollow', 'virtual', 'networked', etc.) appear. But beyond these important organizational design considerations, the new opportunities bring forth a more profound realization. We must not limit our thinking to deal with how best to organize value creation, even if this is crucial. More importantly, we must rethink the very nature of both value creation, and value itself.

In this book, we have thought about value as 'co-produced', not as 'produced'. Value, we have argued, is co-produced by two or more actors with, and for, each other – and with, and for, other actors. *In doing so, the very nature of 'value' as defined in the industrial era is transformed.*

What is value and how is it created? Our basic assumptions need to be questioned.

The most important contribution regarding value creation in the 1980s was by Michael E. Porter, the Harvard Business School professor, who elegantly described the need for companies to consider their contextual differences to position themselves best *vis-à-vis* the competition. Professor Porter also introduced and popularized the concept of the 'value chain' to describe how value gradually is built up during the production process.

The value chain basically depicts a linear, sequential production process that separates tasks and actors according to those tasks. *What has become obvious in the 1990s is that firms face value constellation conditions which are not adequately describable using the chain metaphor.* Such firms are facing interactive, synchronic activities in their value-creating processes.

Thinking about value creation in the form of 'value co-production' liberates us from the constraints of the value-chain model. The co-production model allows us to think of interactions, rather than activities, in which value is not 'added', but rather 'created, recreated [and even] invented'[15] among different groups of actors, including customers.

Defining customers as value creators, not destroyers, is one of the fundamental differences between the old and new models. Another is freeing actors in the value-creation process from the (single) assigned tasks and (rigidly) assigned time and space slots of the industrial era.

As we have seen in this book, customers don't just create value. More specifically, they co-create, and/or co-invent, value both with their suppliers and their own customers. Thus, *in this emerging co-production framework, there are no 'final' customers.*

> For example, using Xerox's terms, the 'documenting' which writing this book consists of is not meant to be sent to a 'final' customer – you, the reader. We take it for granted that if you are taking time to read this book, you are doing this because it will help you to create value which others – and you – will profit from. John Wiley & Sons, using Xerox documenting technology, enable us to create value together. Without our writing the book, without your reading it, and without Wiley making it possible for these two activities to be joined, value would not be created. And those with whom you will create value, helped by this book, will help yet others. No 'final' customer is in view in such a process.

MANAGING IGNORANCE

Working with potentials is much more challenging than calculating positions. Potentials may or may not be realized. So this means that the level of uncertainty of the decision-making process will by definition be increased as the firm accepts to adapt the co-productive approach to business. Add to this that as we enter the twenty-first century, we become even more aware that much of what we have come to take for granted regarding value and values, even the very purpose of incorporating into companies, is being thoroughly questioned by new entrants who are challenging successful incumbents. Ralph D. Stacey[16] has explored what such challenges may consist of. He suggests that in highly interactive settings, established approaches to strategic management are simply not relevant. A 'strong' culture in a company ensuring agreement and consensus on issues facing the organization is then of questionable value.

Stacey argues that first analyzing the environment, followed by planning and then implementation is no longer feasible. Belief systems, the interpretation of social interactions that culture permits, group behavior, individual psychology and other psycho-social aspects are bound to determine what actually happens at least as much as 'rational' planning. The sequence of the events in an innovative process is often less clear during the pace of events than what appears afterwards.

A related observation made by Flavio Vasconcellos and Rafael Ramírez,[17] based on the work of French biologist Henri Atlan[18] distinguished two situations relating to decision making under uncertainty. The first involves 'complicated' situations, which include (a) many variables (b) of different dimensions, with (c) different purposes, (d) composing systems with a given purpose. The second type, 'complex' situations, miss at least one of the previous four (a–d) elements. Both types are found in business situations, but they require different approaches to be addressed. Dealing with complicated objects involves managing knowledge while complex situations require managing ignorance.

Managing knowledge involves determining what one should know to achieve a given objective. Managing ignorance involves determining what one does not know, and includes:

- what we know that we do not know – *puzzles*;
- what we cannot define (with words) but feel we know – *tacit knowledge*;

- finding out that what we know does not apply to a situation – *false belief*;
- suddenly discovering we don't know while we thought we did – *surprises*.

Other things being equal, interactivity increases the proportion of complex situations in relation to complicated ones – while most conventional management is designed to deal with complicated situations.

Managing fast, efficient machines (computers, airplanes, high-speed rail networks, GSM wireless phone systems, etc.) today entails addressing situations which are more complicated than complex. But developing value with customers one has never served before, and with technologies that one understands as they are created, requires hunches, intuition, guessing, sensing, feeling, creativity. Addressing complexity often involves redefining which are the relevant variables in a given situation, doing figure–ground reversals, challenging implicit assumptions. Such problems require the management of ignorance, for which conventional organizing is not well suited.

Dealing with complication means finding the best solution to a given problem. Conversely, dealing with complexity means defining, developing, and constructing the right problem. Organizations need to be designed so they can learn not only how to manage knowledge, but also how to manage ignorance.

Stacey questioned the twentieth-century view whereby management keeps an organization adapted to its changing environment through negative feedback and reinstating stable equilibrium.[19] The results of this feedback are institutionalized in the form of a shared culture that 'fits' environmental conditions as well as possible. Instead, Stacey suggests, we must follow Karl Weick's[20] notion of loosely coupled systems, which he argues better relate to the interactivity we are now embedded in.

Loosely coupled system organizations are less efficient, but more flexible. Such an organization:

- values improvisation more than forecasts;
- dwells on opportunities rather than constraints;

- invents solutions rather than borrows them;
- cultivates impermanence instead of permanence;
- values argument more highly than serenity;
- relies on diverse measures of performance rather than on accounting systems alone;
- encourages doubt rather than removes it;
- continuously experiments rather than searches for final solutions;
- seeks contradictions rather than discourage them.

With this view of organizing (note, 'organization' is now a verb, not a noun), Stacey[21] proposes that a group of people does not necessarily have to have a shared, common goal defined as a state in order to be a group. Individuals can form groups before they have an explicit, tested, common goal. They would do so because they find they have interdependent requirements which can be met through their interacting. Mutually interesting means, not common ends, join these individuals. If a common purpose emerges at all, it does so much later.

In such conditions, Stacey suggests,

- Charismatic leaders and the strong cultures of dependence they provoke in followers may well be extremely unhealthy for organizations.
- A cohesive team of managers may not be a healthy phenomenon at all.
- The idea of the group or the management team may itself be a defense mechanism (against the anxiety of differentiating).
- Groups or teams are a two-edged sword – they contribute to establish individual identity, they enhance operating efficiency, but they can also de-skill members.

In highly interactive settings, then, a common purpose or even a task is not required to function as a group. This corresponds to the value constellation approach we have explored in this book. As mentioned, actors coming together to co-produce value can do so for different purposes. Priority, we maintained, had to be actor centered, and defined only from the specific actor's point of view.

In other words, the value-creating framework we present in this book is well prepared for the conditions Stacey has studied. To be successful in the type of situations that Stacey describes, one has to be able to manage the relationship with one's environment, attending to the changing nature of the boundary. As we saw with the help of Smith's AIC framework, important factors in this respect are the nature and use of power, the level of mutual trust, and time pressures. Creating conditions which are psycho-socially maturing for people,[22] in which people can, individually or in groups, address defenses, test reality, avoid indulging in fantasy, and achieve developmental and complex learning becomes key for success.

The implications of Stacey's analysis is that both a very strong shared culture, and the failure to share culture at all, entail organizational conditions which prevent complex learning by being too tight or too loose. Weakly shared and, thus, multiple cultures generate instability, as each culture attempts to persuade others to follow its own values. Excessive tightness on the other hand disallows questioning. Nokia, for example, works at finding the middle ground by shifting the roles key members occupy so as to avoid established structure, and the values of its leaders, to become overly rigid.

In July 1998 Jorma Ollila, CEO switched the jobs of his three closest executives. Matti Alahuhta, in charge of Nokia Telecommunications, was rotated from his *'customer-schmoozing position into the marketing vortex of handsets'*. Asia-Pacific chief Sari Baldauf became responsible for Nokia Tele-communications. And former Nokia Mobile Phones chief Pekka Ala-Pietilä, became vice-chairman, charged with exploring new ventures.[23] The reason behind these transfers of responsibilities was explained by Ollila as a need to transfer knowledge and experiences from one business to another, and to move people away from their 'comfort zones'.

CHANGING THE BUSINESS MODEL TO REMAIN A PRIME MOVER

From our re-evaluation of the meaning of purpose, how business modeling is being transformed, and the changing nature of value in the above sections of this chapter, it follows that the principles for organizing work cannot remain unchanged. What we see happen is that prime-mover firms go through constant shifts between periods of fairly stable conditions alternating with times of radical change. The challenge is thus to be able to shift the mode of organizing in pace with these requirements.

Wallin[24] investigated in depth seven cases of fundamental business model change (one of which was ABB Fläkt). He was able to identify four paths leading to the change:

1   The emergent path.
2   The crisis management path.
3   The champion path.
4   The structural path.

The *emergent path* is one where the process starts with the decision makers identifying emerging opportunities to improve competitiveness. In this approach management acts proactively and applies initially extraordinary measures to move the process forward. Learning takes place in the interaction between the firm and its customers. This learning enables management to understand better what future offerings could strengthen the relationships between the firm and its customers. At the end of this process an offering vision has emerged. For the final stage the process shifts into a visionary path. One possibility is to develop parallel operations that involve co-productive activities that appear alongside the company's traditional structures and processes. In some cases, these innovative operations appear in an *ad hoc* manner: An entrepreneur within the company might develop a co-productive relationship as part of an independent project, as was the case of Tetra's first appearance within Åkerlund & Rausing, before it was spun out.

Further complicating the challenge of change are the different types of leadership involved between a parallel function and the formal organization. The formal organization is often headed by authoritarian, control-oriented 'managers' at the head of a vertical hierarchy. Parallel functions or processes are headed by 'leaders' who have a more collegial, 'influencing' and 'appreciating' role, experienced as a more horizontal relationship with the other members of the 'team'. Splitting leadership from management presents a number of serious problems, according to Thomas Gilmore and James Krantz.[25] First, the 'leaders' without formal organizational authority are little more than cheerleaders. Meanwhile, managers, separated from the innovation process, often end up killing good ideas. Another risk is that parallel ('temporary') processes might be used 'to bypass, not to work through, the difficulties that a particular organization is facing'.

The *crisis management path* is dominated by the urgency to find a way out of the crisis. This requires management quickly to come up with a solution. This solution is communicated as a very concrete mismatch between the performance of the firm and its future objectives. The future envisaged state is described, including a vision of new offerings. Based on this vision the approach to change is reactive, and ordinary management is the implementation mode. At the same time some new offering elements are developed. The crisis management path may also include structural measures in order to provide the foundations for the new offering(s). The Xerox story illustrates this.

The *champion path* is one in which an individual starts a change process with a fairly clear personal vision of a future offering in mind, but this vision is not yet shared by the whole management and board. The process will be driven by this personal perception of a gap between the present and the future envisaged state of the firm. In this type of change process the focus is on building the capabilities necessary to provide the customers with the envisaged offering. Tetra Pak, Nokia, and Xerox each exhibited an example of this path at different stages of their development.

The *structural path* has similarities to the champion path. The difference is that to achieve the envisaged future state of providing the new offering(s), some structural changes are needed in addition to organic internal changes. For example, an acquisition may be needed to secure the resources necessary for developing the new offering.

The crisis management, champion, and structural approaches can all be called visionary processes in comparison with the emergent approach, which initially is lacking a strong vision as driver of the process.

MANAGING THE CO-PRODUCTIVE VALUE CREATION OF PRIME MOVERSHIP

As is evident from the comments in this chapter, co-production is a much more comprehensive notion than production. As it offers greater strategic advantage, *shifting organizations from production to co-production becomes a high priority agenda item for any board or top management team.* Fundamental change is not easy, especially in well-established and successful companies. One of the major challenges facing management teams joining the co-production logic is the increased need to handle ever increasing information flows. To cope with this there are two activities within the firm, which are asking for special attention: Information Management and Dialogue.

Information management. Our study of Xerox's documenting offerings illustrated the importance which information has in managing 'higher resolution' capabilities, and in allowing co-learning. In Caterpillar, VISA, and Nokia, information transparency allows universal real-time access to all critical codified business within the company, thus increasing speed, global integration, and local responsiveness simultaneously. Nokia's information management architecture is built according to different value-creation layers. The 'bottom layer' includes a transparent information management platform for transaction processing of codified data and information. The second layer is for planning and decision making based on the transparent information. The third layer is for informal communication and sharing of knowledge related to the internal and external world.[26]

Dialogue. Whereas industrial-era companies integrated by instituting organization-wide homogeneity, co-productive organizing draws strength from the diversity, and even incompatibility, among actors and relationships (see Stacey's analysis above). But such incompatibility must be managed so that it becomes a source of creativity, not a source of destruction. Dialogue thus becomes the principle integration tool of co-productive organizing. A first crucial dialogue is the one between the firm and its customers. A second dialogue is with the futures that challenge it. The companies we studied exhibit numerous examples of this, such as Caterpillar's continuous dialogue with its dealers both about the present but also about designing future offerings that match both Caterpillar and dealers' value-creating processes. In the dialogue with the future, tacit knowledge reflecting the perceptions of management, front-line personnel and even outside stakeholders, primarily customers, is crucial – as the Tetra Pak example illustrates. Nokia shows that the emergence of individual and organizational tacit knowledge may be intentionally accelerated if the company offers opportunities for individuals to learn and experience demanding new things through stretching.

The findings from our studying prime movers confirm Larry Hirschhorn and Thomas Gilmore's research[27] to the effect that in co-productive value-creation *boundaries are assets, not liabilities.* Co-production has radically redefined the boundaries that exist between organizations – and between units within them. In the industrial era, organizations related to each other according to a simple make/buy dichotomy; one actor was the 'maker' or supplier, the other was the buyer or customer. As seen above, however, firms are related to each other in a myriad of ways. In the case of Caterpillar we showed how one supplier, Tamrock, actually was also a customer, and at the same time used one of Caterpillar's dealers as its own dealer. The boundary between two firms is therefore no longer a simple make/buy connection. It is an ever-changing, permeable, and overlapping junction involving dynamic and multiple relationships. Because of the very nature of co-production, this junction is an asset to be managed by the firms. The intuitions and feelings that actors have regarding these relationships become resources that can lead to new adventures or opportunities for creating values, or signal dangers to be reckoned with. Boundaries are not liabilities that must be breached or avoided. Nokia changed its boundaries in Japan – between itself and Mitsui, its distributor – into an asset as it persuaded its counterpart to join Nokia in promoting a joint European and Japanese effort to develop the third-generation mobile telecommunications standard.

At the same time as boundaries becomes assets, firms to an increasing degree show flexibility in their relationships to other actors affecting their value constellation. Many of today's requirements for competitive success cannot be achieved by a single firm. We thus saw Nokia fighting against

Motorola in the battle for standards, yet forming the Symbian joint venture with, among others, Motorola, to develop the operating system for the new media phone which could free it from dependence on Microsoft.

What we can be certain about is that organizing for effective business modeling in high interaction settings will involve a very different pattern than that which the industrial era produced. In the co-productive world adaptation and flexibility combined with understanding and learning form the building blocks based on which future leadership will be built.

Managers' interest in organizational learning reflects a search for different approaches that will help experimental, parallel initiatives to inform, reform, and transform the organization – and their own management practices. Managers are even forced to create new language to describe the new processes that they are inventing to develop their business (and to separate these new processes from the traditional, formal practices and processes of the organization). Thus, one of the authors was told by an executive in charge of transforming a production-oriented business unit into a more co-production-oriented one:

> [The change] is being 'co-ordinated' [not 'managed'] by 'mentors' [not 'project managers'] who will 'clarify' [not 'define'] the 'movement' [not 'business problems'] that the corporation has been living with. The 'mentors' will do this through several 'processes' [not 'management measures'] which will 'map' [not 'determine'] the 'concept' [not 'vision' or 'mission'] which the movement will articulate.

Creating language with which to depict the alternative is thus an important part of this transformative managerial task. Such terms reduce the anxiety that the change poses, and articulate the difference that is being sought.

Creating language is part of what this book does, to help managers succeed in the transition.

TO FINISH

Offerings, we have said, reverse the ground of attention to which strategists have given priority. Instead of actors, we suggest that interactions should be considered as the focus. Instead of companies, it is relationships. Instead of positioning within a given context, it is the process of enlarging and redefining environments which we suggest can deliver more effective companies, helping their customers to become more effective value creators, ultimately making up better value constellations.

Previous analyses of the need to 'stake out' the environment with which one is to deal have centered on either the figures (actors, stakeholders, counterparts) or the background which these figures share. Building a common background has proven to be a good way of containing and addressing the complexity firms in co-productive environments must face. Both Charles Perrow and Eric Trist[28] noted that the background of an economic system provides *common* ground(s) enabling actors to collaborate. As Eric Trist put it: 'a common figure we may not find. Common ground we may.'

Common ground offers coherence and congruence. Thus we see top managers striving to manage the complexity of today's business world by defining their organization's (or corporation's) values in ways that can be related to the values of others with whom they seek to co-create value. In so doing, they become or remain prime movers.

It is in this co-productive spirit that we offer this book.

Notes

Chapter 1

1 The notion of 'referent' organization, was developed by Trist ('Referent Organizations and the Development of Inter-organizational Domains', *Human Relations* 36, no. 3 (1983): 269–84).

2 See full case in Normann and Ramírez, 1998.

3 ibid.

4 'Capabilities', which are further explored in Chapter 6, is what produces competence. Competences are thus *ex post* results. We thus use the notion of capability in this book, as it is what allows managers to determine how to produce the competence that will have rendered their business successful.

5 Conventional wisdom has it that for the business to be commercially viable over time, the cost of capabilities must be lower than the price customers are willing to pay for offerings. Yet many Silicon Valley start-ups which have never delivered on this conventional wisdom have been sold at a very high premium. These start-ups have put a twist on conventional wisdom; their track record in effect suggests that one does not (f)actually need to 'prove' that the cost of capabilities must be lower than the price customers are willing to pay. Instead, one simply needs to convince someone that one has laid the ground for the conventional wisdom to become a reality at a later date. We will see in Chapter 5, that the relation beween price and cost is transformed as businesses become more relation-based, with business models whose viability depends less on single transactions. As the joke goes in venture capital circles in Silicon Valley: 'profits are for wimps'. That is, if you want to have profits ('too') early, you are not being aggressive enough as a reconfiguer!

6 While we limit our analysis in this book to offerings transacted in 'commercial' markets, where goods, services, and/or information are traded, offerings also compete for customer's attention and money in other types of markets:

- job markets, where positions in firms are offered, and in which candidates offer their distinctive competencies to prospective employers;
- financial markets, where firms offer investors bonds, stocks, and other products;

- technical (or author) markets in which inventors or their agents offer access to their patented or copyrighted creations or discoveries through licenses;
- institutional markets in which firms offer arrangements such as joint-ventures, alliances, franchises, concessions;
- political markets in which lobbyists compete with each other for the attention of policy- and lawmakers, regulators; or candidates for voters' confidence.

A given economic actor – a company – will determine strategies for doing well in each of the markets it competes in. As we see in Chapter 4, the priorities it gives to the different stakeholders with which it interacts (employees, customers, owners, lawmakers, environmentalists) in such markets will be reflected in its (espoused or actual) *values*. These values 'ground' the strategy of the firm, its formulation of 'business' and its way of carrying it out. In other words, values ground value, and its creation.

7   The value constellation framework was originally developed by Normann and Ramírez (1993, 1994, 1998). Wallin and Ramírez have further refined it together and separately (Wallin and Ramírez 1996; Wallin, 1997; Ramírez, 1999).

Chapter 2

1   Fabienne Autier, Denis Bourgeois, and Flavio Vasconcellos collaborated in developing this case study, in research financed by the Fondation HEC.
2   Leonard-Barton, 1992.
3   Miller, 1990.
4   Initially named electrophotography.
5   Convinced that there must be something out of this technology . . . Battelle agreed to spend $3000 on further development work in exchange for three-quarters of any future royalties realized from the idea.
6   Kearns and Nadler, 1992.
7   ibid.
8   More precisely, Xerox copiers exceeded the sales price of existing copying machines by a considerable amount, but they enjoyed a smaller operating cost, since the competing machines used more expensive papers (coated paper), costing typically 10 to 15 cents a copy.
9   Charlie would become a real issue later, when the 9200 was introduced, since this new copier addressed his core business: the high volume copying that had been done in a centralized way.
10   See Kearns and Nadler, 1992.
11   Normann et al., 1989.
12   Schön, 1971.
13   Leonard-Barton, op. cit.
14   Selznick, 1957.
15   There had been other efforts to look at the future, especially technology, in

previous years, but not as part of a formal strategic direction-setting exercise.

16   Roger Levien, Head of Corporate Strategy. Interview in Stamford, Connecticut. 26 November, 1996.

17   Paul Allaire, *Business Week* (22 June 1987).

18   ibid.

19   Roger Levien, Head of Corporate Strategy. Interview in Stamford, Connecticut. 26 November 1996.

20   Len Vickers, Senior VP Corporate Strategic Development and Communications; Interview at Young and Rubicam, New York. 20 November 1996.

21   ibid.

22   The commercial they shot for the occasion involved a story of a mother and her daughter at home.

The father returns.

The daughter says: 'Hey Daddy, I got a gold star today'.

The father: 'Terrific!'

The daughter: 'Daddy, what did you do at the office today?'

The father: 'I made phone calls, I was in meetings . . .'

The daughter: 'No Daddy, what did you *make*, Daddy?'

The father answers by showing documents. The daughter remarks: 'Maybe you will have a gold star also'.

23   He in fact retired in 1998.

24   *USA Today* (7 November 1994).

25   It is interesting to note that it was released prior to when the Document Company Strategy was made public, yet some people mentioned the great help the new strategy offered to position and market the product. We see here the interaction between the reality and the wording.

Chapter 3

1   Reichheld, 1996.

2   In turn, of course, the seller of the shirt is able to realize a part of this value creation in the form of the price to be paid for the shirt.

3   An earlier version of this sub-section originally appeared in Wallin, J. 'Competence Driven Offering Design', presented at the Fourth International Conference on Competence Based Management in Oslo, 18–20 June 1998.

4   *The Economist* (7 September 1996).

5   *The Economist* (5 July 1997).

6   Note that the marketplace will not always accurately measure the worth or value of a product through the price the offering can command. For example, the realized price is not a reliable guide to the amount of value created if the customer is able to exercise bargaining power and force the price down. He or she might be willing to pay more to get the benefits but is able to exploit weaknesses among the suppliers. Wharton Professor George Day (1984, 1990) has defined relative value in use (RVU) as a way

to deal with this situation. The relative value in use is the maximum amount a customer should be willing to pay for the firm's product, assuming he or she is fully informed about the firm's product and the offerings of the competitors. The reference point for RVU analysis is the life-cycle cost (which is equal to all costs related to the purchase and use of the product throughout its whole life-cycle) of the closest competitive alternative. The RVU will differ from the purchase price of this reference product by the amount of perceived savings in start-up and prepurchase costs, and any augmented value, including learning, that the firm's product provides.

7   Often represented by the supplier's individual sales person.

8   Pricing can be either transaction- or relationship-based. The maximum possible price is:.

$$P < NSC - C2 - C_3 - C_4 - R + L.$$

Note that the purchasing price and the costs can exceed the NSC if the learning element (L) has an important positive value.

9   Again, often perceived and based on individual relationships.

10   Schlender, 1995.

11   Jeff Bailey, 'Why Customers Trash the Garbage Man', *Wall Street Journal* (17 March, 1993): p. B1.

12   Timmins, 1997.

13   Corey, 1975.

14   Levitt, 1980.

15   Normann and Ramìrez, 1993a, 1994, 1998.

16   Adapted from Wallin, 1997.

17   ibid.

18   The notion of scope in Figure 3.2 indicates that individual customers can have different priorities in respect of how they value different offering elements. For example, in the physical content element, some customers are more interested in high quality than in scope (they just want the core features to be 100 percent dependable, as opposed to a broad range of different features). Other customers may be interested in a breadth of features, but are not so demanding in respect to quality. Whether scope or quality is emphasized by a customer is not indicated on this chart, since one measurement is used for both factors.

19   Note in addition that the firm not only needs to consider to what extent the offering provides value to potential customers in the short term. It must also reflect on how the established value constellation can be leveraged for later value creation.

20   Levien, 1989a.

21   The Finnsugar Bioproducts case was originally presented in the 17th Annual International SMS Conference in Barcelona, 5–8 October 1997 in a paper called 'Context Specific Customer Orientation' by Johan Wallin.

22   Herring, 1997.

Chapter 4

1 The ABB case was originally analyzed by Johan Wallin in Aimé Heene and Ron Sanchez, eds., *Competence-based Strategic Management* (New York: Wiley, 1997). The original analysis is here somewhat extended.

2 Barnevik, 1990.

3 The value creation framework from Chapter 3 (Figure 3.1) provides some interesting findings regarding 'firm-specific' and 'firm-addressable' resources.

First, there is an issue relating to the *unit of analysis* within a large corporation. The notion of business model is applicable for a company within a larger corporation (for example, ABB Fläkt Group), for a division or business area (like the Air Pollution Control business area within the ABB Fläkt Group), for a country organization (such as ABB Finland) or for a single business unit (such as the industrial division within ABB Fläkt in Finland). This means that the notion of 'The Firm' and 'Firm-addressable Resources' in Figure 3.1 has to be defined based on which is the unit of analysis.

In the case of implementing 'Customer Focus' at ABB Fläkt the role of the business unit within the context of the corporation was relevant. As the industrial division faced reduced demand for its offerings within the existing customer base, its interest in addressing corporate resources shifted from domestic resources within the Finnish ABB Group to foreign resources within the global ABB Group. When developing its new export-focused priority it was able to draw on corporate resources to leverage its capabilities.

Note that there may be firm-specific resources within the corporation which, from the business unit point of view, are less addressable than external firm-addressable resources. When the corporate culture favors internal competition, as is the case in ABB, the preferred addressable resource may prove to be external. Thus in export projects the industrial division was in certain cases competing with other ABB units. Putting together project specific alliances could in such a case, from the point of view of the business unit, favor co-operation with external partners instead of internal co-operation. Whether this is 'good' or 'bad' has to be related to other advantages/disadvantages within the existing mode of operation.

One advantage of the ABB way of working is that efficiency is measured all the time, and each unit had to perform as if it was a stand alone business. However, one disadvantage is that from the customers' point of view little co-ordination is evident, and entertaining multiple ABB salespeople had been seen in many occasions to be a nuisance. Therefore one ambition stressed by ABB management when launching the 'Customer Focus' initiative was to increase cross-business unit co-operation. This was a real challenge within an organization that favored internal competition and a high degree of decentralization, and emphasized competitive priorities based on products and technical skills.

4 To move the organization to 'strategic partnerships' involves multiple steps. The ultimate goal, a truly customer-focused organization, bases its long-term direction on individual customer priorities and plans (Schulmeyer, 1992).

5   The first version of the model of the firm as an open system was presented by Johan Wallin and Rafael Ramírez in a paper called *Value Constellations and Competence Development*, 1996. The here further developed version is derived from J. Wallin, *Customer Orientation and Competence Building*, doctoral dissertation, Helsinki University of Technology, 2000. The authors acknowledge the work of professors Ron Sanchez and Aimé Heene (1996) in the development of this model of the firm as an open system. The model we present here is an extension of their original model.

6   Bohm, 1980.

7   Ackoff, 1970.

8   van der Heijden, 1996, pp. 2–5.

9   See R. Sennet (1998) for a full analysis.

10   *Information Strategy,* May 1997, p. 18.

11   idem.

12   Zetterberg, 1992.

13   Wallin, 1998c

14   de Geus, 1997.

15   de Geus, 1997; Senge, 1990.

16   Bogaert, Martens, van Cauwenbergh, 1994.

17   A. Solé, 1996.

18   In particular, the definitions we use are derived from Sanchez, Heene, and Thomas, 1996; see also Prahalad, and Hamel, 1990, Teece et al., 1990.

19   According to competence-based authors Sanchez, Heene and Thomas (1996), a combination of capabilities enabling sustained delivery of offerings with above-average customer and exchange value constitutes a *competence*.

20   Argyris and Schon, 1978.

21   For the industrial division, a customer-orientation business model could have implied further refining its service offerings for existing big Finnish pulp and paper factories, or developing new, even more effective, pollution-control solutions for the Finnish steel producers. Such new, technically enhanced offerings would have required substantial capability-building efforts.

22   Kulkki and Kosonen, 1999.

Chapter 5

1   Grönroos, 1990, p. 138.

2   Håkansson and Snehota, 1995, pp. 384–85; Blankenburg et al., 1999.

3   Schlender, 1996.

4   The notion of customer as 'king' is not accidental. Weber established that there were two forms of legitimacy: a charismatic one which over time became institutionalized as a traditional one, for example by royalty, and the 'rational' one which bureaucracy and its governing rules could offer. The role of customer as 'king' means that customer is now invoked as a guarantor of legitimacy when rational arguments would fail to convince.

5 For example, parts of merchant or investment banking have 'fatter' fees in developing new projects and offerings with sophisticated customers than in 'commoditised' activities.

6 Magnet, 1994.

7 Lang, 1997.

8 Construction put in place during April 1999 in the US alone was estimated at a seasonally adjusted annual rate of $700 billion, according to the US Commerce Department's Bureau of the Census. The figure represents an 8 percent increase over April 1998. Improvements accounted for 67 percent of the 1998 estimate. The remaining 33 percent was spent on maintenance and repairs. When adding maintenance and improvement, the volume is estimated to be more than $865 billion. The industry is estimated to include 650,000 firms and employ 5.7 million people according to the advance summary statistics for United States (1997 NAICS Basis): 1997.

9 According to a study published by Associated Equipment Distributors and Associates, the business of renting construction equipment grew from $614 million in 1982 to $16.2 billion in 1996. Nearly 15,000 outlets today rent equipment in the US market, divided roughly between 3,000 distributor locations engaged in both rent-to-rent and rent-to-sell activities, and 12,000 outlets engaged only or primarily in the rent-to-rent business.

10 Porter, 1980.

11 *Harvard Business Review* (March–April, 1996).

12 Urwick, 1943. Urwick is quoted in Lampel and Mintzberg, 1996.

13 Taylor, 1997.

14 Quinn, 1992, p. 439.

15 A European car manufacturer, through its customer surveys, found that there is no clear correlation between high customer satisfaction and loyalty (as measured by repurchases) in some European countries. An explanation for this phenomenon could be that preferences for different types of cars, including different brands, evolve as customers age. A car that perfectly matches the preferences of a 25-year-old will not in many cases match the preferences for the same individual once he or she has reached 35; or 50, or 70. The customer's conception of 'status' evolves with age; and status will have a different position in relation to other value-creating aspects; for the importance of counterparts itself changes with time. The car as an offering may therefore become a victim of the role of values in the customer value equation. For certain customer segments, this implies that customer relationships cannot be maintained more than for a certain period of the customer's lifetime.

16 Information technology has been used to increase safety and expand the functions of the car. Cars have become communications centers (with mobile phones and Internet access), audio studios (with radio, cassette recorder, and CD players) and to a certain degree the car is relieving the driver from his job (for example, through cruise control and Global Positioning Systems connected to local maps). All these changes can be seen in the physical product.

17   Such as extended warranties, different forms of financing, insurance packages, membership in service pools, etc. These expanded services require sophisticated computer systems to keep track of each individual car as well as the car owner. At the same time they enable the service provider (either the original car producer or an authorized dealer) to collect extensive information about its customer to use this information further to improve the customer service.

Chapter 6

1   This idea is Andreu Solé's, a Professor at HEC. See Solé (1996).

2   A first classification similar to the one here presented was developed by Richard Normann and Rafael Ramírez when they both worked with an SMG multi-client project in the late 1980s. The ideas were further developed by Johan Wallin, and applied in his consulting assignments with ABB Fläkt and other companies. A more detailed discussion related to these four capabilities can be found in J. Wallin, 'Customers as the Originators of Change in Competence Building: A Case Study,' and R. Sanchez, R. and A. Heene, 'Competence-based Strategic Management: Concepts and Issues for Theory, Research, and Practice.' Both articles appear in A. Heene and R. Sanchez, (eds.), *Competence-based Strategic Management* (New York: Wiley, 1997).

3   Offering design and development should not be confused with innovation. Innovation is the creative process located within 'generative' capabilities. Offering design and development acts as a conduit for innovation, responding to the voices and views of customers, and linking these to employees and capital investments (Gorb, 1990).

4   Tasks are the units of analysis used in studies and interventions by Tavistock Institute authors, such as Emery and Trist, particularly in the socio-technical systems tradition. Activities were rendered popular by Porter (1985), but have a long tradition, arguably going back to Lawrence and Lorsch's seminal studies.

5   McCann and Gilmore, 1983; Gilmore and Kazanjian, 1988; Gilmore, 1988.

6   The notion of absorptive capacity was first presented by Cohen and Levinthal, 1990.

7   Hamel and Prahalad, 1994, p. 76.

8   Schein, 1996, 1997.

9   Nonaka and Takeuchi, 1995.

10   idem.

11   G. Bateson, *Steps to an Ecology of Mind* (New York: Chandler, 1972).

12   *Financial Times* (27 July 1999).

13   Some studies show that people need a vision in which they can believe and role models that show them the way (Zeithaml et al., 1991).

14   See for instance, Jones et al., 1997.

15    $EV = P - RC \pm B \pm G - R + L$, found in Chapter 3.

16   Jenkins and Floyd, 1998.

17   Abell (1994) has noticed that 'The firm has to accomplish two interrelated tasks; it has to manage its current operations effectively and it must be able to change these operations, to meet continually shifting future demands.'

18   This example elaborates a study by Lorino and Tarondeau (1998) that has been further discussed with Lorino (1999). The name of the company is disguised, as originally done by Lorino and Tarondeau. We acknowledge the help of our SMG colleague, Mikael Huhtamäki, in re-presenting Port-Express according to our own framework.

19   Stabell and Fjedlstad, 1998.

20   Normann, 1994.

21   Sanchez, 1995.

22   Again, these names camouflage those of the real companies.

23   van der Heijden, 1993.

24   Commitments to the future IT architecture need to be left open for as long as possible.

25   $EV = P - RC \pm B \pm G - R + L$, found in Chapter 3.

Chapter 7

1   Emery and Trist, 1965.

2   This is because living entities survive by importing certain materials and energy sources from their environment. They transform these in accordance with their own system characteristics, and export other types of energy and material outputs back into the environment.

3   Emery and Trist, 1965.

4   Maturana and Varela, 1980.

5   Schwartz, 1997; van der Heijden, 1993.

6   Smith, W.E.: 'Wholeness: A Theme for the New Generation of Systems Application', paper prepared for the Social Systems Science 1998 meeting (found at the odii web-site).

7   Garud and Kumaraswamy, 1993.

8   This case has been derived from company annual reports 1985–98; the story which ran in the *Helsingin Sanomat* newspaper during July 1999; and M. Mäkinen, *Nokia Saga* (Gummerus, 1995).

9   Mullins, S., 1997, 'Cellular Success, Made in Scandinavia' *Telecommunications Online* (October 1997). (http://www.telecoms-mag.com/issues/199710/tci/mullins.html).

10   For a more detailed discussion of the role of a 'guarantor' in systems terms, see Churchman, 1979.

11   Hamel and Prahalad, 1994.

Chapter 8

1   See Chapter 7 for a discussion of this model.

2   A practice which to date (1999) the Groupement Cartes Bancaires in France has refused to implement.

3   John Authers, 'MasterCard to Allow Banks to Move its Logo', *Financial Times* (26 June 1999): 26.

4   We gratefully acknowledge the help of Flavio Vasconcellos in developing this case study. A version of it was used in a paper by F. Vasconcellos and R. Ramírez presented at the 17th Strategic Management Society Annual International Conference in Barcelona in October 1997, entitled: 'Domain Definition: How Value Propositions Induce Strategic Innovation and Organizational Change'. Jagdeep Kapoor updated some of the figures on the original case. His help is here also gratefully acknowledged.

5   At the time of this writing, nine banks represented at CB's Board of Directors are: BNP, the Banques Populaires group, Caisse d'Epargne, CCF, CIC, Crédit du Nord, Crédit Lyonnais, La Poste, and Société Générale.

6   It is called a '*Groupement*' because its legal constitution is in the form of a French '*Groupement d'Intérêt Economique*' (GIE), or non-profit business organization.

7   B.N.P., Crédit Lyonnais, Société Générale, CIC, and CCF.

8   Interview with Jean Pierre Camelot, CB Director, London, March 1997.

9   Banque Nationale de Paris, Société Générale, Crédit Industriel et Commercial, Crédit Commercial de France, Crédit Lyonnais, Banques Populaires, Crédit du Nord, Caisses d'Epargne, and *La Poste* (The Post Office).

10   Interview with Jean Pierre Camelot, CB Director, London, March 1997.

11   VISA and Mastercard however, do not issue non-CB cards in France.

12   Interview with Jean Pierre Camelot, CB Director, London, March 1997.

13   'French Banking Association'.

14   The French central bank, responsible for the country's monetary policy.

15   An estimated 1 billion smart cards were shipped in 1998, and the world market is expected to go from $722 million (1998) to $4.8 billion in 2002.

16   Interview with Jean Pierre Camelot, CB Director, London, March 1997.

17   Non-French banks operating in France who are members of the GIE CB will profit from the same advantages.

18   Interview with Jean Pierre Camelot, CB Director, London, March 1997.

19   A trend for the players in the virtuous circle is that the one that is furthest ahead will get even further ahead.

20   Interview with Jean Pierre Camelot, CB Director, London, March 1997.

21   Max Auriol, 'Les Cles de l'Interbancarité', GIE-CB Internal Document, 1994.

22   Interview with Jean Pierre Camelot, CB Director, London, March 1997.

23   Visa, MasterCard, Microsoft, etc.

24   Interview with Claude Menesguen, GIE-CB President, Paris, May 1997.

25   Interview with Jean Pierre Camelot, CB Director, London, March 1997.

26   Interview with Claude Menesguen, GIE-CB President, Paris, May 1997.

27   Interview with Jean Pierre Camelot, CB Director, London, March 1997.

Chapter 9

1   L. Leander, *Tetra Pak, Visionen som blev verklighet* (1995): 21–22; (translation from Swedish by the authors).
2   'Wholeness' paper, oddii.com www site.
3   The process developed to produce liquid eggs had been developed by Leche Pascual in close co-operation with Tetra Pak in 1993.
4   See Churchman, 1979.
5   ibid.
6   Leonard-Barton, 1992.

Chapter 10

1   *Business Week* (4 May 1998) and *Business Week* (10 August 1998).
2   Jorma Ollila, CEO, presentation at the Finnish Strategic Management Society 10th Anniversary, 20 January 1999.
3   Mr Ollila did not mention, in this context, the importance of values and corporate culture, even if he in other connections (see Chapter 7) very firmly has attributed these a substantial role of the success of Nokia.
4   Simon, 1960.
5   Section adapted from Ramírez, 1999.
6   Ramírez, 1999.
7   de Geus, 1997.
8   Roth, 1999.
9   Rafael Ramírez: 'Redefining Tacit Knowledge', 4th International Conference on Competence-Based Competition, 18–20 June, 1998, Norwegian School of Management, Oslo, Norway.
10   Normann and Ramírez, 1989; 1993a.
11   Wallin, 1997.
12   Ackoff, 1970.
13   van der Heijden, 1996; van der Heijden refers to Jay Ogilvy's metaphor of scenarios as test conditions in a windtunnel for designing strategic success as the origin for his own use of the notion of windtunneling.
14   This example is adapted from Ramírez (1999).
15   Normann and Ramírez, 1993a.
16   Stacey, 1993.
17   Flavio Vasconcellos and Rafael Ramírez, 'Competences and Complexity: An Exploration', *Organizational Learning Symposium*, Lancaster University, 1996; and 'Managing Knowledge and Ignorance: A Co-evolutionary Perspective', *Strategic Management Society Conference*, Berlin, 1999.

18   Atlan, 1979; Atlan, 1991.

19   The change process these go through involves a sequence of unfreezing, of reformulating the management recipe, and then refreezing, so that people are converted and persuaded to accept the new recipe. After refreezing the organization thus returns to a state of harmony and stability characterized by all sharing the same culture.

20   Weick, 1979.

21   Stacey, 1993, p. 166.

22   Denis Bourgeois, PhD thesis, 2000.

23   *Business Week*, 10 August 1998.

24   Wallin, Johan, 'Customer Orientation and Competence Building', doctoral dissertation, Helsinki University of Technology, 2000.

25   Gilmore, T. and J. Krantz (1991) 'Innovation in the Public Sector: Dilemmas in the Use of *ad hoc* Processes', *Journal of Policy Analysis and Management* 10, no. 3: 455–68.

26   Kulkki and Kosonen, 1999.

27   Ramírez, 1999.

28   Perrow, 1979; Trist, 1973.

References and further reading

Abell, D. F. (1978) 'Strategic Windows'. *Journal of Marketing* (July): 21-26.

Abell, D. F. (1994) *Managing with Dual Strategies: Mastering the Present, Preempting the Future*. New York: The Free Press.

Ackoff, R. L. (1970) *A Concept of Corporate Planning*. New York: Wiley.

Ala-Pietilä, P. (1998) Speech at the SMS conference, Orlando, Fla., 4 November.

Argyris, C., and D. A. Schön (1974) *Theory in Practice: Increasing Professional Effectiveness*. San Francisco: Jossey-Bass.

Argyris, C., and D. A. Schön (1978) *Organizational Learning*. London: Addison-Wesley.

Arthur, B. W. (1996) 'Increasing Returns and the New World of Business'. *Harvard Business Review* (July–August): 100–9.

Atlan, H. (1979) *Entre le Cristal et la Fumée: Essai sur l'Organisation du Vivant*. Paris: Editions du Seuil.

Atlan, H. (1991) 'L'intuition du complexe et ses théorisations', in F. F. Soulié (ed.), *Les théories de la complexité*. Paris: Editions du Seuil.

Attali, J. *Les Trois Mondes*. Paris: Fayard, 1981.

Bailey, J. (1993) 'Why Customers Trash the Garbage Man'. Wall Street Journal (17 March): B1.

Barnevik, P. (1990) *Customer Focus*. Internal ABB document.

Bastiat, F. (1851) *Harmonies économiques*. Paris: Guillaumin.

Bateson, G. (1972) *Steps to an Ecology of Mind*. New York: Chandler.

Blankenburg H. D., K. Eriksson and J. Johanson (1999) 'Creating Value Through Mutual Commitment to Business Network Relationships'. *Strategic Management Journal* 20: 467–86.

Bell, D. (1973) *The Coming of Post-Industrial Society: A Venture in Social Forecasting*. New York: Basic Books.

Berger, P., and T. Luckmann (1967) *The Social Construction of Reality*. New York: Anchor Books.

Bogaert, I., R. Martens, and A. van Cauwenbergh (1994) 'Strategy as a Situational Puzzle: The Fit of Components'. In *Competence-Based Competition*, edited by G. Hamel and A. Heene. New York: Wiley.

Bogner, W. C., and H. Thomas (1996) 'From Skills to Competences: The "Play-Out" of Resource Bundles Across Firms'. In *Dynamics of Competence-Based Competition*, edited by R. Sanchez, A. Heene, and H. Thomas. Oxford: Elsevier.

Bohm, D. (1980) *Wholeness and the Implicate Order*. London: Routledge and Kegan Paul.

Boisguilbert, P. L. (1966) *Factum de la France*. Paris: National Institute of Demographic Studies, (1707).

Brender, A., A. Chevalier, and J. Pisani-Ferry (1980) *Etats-Unis: Croissance, Crise et Changement Technique dans une Économie Tertiaire*. Paris: CEPII-La Documentation Française.

'The CEO as an Organizational Architect, Interview with Paul Allaire' (1992) *Harvard Business Review* (September–October).

Christensen, C. M. and J. L. Bower (1996) 'Customer Power, Strategic Investment, and the Failure of Leading Firms'. *Strategic Management Journal* 17, no. 3: 197–218.

Churchman, C. W (1968) *The Systems Approach*. New York: Dell Publishing.

Churchman, C. W. (1979) *The Systems Approach and its Enemies*. New York: Basic Books.

Churchman, C. W., R. L. Ackoff, and E. L. Arnoff (1957) *Introduction to Operations Research*. New York: Wiley.

Cohen, W. M., and D. A. Levinthal (1990) 'Absorptive Capacity: A New Perspective on Learning and Innovation'. *Administrative Science Quarterly* 35: 128–51.

Corey, E. R. (1975) 'Key Options in Market Selection and Product Planning'. *Harvard Business Review*. (September–October): 119–28.

Crozier, M. (1964) *The Bureaucratic Phenomenon*. London: Tavistock Publications.

D'Aveni, R. (1994) *Hypercompetition: Managing the Dynamics of Strategic Maneuvering*. New York: Free Press.

Day, G. S. (1984) *Strategic Market Planning: The Pursuit of Competitive Advantage*. St Paul, MN: West Publishing Company.

Day, G. S. (1990) *Market Driven Strategy*. New York: The Free Press.

de Bandt, J., and J. Gadrey, eds. (1994) *Relations de service, marchés de service*. Paris: CNRS Editions.

de Geus, A. (1997) *The Living Company*. Boston: Harvard Business School Press.

Delaunay, J. C., and J. Gadrey (1992) *Services in Economic Thought, Three Centuries of Debate*. London: Kluwer Academic Publishers.

Eisenhardt, K. E, and S. L. Brown (1998) 'Time Pacing: Competing in Markets That Won't Stand Still'. *Harvard Business Review* (March–April): 59–69.

Emery, F., and Trist E. (1965) 'The Causal Texture of Organizational Environments'. *Human Relations* 18: 21–32.

Ennerfelt, S., M. Paltschik, and E. Tillberg (1996) *Verktyg för framtiden*. Stockholm: Ekerlids förlag.

Fites, D. V. (1996) 'Make Your Dealers Your Partners'. *Harvard Business Review* (March–April): 84–95.

Forrester, J. W. (1971) 'Behavior of Social Systems'. In *Hierarchically Organized Systems in Theory and Practice*, edited by P. A. Weiss, 81–122. New York: Hafner.

Fourastié, J. (1949) *Le grand espoir du XXeme siècle*. Paris: PUF.

Fuchs, V. (1965) *The Growing Importance of the Service Industries*. Occasional paper no. 96. Washington: National Bureau of Economic Research.

Fuchs, V. (1968) *The Service Economy*. New York: Columbia University Press.

Garud, R., and A. Kumaraswamy (1993) 'Changing Competitive Dynamics in Network Industries: An Exploration of Sun Microsystems' Open Systems Strategy'. *Strategic Management Journal*, 14: 351–69.

Garvin, D. A. (1995) 'Leveraging Processes for Strategic Advantage'. *Harvard Business Review* (September–October): 77–90.

Gershuny, J. (1978) *After Industrial Society? The Emerging Self-Service Economy*. London: Macmillan.

Gershuny, J., and I. Miles (1983) *The New Service Economy: The Transformation of Employment in Industrial Societies*. London: Frances Pinter.

Gilmore, T. (1988) *Making a Leadership Change*. San Francisco: Jossey Bass.

Gilmore T. and R. Kazanjian (1988) 'Clarifying Decision Making in High-Growth Ventures: The Use of Responsibility Charting'. *Journal of Business Venturing* (October).

Gilmore, T., and J. Krantz (1991) 'Innovation in the Public Sector: Dilemmas in the Use of Ad Hoc Processes'. *Journal of Policy Analysis and Management* 10, no.3.

Glaser, B. G., and A. L. Strauss (1967) *The Discovery of Grounded Theory*. Chicago: Aldine de Gruyter.

Gomes-Casseres, B. (1994) 'Group Versus Group: How Alliance Networks Compete'. *Harvard Business Review* (July–August 1994): 62–94.

Gomes-Casseres, B. (1996) 'Competing in Constellations: The Case of Fuji Xerox'. Based on his book, *The Alliance Revolution: The New Shape of Business Rivalry*. Boston: Harvard University Press.

Gorb, P. (1990) 'Design as a Corporate Weapon'. In *Design Management*, edited by P. Gorb. London: London Business School.

Gore, W. L. (1985) 'The Lattice Organization: A Philosophy of Enterprise'. *Networking Journal* (Spring-Summer): 24–8.

Grant, A. W. H., and L. A. Schlesinger (1995) 'Realize Your Customers' Full Profit Potential'. *Harvard Business Review*, (September–October).

Grönroos, C. (1983) *Strategic Management and Marketing in the Service Sector*. Marketing Science Institute.

Grönroos, C. (1990) *Service Management and Marketing*. Lexington, MA: Lexington Books.

Gulati, R. (1998) 'Alliances and Networks'. *Strategic Management Journal* 19: 293–317.

Haanes, K., and Ø. Fjeldstad (Forthcoming) 'The Strategic Link Between Competition and Competences'. In *Formulating Competence-Based Strategy,* edited by R. Sanchez, and A. Heene.

Håkansson, H., and I. Snehota (1995) *Developing Relationships in Business Marketing*. London: Routledge.

Hamel, G., and A. Heene, eds. (1994) *Competence-Based Competition*. Chichester: Wiley.

Hamel, G., and C. K. Prahalad (1994) *Competing for the Future*. Boston: Harvard Business School Press.

Hastings, C. (1993) *The New Organization: Growing the Culture of Organizational Networking*. London: McGraw Hill.

Hedlund, G., and I. Hägg (1978) 'Case Studies in Social Science Research.' Working paper No. 78-16, EIASM, Brussels.

Heene, A., and R. Sanchez, eds. (1997) *Competence-Based Strategic Management*. New York: Wiley.

Herring, P. (1997) 'Putting Value at the Heart of Your Business Plan'. *Cultor World* (March).

Heskett, J. L., W. E. Sasser, and L. Schlesinger (1997) *The Service Profit Chain*. New York: The Free Press.

Hirschhorn, L. (1984) *Beyond Mechanisation*. Boston: MIT Press.

Jarillo, C. (1988) 'On Strategic Networks'. *Strategic Management Journal* 9: 31–41.

Jenkins, M., and S. W. Floyd (1998) 'Knowledge, Resources and Advantage in Formula One Racing.' Paper presented at the 18th Annual International SMS Conference, Orlando, FL, 1–4 November.

Jones, C., W. S. Hesterly, and S. P. Borgatti (1997), 'A General Theory of Network Governance: Exchange Conditions and Social Mechanisms'. *Academy of Management Review* 22, no. 4.

Kaplan, R. S., and D. P. Norton (1996) *The Balanced Scorecard: Translating Strategy into Action*. Boston: Harvard Business School Press.

Kearns, D. and D. Nadler (1992) *Prophets in the Dark – How Xerox Reinvented Itself and Beat Back the*

Japanese. New York: HarperCollins,.

Kennedy, C. (1989) 'Xerox Charts a New Strategic Direction'. *Long Range Planning* 22, no. 1.

Kotter, J., and J. Heskett (1990) *Corporate Culture and Performance*. New York: The Free Press.

Kulkki, S., and Kosonen, M. (1999) 'How Tacit Knowledge Explains Organizational Renewal and Growth: Case Nokia'. In *Knowledge Creation and the Firm* by I. Nonaka and D. Treece. Oxford: Oxford University Press.

Lampel, J., and H. Mintzberg (1996) 'Customizing Customization'. *Sloan Management Review* 38, no. 1: 21–9.

Lang, J. W. (1997) 'Leveraging Knowledge Across Firm Boundaries: Achieving Strategic Flexibility Through Modularization and Alliances'. In *Strategic Learning and Knowledge Management*, edited by R. Sanchez, and A. Heene. New York: Wiley.

Lazzarato, M., Y. Moulier-Boutang, A. Negri, and G. Santilli (1993) *Des Entreprises Pas Comme Les Autres: Benetton en Italie, Le Sentier à Paris*. Paris: Editions Publisud.

Leander, L. (1995) *Tetra Pak, Visionen som blev Verklighet*. Lund: Tetra Pak (internal publication): 21–22.

Leonard-Barton, D. (1992) 'Core Capabilities and Core Rigidities: A Paradox in Managing New Product Development'. *Strategic Management Journal* 13 (Summer): 111–25.

Levien, R. E. (1987) 'Electronic and Systems Reprographics: Technological Revolution in Xerox' Core Business'. *Xerox Corporation* (August).

Levien, R. E. (1989a) 'The Civilizing Currency: Documents and Their Revolutionary Technologies'. Xerox Corporation (August).

Levien, R. E. (1989b) 'Making Strategic Concepts Work'. In *Information Technology and Management Strategy* by Kenneth Laudon, and John Turner. Englewood Cliffs, NJ: Prentice Hall.

Levitt, T. (1960) 'Marketing Myopia'. *Harvard Business Review* (July–August): 24–47.

Levitt, T. (1965) 'Exploit the Product Life Cycle'. *Harvard Business Review* (November–December): 81–94.

Levitt, T. (1980) 'Differentiation of Anything'. *Harvard Business Review* (January–February).

Lewin, K. (1947) 'Frontiers in Group Dynamics'. *Human Relations* 1: 5–41.

Lorino, P. (1999) Personal communication. Copenhagen, 22–23 February.

Lorino, P., and J.-P. Tarondeau (1998) 'From Resources and Competences to Processes in Strategic Management'. Research paper presented at the 4th International Conference on Competence-Based Management in Oslo, 18–20 June.

Löwendahl, B. R., and K. Haanes (1997) 'The Unit of Activity: A New Way to Understand Competence Building and Leveraging'. In *Strategic Learning and Knowledge Management,* edited by R. Sanchez, and A. Heene. (New York: Wiley.)

Magnet, M. (1994) 'The New Golden Rule of Business'. *Fortune* (21 February).

Mäkinen, M. (1995) *Nokia Saga,* Helsinki: Gummerus.

Maruyama, M. (1963) 'The Second Cybernetics: Deviation-Amplifying Mutual Causal Processes'. *American Scientist* 51: 164–79.

Marx, K. (1974) *Théories sur la Plus-value*. Paris: Editions Sociales.

Maturana, H., and F. Varela (1980) 'Autopoiesis and Cognition'. *Boston Studies in the Philosophy of Science* 42, Reidel.

McCann, J. and T. Gilmore (1983) Diagnosing Organizational Decision Making through Responsibility Charting'. *Sloan Management Review* 24, no. 2 (Winter).

McHugh, P., G. Merli, and W. A. Wheeler (1996) *Beyond Business Process Redesign: Towards the Holonic Enterprise*. Chichester: Wiley.

Mill, J. S. (1852) *Principles of Political Economy*. 3rd edn., London: John W. Parker and Sons.

Miller, D. (1990) *How Exceptional Companies Bring Their Own Downfall*. New York: Harper.

Mintzberg, H. (1978) 'Patterns in Strategy Formation'. *Management Science* 24: 934–48.

Mintzberg, H. (1990) 'The Design School: Reconsidering the Basic Premises of Strategic Management'. *Strategic Management Journal* 11: 171–95.

Mintzberg, H., and J. A. Waters (1985) 'Of Strategies, Deliberate and Emergent'. *Strategic Management Journal* 6: 257–72.

Moore, J. F. (1993) 'Predators and Prey: A New Ecology of Competition'. *Harvard Business Review* (May–June): 75–86.

Moore, J. (1996) *The Death of Competition: Leadership and Strategy in the Age of Business Ecosystems*. Chichester: Wiley.

Mosakowski, E., and W. McKelvey (1997) 'Predicting Rent Generation in Competence-Based Competition'. In *Competence-Based Strategic Management*, edited by A. Heene, and R. Sanchez. New York: Wiley.

Nadler, D. A., and M. L. Tushman (1989) 'Organizational Framebending: Principles for Managing Reorientation'. *Academy of Management Executive* 3, no.3: 194–204.

Naville, P. (1963) *Cahiers d'Études des Sociétés Industrielles et de l'Automatisation* 5. Paris: Centre de recherche d'urbanisme.

Naville, P. (1965) *Cahiers d'Études des Sociétés Industrielles et de l'Automatisation* 7. Paris: Centre de recherche d'urbanisme.

Nonaka, I., and H. Takeuchi (1995) *The Knowledge-Creating Company*. Oxford: Oxford University Press.

Normann, R. (1969) *Variation och Omorientering*. Stockholm: SIAR Dokumentation AB (SIAR-S-21).

Normann, R. (1975) *Skapande Företagsledning*. Stockholm: Aldus.

Normann, R. (1976) *På Spaning efter en Metodologi*. Stockholm: SIAR Dokumentation AB (SIAR-S-69).

Normann, R. (1977) *Management for Growth*. Chichester: Wiley.

Normann, R. (1978) *Utvecklingsstrategier för Svenskt Servicekunnande*. Stockholm: SIAR.

Normann, R. (1983) *Service Management*. Stockholm: LiberFörlag.

Normann, R. (1994) *Service Management*. 2nd ed. Chichester: Wiley.

Normann, R. (1998) Presentation at the Business Concept Innovation Conference, Zurich, 6–7 November.

Normann, R., and R. Ramírez (1989) 'A Theory of the Offering: Toward a Neo-industrial Business Strategy'. In *Strategy, Organization Design and Human Resource Management*, edited by C. C. Snow. Greenwich, CT: JAI Press.

Normann, R., and R. Ramírez (1993a) 'Designing Interactive Strategy: From Value Chain to Value Constellation'. *Harvard Business Review* (July–August): 65–77.

Normann, R., and R. Ramírez (1993b) 'Strategy and the Art of Reinventing Value', Perspectives Section. *Harvard Business Review* (September–October).

Normann, R., and R. Ramírez (1994) *Designing Interactive Strategy*. Chichester: Wiley.

Normann, R., and R. Ramírez (1998) *Designing interactive strategy*. 2nd edn., Chichester: Wiley.

Normann, R., J. Cederwall, L. Edgren, and A. Holst (1989) *Invadörernas dans – eller den oväntade konkurrensen*. Stockholm: Liber.

Pascale, R. T. (1984) 'Perspectives on Strategy: The Real Story Behind Honda's Success'. *California Management Review* (Spring): 47–72.

Penrose, E. (1959) *The Theory of the Growth of the Firm*. Oxford: Basil Blackwell.

Perrow, C. (1972, 1979) *Complex Organizations: A Critical Essay.* Glenview, Ill.: Scott Freeman and Company.

Pfeffer, J., and G. R. Salanick (1978) *The External Control of Organizations: A Resources Dependence Perspective.* New York: Harper & Row.

Polanyi, M. (1996) *The Tacit Dimension.* New York: Doubleday.

Porter, M. E. (1980) *Competitive Strategy.* New York: Free Press.

Porter, M. E. (1985) *Competitive Advantage.* New York: Free Press.

Porter, M. E. (1987) 'From Competitive Advantage to Corporate Strategy'. *Harvard Business Review* 65, no.3: 43–59.

Porter, M. (1996) 'What is Strategy?' *Harvard Business Review* (November–December): 61–78.

Prahalad, C. K., and G. Hamel (1990) 'The Core Competences of the Corporation'. *Harvard Business Review* 68, no.3: 79–93.

Prigogine, I., and I. Strengers (1984) *Order Out of Chaos: Man's New Dialogue With Nature.* London: Bantam.

Quinn, J. B. (1978) 'Strategic Change: Logical Incrementalism'. *Sloan Management Review* (Fall): 7–21.

Quinn, J. B. (1980) *Strategies for Change. Logical Incrementalism.* Burr Ridge: Irwin.

Quinn, J. B. (1992) *Intelligent Enterprise.* New York: The Free Press.

Ramírez, R. (1983) 'Action Learning: A Strategic Approach for Organizations Facing Turbulent Conditions'. *Human Relations* 36, no. 8.

Ramírez, R. (1999) 'Value Co-production: Intellectual Origins and the Implications for Practice and Research'. *Strategic Management Journal* 20: 49–65.

Reichheld, F. F. (1996) *The Loyalty Effect.* Boston: Harvard Business School Press.

Roth, D. (1999) 'The Value of Vision'. *Fortune*, May 24.

Sanchez, R. (1995) 'Strategic Flexibility in Product Competition'. *Strategic Management Journal* 16 (Summer): 135–59.

Sanchez, R. (1997) 'Managing Articulated Knowledge in Competence-Based Competition'. In *Strategic Learning and Knowledge Management*, edited by R. Sanchez, and A. Heene. New York: Wiley.

Sanchez, R. and A. Heene (1996) 'A Systems View of the Firm in Competence-Based Competition'. In *Dynamics of Competence-Based Competition*, edited by R. Sanchez, A. Heene, and H. Thomas. Oxford: Elsevier.

Sanchez, R. and A. Heene eds. (1997a) *Strategic Learning and Knowledge Management.* New York: Wiley.

Sanchez, R. and A. Heene (1997b) 'Competence-Based Strategic Management: Concepts and Issues for Theory, Research, and Practice'. In *Competence-Based Strategic Management*, edited by A. Heene, and R. Sanchez. New York: Wiley.

Sanchez, R. and H. Thomas (1996) 'Strategic Goals'. In *Dynamics of Competence-Based Competition*, edited by R. Sanchez, A. Heene, and H. Thomas. Oxford: Elsevier.

Sanchez, R., A. Heene, and H. Thomas, eds. (1996) *Dynamics of Competence-Based Competition.* Oxford: Elsevier.

Sauvy, A. (1949) 'Progrès Technique et Repartition Professionelle de la Population'. *Population* 1–2.

Schein, E. H. (1996) 'Three Cultures of Management: The Key to Organizational Learning'. *Sloan Management Review* 38, no. 1: 9–20.

Schein, E. H. (1997) *Organizational Culture and Leadership.* Paperback edition. San Francisco: Jossey-Bass.

Schlender, B. (1995) 'What Bill Gates Really Wants'. *Fortune* (16 January): 16–33.

Schlender, D. E. (1996) 'Use Strategic Market Models to Predict Customer Behavior'. *Sloan Management Review* 37, no.3 (Spring): 85–92.

Schneider, A. V., and H. W. Ebeling (1992) 'Targeting a Company's Real Core Competences'. *Journal of Business Strategy* 13, no. 6 (November-December): 26–32.

Schön, D. (1971) *Beyond the Stable State*. New York: Random House.

Schön, D. A. (1994) Foreword to *Designing Interactive Strategy* by R. Normann and R. Ramírez. Chichester: Wiley.

Schulmeyer, G. (1992) 'Customer Focus: An Organisational Imperative'. Internal ABB Document.

Schwarz, P. (1997) *The Art of the Long View*. Chichester: Wiley.

Seely Brown, J. (1991) 'Research That Reinvents the Corporation'. *Harvard Business Review* (January–February).

Selznick, P. (1957) *Leadership in Administration*. New York: Harper & Row.

Senge, P. (1990) *The Fifth Discipline: The Art and Practice of Organizational Learning*. New York: Doubleday.

Sennet, R. (1998) *The Corrosion of Character: Personal Consequences of Work in the New Capitalism*. New York: W. W. Norton.

Simon, H. A. (1960) *The New Science of Management Decision*. Englewood Cliffs, N J: Prentice Hall.

Smith, A. (1776) *An Enquiry Into the Nature and the Causes of the Wealth of Nations*.

Solé, A. (1996) 'La Décision: Production de Possibles et d'Impossibles'. In *Traité d'ergonomie*, edited by P. Cazamanian, F. Hubaut and M. Noulin. Paris: Octares Editions, Collection Travail: 573–636.

Sole, T., and R. Marshall (1998) *Nearly Impossible Brain Bafflers*. New York: Sterling Publications.

Stabell, C., and O. D. Fjedlstad (1998) 'Configuring Value for Competitive Advantage: on Chains, Shops, and Networks'. *Strategic Management Journal* 19 no. 5: 413–38.

Stacey, R. D. (1993) *Strategic Management and Organizational Dynamics*. London: Pitman Publishing.

Stanback, T. M. (1980) *Understanding the Service Economy*. Baltimore: Johns Hopkins University Press.

Stoffaes, C. (1981) 'L'emploi et la révolution informationnelle'. Informatisation et emploi, menace ou mutation. Paris: La Documentation française.

Storch, H. (1815, 1823) *Cours d'Economie Politique ou exposition des principes qui détérminent la prospérité des nations*. Paris: Aillaut.

Taylor, A. (1997) 'How Toyota Defies Gravity'. *Fortune* (8 December): 38–44.

Timmins, M. (1997) 'A £130m loss leader'. *Financial Times* (19 June)

Treece, D. J., Pisano, G., and Shuen, A. (1990) 'Firm Capabilites Resources, and the Concept of Strategy'. CCC Working Paper 90-8, University of California at Berkeley.

Trist, E. L. (1973) 'Task and Contextual Environments for New Personal Values'. In *Towards a Social Ecology: Contextual Appreciations of the Future in the Present* edited by F. Emery and E. L. Trist. London: Plenum.

Trist, E. L. (1976) 'A Concept of Organizational Ecology'. *Australian Journal of Management* 2: 161–75.

Trist, E. L. (1979) 'New Directions of Hope: Recent Innovations Interconnecting Organizational, Industrial, Community, and Personal Development'. *Regional Studies* 13: 439–51.

Trist, E. L. (1983) 'Referent Organizations and the Development of Inter-organizational Domains'. *Human Relations* 36, no. 3: 269–84.

Urwick, L. (1943) *Elements of Administration*. London: Pitman.

Utterback, J. M. (1994) *Mastering the Dynamics of Innovation*. Boston: Harvard Business School Press.

van der Heijden, K. (1993) 'Comment in: 'Strategies and the Art of Reinventing Value'.' Perspectives Section, *Harvard Business Review* (September–October).

van der Heijden, K. (1996) *Scenarios: The Art of Strategic Conversation*. New York: Wiley.

Wallin, J. (1997) 'Customers as the Originators of Change in Competence Building: A Case Study'. In *Competence-Based Strategic Management*, edited by A. Heene, and R. Sanchez. New York: Wiley.

Wallin, J. (1998a) 'Competence Driven Offering Design'. Paper presented at the 4th International Conference on Competence Based Management in Oslo, 18–20 June.

Wallin, J. (1998b) 'Customer Orientation and Data Warehousing'. *Journal of Data Warehousing* 3, no.2: 24-32.

Wallin, J. (1998c) 'Corporate Values As A Driver For Priority Development', paper presented at the 18th SMS Conference, Orlando, FLA, 1–4 November.

Wallin, J., and R. Ramírez (1996) 'Value Constellations and Competence Development'. Paper presented at the 16th Annual International Conference of the Strategic Management Society, 5–8 October in Phoenix, Arizona.

Webster, F. E. (1993) Presentation at the 1993 American Marketing Association Educators' Conference (August), Boston, Massachusetts (in M. D. Hutt and T. W. Speh *Business Marketing Management*)

Weick, K. (1979) *The Social Psychology of Organizing*. Reading, Mass.: Addison-Wesley.

Wheatley, M. (1992) *Leadership and the New Science*. San Francisco: Berret-Koehle

Whitney, D. E. et al. (1997) 'Fast and Flexible Communication of Design Information in the Aerospace and Automobile Industries: A Project Conducted by MIT and Lehigh University'. *Agility & Global Competition* 1, no.1: 30–42.

Zeithaml, V. A., A. Parasuraman and L. L. Berry (1991) 'Refinement and Reassessment of the SERQUAL Scale', *Journal of Retailing* 67, no. 4: 420–50.

Zetterberg, H. (1962) *Social Theory, Social Practice*. New York: Bedminster Press.

Zetterberg, H. (1992) 'The Study of Values'. Paper originally presented at the 87th Annual Meeting of the American Sociological Association, 20–24 August in Pittsburg, Pennsylvania.

Index